This is Only the Beginning

This is Only the Beginning

The Making of a New Left, From Anti-Austerity to the Fall of Corbyn

Michael Chessum

BLOOMSBURY ACADEMIC
LONDON • NEW YORK • OXFORD • NEW DELHI • SYDNEY

BLOOMSBURY ACADEMIC
Bloomsbury Publishing Plc
50 Bedford Square, London, WC1B 3DP, UK
1385 Broadway, New York, NY 10018, USA
29 Earlsfort Terrace, Dublin 2, Ireland

BLOOMSBURY, BLOOMSBURY ACADEMIC and the Diana logo are trademarks
of Bloomsbury Publishing Plc

First published in Great Britain 2022

A catalogue record for this book is available from the British Library.

A catalog record for this book is available from the Library of Congress.

ISBN: HB: 978-0-7556-4128-4
ePDF: 978-0-7556-4130-7
eBook: 978-0-7556-4129-1

Typeset by Deanta Global Publishing Services, Chennai, India
Printed and bound in Great Britain

To find out more about our authors and books visit www.bloomsbury.com and
sign up for our newsletters.

To the crowd of misfits, troublemakers and idealists, who smashed the plate glass of Conservative Party headquarters and the consensus that enveloped the world we lived in; who were ridiculed, beaten and incarcerated; who never apologised, and never should.

Contents

Preface and Acknowledgements

From the roof of Millbank Tower as it bristled with red and black flags, on picket lines of public sector workers as they struck for their pensions and in frantic assemblies of the newly politicized outside St Paul's Cathedral, one string of words was ever-present. I heard it again ten years later as Black Lives Matter took over Parliament Square, and in the spring of 2021 when a feminist-led movement sprang up in response to the new Policing Bill and the murder of Sarah Everard. That November, when I interviewed activists in Santiago ahead of the elections that put the Chilean left in power for the first time since Salvador Allende's victory in 1970, the same sentiment echoed back, word for word.

'This is only the beginning' captures something innate about movements that fight to change the world. It expresses not just a sense of optimism and determination but also a collective understanding that is necessary for any movement to function: that while this moment might be fleeting, and its immediate objectives might be defeated, it is part of a bigger whole whose long-term ramifications we cannot know. That much was certainly the case for those of us who were part of the youth uprising of 2010 and the anti-austerity movements that followed it, whose seemingly abject defeat prepared the ground for Jeremy Corbyn's rise and the re-emergence of the left as a mainstream force in British politics.

The first draft of this book was written over the course of four hectic months, though it is in reality the culmination of a whole decade of frantic mobilization, defeats, surprises, triumphs, breakdowns and mistakes. Those who read it will find not an academic text but a version of history, and a perspective on the future, from the inevitably incomplete and partial perspective of an activist and a protagonist. I make no apologies and seek no forgiveness for the fact that it 'takes sides' – that is the point of it – but I have also tried to be fair to those with whom I disagree and to give time to differing perspectives. I also hope that, in its account of social movements and the British left, it stands up as a historical document for the years it covers and that those who read it will find the story it tells as full of natural laughs and entertainment as it seemed to me, both at the time and while writing it.

Looking back on the years that built this book, despite all the pain and disappointment, my main sensation is one of luck and gratitude. The eventful decade of the 2010s coincided almost exactly with my twenties. Like a lot of my generation, I spent much of the decade stressed, overworked or hard up, but I was also given the privilege of spending much of it in paid work for 'the movement', in campaigns such as 'Another Europe is Possible' and in student unions. From very early on, I had a public platform because of my role in the student protests, and even after I became a dissident outcast within Corbynism, I still had a platform to write and campaign.

It is rare, in fact vanishingly so, to be given the opportunity to write up both your twenties and a pivotal moment in British politics in the neat form of a book. And so the first people I must thank are Tomasz Hoskins, Nayiri Kendir, Atifa Jiwa and everyone else at Bloomsbury Publishing, who took a punt on an unsolicited pitch from an unpublished author in the summer of 2020. I must also thank my partner, Kelly Rogers, whose dedication to the struggle for social justice and achievements as an organizer have always inspired me, and without whose love, patience and intelligent criticism I would never have got through the process of writing all this down. My parents, Richard Chessum and Emma Witney, should also get a mention, not just for sentimental reasons but because, as veteran activists of a previous era, they have always been a source of wisdom and had a substantial influence on my political and intellectual outlook in the period that the book covers.

No author writes in a vacuum, and writing about mass movements and the left makes you especially dependent on the collective wisdom of those around you. Aside from the influences of a number of other books and oral histories, which are referenced in the running text, three people in particular should be mentioned for providing inspiration for specific sections of the book. In the bleak winter of 2020–21, I sat down with Jon Moses, an old friend and flatmate in the formative years of 2010 and 2011, who still writes and campaigns. Over a number of ales we dissected the political experience of our generation and contemporaries, and Chapter 2 owes much to this single, day-long conversation. Sections of Chapter 3, my history of the anti-austerity movement, are indebted to a number of exchanges, with Simon Hannah, a good friend and an accomplished author in his own right. Then there is Ed Maltby, still a close friend, ally and prolific organizer, whose uncanny ability to bring clarity and wit to a situation I could rely on both in the moment and when writing about it, especially in the first half of the book. Neither they nor any of the other people who are quoted, cited or otherwise acknowledged bear any responsibility for my errors and opinions.

There are almost innumerable others who I should thank, and I will not make the mistake of attempting to list them all, running the almost certain risk of forgetting and offending them. Many are interviewed and quoted, and many of the rest know who they are.

The world has changed a lot since I started writing this book, though in many ways it hasn't. The pandemic created a new reality, but one of the deeper arguments that I want to make is that many of the roots of the political and economic crises we now face can be traced to the way in which the global ruling class responded to the 2008 financial crisis in the decade that followed it and to the social and political movements that sprung up in response. As popular support for neoliberalism collapsed, the world polarized between visions of the future based on environmental sustainability, economic radicalism and social progressivism on the one hand, and nostalgia, climate denialism, border-building and authoritarianism on the other. We are, to a great extent, still stuck in the waiting room after that moment: the old centre cannot hold, but what will replace it remains unclear. Whether progressives win or lose will depend much on our ability to understand what happened in the 2010s and to learn the lessons the decade contains.

Introduction

There is nothing so wrenching, and yet so familiar, as the sound of collective dreams colliding with reality. Just ask anyone who supported the miners' strike on the day they went back to work in 1985 or the young activists in the streets of Athens in 2015 as the Third Bailout Package was signed. In December 2019, that same sensation was visited on the whole of the British left, as Jeremy Corbyn's Labour Party was comprehensively defeated at the ballot box, paving the way for the hardest of Brexits under the leadership of an increasingly authoritarian and rightward-moving Conservative Party. There is a neat but tragic symmetry to the fact that a decade that began with such hope, with a political awakening and a series of mass revolts, ended with such an earth-shattering and seemingly total defeat. The new Labour left, which had rammed socialist ideas into the political mainstream for the first time in decades, fell apart. Across the Atlantic, Bernie Sanders failed for the second time to win the Democratic nomination. The Arab Spring was long dead. The Greek left was in disarray. Podemos stagnated.

And yet, in Britain and across most of the Western world, the radical left is today in a far stronger position than it was in the immediate aftermath of the financial crisis in 2008. Millions of people identify with socialist and social democratic ideas, and many of them have been brought into active politics in one way or another, despite all of the setbacks they have suffered. The history of progressive politics is often, if we are honest, a history of defeats and limitations – of the power and determination of ordinary people coming up against immovable barriers and enemies so well equipped that it takes a subjective leap of faith in order to believe that the victory of a political project, a strike or a protest movement is even possible. The point is that between the moments of defeat are a million tiny strides forward and a million moments of hope in which the boundaries of what seems possible split open at the seams.

Those moments are what this book is about. This is the story of how the British left came to life again in the 2010s: of a generation that exploded in revolt when no one thought they were capable of doing so, a mass movement that broke the austerity consensus and an electoral project that transformed politics. It is also the story of what went wrong: the institutional failures, the lack of pluralism and internal democracy, the culture of loyalism and the failure to successfully confront the rise of right-wing nationalism. In 2010 and the years that followed it, I was an organizer in the student movement and the wider anti-austerity movement. When Momentum first established democratic structures, I was elected onto its Steering Committee and saw first-hand many of the tensions and contradictions within the Corbyn project. I spent most of the following years organizing movements for migrants' rights and against Brexit, campaigns which put me in the awkward position of going head-to-head with a Labour leadership which I continued, in a broad sense, to support. My perspective is inevitably partial, controversial and based on my own experiences, and it is from this perspective that I will attempt to set out what we, the left, need to do now that both our mass movements and our electoral projects appear to have run aground.

This book is my account of the rise of a new left in British politics, a force created by the specific experiences of the social movements and political upheavals of the 2010s but which can also trace a lineage to the movements and new lefts of previous eras. The emergence of Corbynism not only gave the movements of the 2010s a greater platform but also limited their horizons, as many of their adherents came to identify not as partisans of a distinctive new left politics but as supporters of the Labour leadership. And yet as we emerge from the pandemic into a new era, it is this force that holds the key to the progressive renewal of politics, if only it can cohere itself.

*   *   *

Over the course of the 2010s, Britain became a meaner, nastier place, and for most people a poorer one. In the seven years up to 2015, median earnings fell by 10.6 per cent, a drop second in the developed world only to Greece, and had still not recovered by 2020.[1] By the end of the decade, child poverty had increased to 4.2 million, meaning that one in every three children lived in households which struggled with basics like food, shelter and heating.[2] Rates of homelessness and rough sleeping rocketed. The Trussell Trust, Britain's main but by no means only food bank provider, handed out 40,898 food parcels in the financial year 2009–10; in 2019–20, it handed out 1.9 million.[3]

The pandemic has provided governments with a never-ending source of excuses for poor health outcomes. But the truth is that by the time Covid-19 struck in early 2020, NHS waiting lists were already at record highs and Britain was already in the grips of a chronic crisis in public health. For a whole century prior to the 2010s, life expectancy increased by around three years every decade, but over the course of this decade it went up by just 0.7 years. In some of the most deprived areas of the country, it went down.[4] Infant mortality began to rise after a century of continuously falling.[5] A report released by the IPPR think tank in 2019 estimated that, between 2012 and 2017, a stalling in the rate of improvement of public health was responsible for something like 131,000 preventable deaths.[6] The dramatic rise in poverty and precarious work also led to a crisis in mental health. In 2008, 36 million prescriptions were issued for antidepressants; by 2018, that figure stood at 70.9 million, and 17 per cent of the entire adult population was on them.[7]

These were the social conditions from which the radical left in Britain regrew and became a major political force for the first time since the 1980s. Its resurgence was a response to an all-out assault on what remained of the post-war welfare state and on the incomes and living standards of the majority of people.

There was once a time when you didn't really need to understand the left in order to make sense of what was happening in politics. Some people, and these people can be found in high concentration within the media and the political commentariat, still live in this era. Many more still want to live in it and can often be found engaging in wishful thinking on our television screens and in the pages of broadsheet newspapers. The rebirth of the left, they say, is a historical aberration, a collective moment of madness. Soon enough, equilibrium will be restored, and the utopian ideas that briefly took flight in the wild decade of the 2010s will once again be quaint relics. Time will tell, of course, if they are right, but in a world of radicalized youth, ecological crisis and intensifying exploitation and economic injustice, it is difficult to see how they could be.

It is not just the opponents of the left's renaissance that have attempted to define it, of course. There has been no shortage of accounts written or produced on the Corbyn project in recent years, which have sought to talk about its achievements and offer explanations for its successes and failures. Many of these accounts are essential reading for anyone who wants to understand British politics today. Most of them are limited, however, to telling an inside story of political intrigue. Despite their belief in mass politics, so many left-wing writers remain preoccupied with court histories and the telling and retelling of the moment in which the radical left briefly vanquished the centrist political establishment of the Labour Party. Just as the new Labour left's activists were entrusted with doorknocking rather than setting policy or collectively deciding strategy, so many histories of the project seek to suck all of the agency upwards. The history of the new Labour left is, accordingly, viewed in terms of clever (or stupid) political management, dramatic decisions taken by plucky aides and deals hammered out in smoky backrooms. It is almost as if, when it comes to analysing Corbynism, the left is uninterested in asking the questions it would ask of any other electoral project: Where did this moment come from, what can it teach us and what were its deeper roots – not just in terms of a painting-by-numbers narrative about social injustice, but in terms of mass movements and 'politics from below'?

The British left has generated no shortage of policy in the time since Jeremy Corbyn became Labour leader. The Labour Party's manifestos in 2017 and 2019 laid out a real blueprint for what a truly transformational government might do. Much of its programmes – massive public investment, building council houses and the renationalization of the NHS, rail and utilities – would have been familiar to a Labour activist of the mid-twentieth century. Other aspects were qualitatively more radical: in office, a Corbyn government would have created new integrated public services for social care and education and led the world in decarbonization. It tentatively took up the cause of the four-day working week, universal basic income and the expansion of the franchise to millions of migrants living in the UK. Hundreds of thousands were so inspired by the prospect of these ideas becoming reality that they joined the Labour Party, and tens of thousands hit the doorsteps. Their combined effort in December 2019 was not enough to compensate for Labour's sharp electoral decline in the north of England and the Midlands and a moment of polarization in which the party lost almost two million voters on each side of the Brexit divide.[8]

What the left lacks, then, is neither a governmental programme nor the people to support it but a means of cohering a genuinely thriving, democratic movement which can mobilize outside of election periods. Until now, this has been difficult. From the moment that the left won the Labour leadership in 2015 to the moment it crashed and burned in the leadership election of 2020, it developed under siege. Its momentum was held together by a constant patchwork of elections, leadership challenges, internal crises and scandals both real and manufactured.

There is a version of history in which the left won basically by accident: the Labour Party establishment ran out of ideas; Jeremy Corbyn won the Labour leadership after Ed Miliband accidentally created an electoral system which favoured him; and then, by virtue of genius political positioning by a handful of chess-playing experts, we would scrape a plurality of the vote which, because of Britain's dysfunctional electoral system, would hand us a parliamentary majority which we would use to legislate socialism from above. This world view makes for great television, but I have never subscribed to it, and its prevalence in the minds of many of those at the heart of the project was the cause of a great deal of problems. The 2017 general election, in which Corbyn achieved the greatest increase in Labour's vote share since 1945 and denied Theresa May a majority, was a moment of intoxication from which the leadership never really came down. It seemed to vindicate every decision they had made, from the radical manifesto which Labour put forward, to the repurposing of Momentum into an efficient top-down campaign machine, to the policy of not quite having a policy on Brexit.

Some of these feelings of vindication were justified, and the desperate need for Labour to put forward a bold insurgent programme resonates even more strongly today. Others were not.

Corbynism held out the possibility of fulfilling the historic promise of the Labour left, stretching back to the Benn era in the 1980s and to Bevanism in the immediate post-war period. All of these projects had fought to transform Labour, placing increasing emphasis on opening up the party and building relationships with external movements. Corbynism's promise break from establishment Labourism – with its bureaucracy, lack of democracy and the demobilization of workers – was stronger than any iteration of the Labour left before it.

As we shall see, what actually happened was quite different. Despite claiming the mantle of the mass movements that preceded it, the official leadership of the new Labour left seemed curiously allergic to devolving power to their own activists and failed to democratize the party during their time in office. The manner in which the project was run, with its tendency to centralize decision-making and its deployment of activists as doorknocking foot soldiers rather than thinking participants in a democratic movement, meant that it often resembled a left-wing version of New Labour as much as it did a modernized version of the Bennite tradition. It was a politics for the many but cooked up in a political machine in which the levers of power were held by a tiny few.

The antidote to this situation, and to the often unhealthy atmosphere and culture which prevails alongside it, lies not in the dim and distant past, or the realms of utopian thinking, but in the five years immediately before 2015. Corbynism was built on the back of an explosion of social movements and industrial struggle which opened in late 2010 and peaked in 2011, though they continued simmering for many years afterwards. These mass movements, which I detail in the first three chapters, were an explosive rebuttal of the neoliberal consensus and were, by and large, a revolt against the political establishment as a whole. They were wild, disruptive and uncontrollably bottom-up, at times to the point of being leaderless. Outside of the antics of a few backbench MPs like John

McDonnell and Jeremy Corbyn, they lacked any form of political expression and vested very little hope or trust in the Labour Party which, under the leadership of Ed Miliband, did not really oppose austerity.

The paradox of the Corbyn moment is that it represents an enormous step forward for the British left but also precipitated a step backwards. In the summer of 2015, these movements came together with many older generations of leftists and progressives, and the withered remains of the Labour left, to give birth to Corbynism. The new Labour left which emerged represented, at last, a chance for the movements to break through into politics but presented itself as a kind of mirror image of them. The Corbyn project spoke constantly about 'a new kind of politics', a grassroots rebirth inspired by the social movements that had come before it; and in its rallies and canvassing sessions, it did succeed in bringing about the return of a kind of mass politics. In the end, however, the Corbynite left remained entirely focussed on elections – both internal and external – to the exclusion of building any form of social or industrial power, and it was led from above with very little internal democratic life. The lack of a truly empowered grassroots in the new Labour left was not an accident or an inevitable fact but the result of a series of conscious decisions on the part of its leadership and an unspoken battle of ideas and methods in which the politics of the social movements was, quietly, snuffed out.

The pattern of social movements morphing into electoral projects is not a new one and is not unique to the UK either. Podemos, Syriza, the Bernie Sanders campaign and many others can also trace their roots to street protests, tent cities and strikes. The flipping of the left which occurred in the UK in 2015 produced and showcased all kinds of contradictions and handbrake turns: devout anarchists turned into social democrats, revolutionaries threw themselves into campaigns to get Blairite MPs re-elected and most of the people who spent the first half of the decade telling me off for being a member of the Labour Party spent the second half of the decade telling me off for being too critical of its leadership.

There is a danger that, as the tumultuous decade of the 2010s begins to be written up, the real roots of the left's renaissance are smoothed over and forgotten, and that we begin to see mass movements as mere warm-up acts for the 'real thing'. Conventional electoral politics are, after all, the most easily comprehensible part of the left's output as far as many journalists are concerned and have the most easily measurable successes and failures. Few writers – even those who approach the decade from a left perspective – seem to be that bothered about the movements against tuition fees, austerity and privatization on their own terms.

Their achievements, their limitations, the reasons for the defeats and success are, we are so often told, not that important: they popularized alternative narratives about the economy and created the human material for Corbyn (or Sanders, or Tsipras, or Iglesias) and the rest is history. I think this approach is wrong, not just because it misses out on some of the most inspiring stories and erases the deeper contributions of those who took part but because it misunderstands how history happens and is liable to misprescribe what is needed now if the left is to succeed.

The different versions of Corbynism's origins and demise are far more than just disagreements about the past. The different narratives about why the project happened and why it failed – over the approach towards trade unionism, the question of how to deal with parliamentary politics, the importance of internal democracy, the need for discipline and loyalism, the left's response to Brexit, the role of the nation state and so on – are really questions about what the left should do now. Social movements are by their nature politically and ideologically heterogeneous, but I want to argue that the mass revolt that took place in the early part of the decade can and must be understood as containing the seeds of a new left – less hierarchical and sectarian, more democratic, radical in its tactics and determined to break free of the confines of conventional electoral politics. Within the new Labour left, it was overshadowed and consciously defeated by better-organized institutional tendencies within the party, but that is not the end of its story.

This book is my attempt to answer the question of what happened and what we need to do now. By the time that Jeremy Corbyn decided, reluctantly, to put his name forward to run for Labour leader in the summer of 2015, his leadership campaign already knew that it could draw on a gigantic support base which had been created by the movements and strikes that had gone before it. The people who flocked to his rallies had, mostly, already known hope and disappointment, though many would feel both of those emotions even more keenly in the years that followed. The new British left was not built by professionals, politicians and bureaucrats, and it did not hit a brick wall because of bad personal relationships between top aides, or a badly worded press release or a badly thought-through strategy on a single issue. The 2010s are the story of not one but several mass movements: moments in which people stood up, realized their own strength and fought to change everything, in spite of the inadequacy of their leaders and the crowing of their bosses and the political elite, shocking themselves and the world in what they achieved.

Part I

2010–15

1

Students in a dream world

On Thursday 9 December 2010, just after 5.41 pm, a dull wall of noise echoed across Parliament Square. The House of Commons had voted on the Coalition government's proposal to triple university tuition fees from £3,000 to £9,000. Despite the widespread public opposition and a wave of protest from students and education workers – not to mention the promises on which they had been elected – not enough Liberal Democrat MPs had rebelled. The measure had passed by 323 votes to 302. Britain's higher education sector was on its way to being fully marketized, and it was now one of the most expensive in the world.

Via social media and a collective howl of anger, the news spread quickly to the crowd outside, where thirty thousand people, the vast majority of them school or university students, had mobilized in a last-ditch attempt to stop the proposals. Many had travelled hundreds of miles by coach, some by hitchhiking. Others had risked expulsion or disciplinary action to walk out of school. Some had stayed overnight in the by-now extensive network of campus occupations spread across central London – lecture halls, conference rooms and buildings that had been repurposed as live-in organizing hubs, arts studios, radical seminar rooms, live music venues, banner-making workshops and dormitories for the student movement. The BBC split-screened its coverage of the vote in parliament. On one side was footage of MPs as they took part in the debating rituals of Westminster. On the other was a riot.

The Battle of Parliament Square, as the day became known by many of those who attended, was the culmination of an explosive month of protest, by many measures the biggest student movement in British history. More than a hundred thousand took part in a series of days of action, and forty-six campuses were occupied as part of the revolt. The civil disobedience and direct action that characterized the student protests had been brutally policed. The police euphemistically referred to their preferred tactic, which they had perfected during the G20 protests the previous year, as 'containment'. Everyone else called it kettling, a method which involved forcibly detaining whole protests in the open air for hours, often without access to food or toilet facilities in an attempt to demoralize and subdue the crowd. It had been deployed to great effect throughout the brutally cold autumn of 2010, despite the presence of school students as young as ten.

That night, the crowd had already been penned into Parliament Square and Whitehall from around 3.00 pm. As grime and reggae boomed out from mobile sound systems, protesters danced to keep warm. The burning of placards and wooden benches which began as a gesture of defiance turned into a source of heat. Betrayed by politicians, trapped by the police and chilled to the bone, protesters, some of them in school uniform, stormed into the Treasury building and the Supreme Court and lit fires in the compounds.[1] The police responded by charging horses into the trapped crowd. 'There was this cry of "get out the way"', remembers Owen Jones, then a PhD student at University College London. 'I was standing by Parliament Square and I remember diving out the way as the horses charged. People were genuinely stunned.'

Baton charge after baton charge moved the students down Whitehall and away from Victoria Street, towards the river. The level of police violence in the kettle that night went beyond anything that had been seen on the streets of London in many decades. One student, Alfie Meadows, was batoned and then trapped in the kettle, before being left to wander the streets. He eventually found an ambulance and was rushed to hospital for brain surgery that saved his life, in the nick of time. Another, Will Horner, had his teeth knocked out while running away from PC Andrew Ott, who was, five years later, jailed for eight months. Jody McIntyre, a relatively prominent blogger, was hit with a baton and dragged from his wheelchair across the street in an incident that was filmed live by bystanders.

But aside from the famous cases, the truth is that hundreds of protesters were injured, many of them seriously. Eventually, at around 9.00 pm, the remaining students were herded onto Westminster Bridge, the crowd so tightly packed that many reported almost falling into the river, before being released slowly at around midnight while being filmed by police. Ash Sarkar, then a first-year English student at UCL, spent the evening receiving reports from friends who were trapped on the bridge. 'They were just fucking freezing', she says, 'and they were kids. They weren't hardened protesters who chained themselves to stuff, they were kids who'd barely brought a granola bar with them and who had come out to the demo because they thought it was important.' Doctors who set up a field hospital in Parliament Square later compared the scene to the Hillsborough

Disaster, with some of those on the bridge suffering respiratory problems and symptoms of severe crushing.[2] 'Police charged at us on their horses on Whitehall, near Downing Street', James Greenhalgh, a twenty-year-old politics student at Leeds University, told the BBC. 'People were trying to get out of the way, but there was nowhere to go. Christmas shoppers were caught up in it all – they couldn't get out.'

Those who could escape the bridge either ran around central London blocking traffic or drifted off to their homes or university occupations to regroup, debrief and get drunk. In Bloomsbury, the occupations were full of shaken, injured students, some clutching bottles of wine and others contemplating trips to A & E. One occupier at the School of Oriental and African Studies had lost a finger.[3] Another, a friend of mine at UCL, was drinking heavily and grimacing with pain after being batoned from behind while kneeling down to tie his shoelaces. 'Oh', he told me a few days later, 'I've had an X-ray. It turns out they broke my ribs.' It was, in retrospect, astonishing that no one died that night.

The following morning, the media was awash with choreographed outrage. Protesters had broken the windows of government buildings and done the same to various shops on Oxford Street and Regents Street, including Topshop which was famous for its corporate tax avoidance. Graffiti – some of it political, some of it situationist and some of it just sweary – had been daubed all over Westminster. The *Daily Mail* frothed at the 'baying rabble of masked and hooded troublemakers' who had urinated on the statue of Winston Churchill and swung from the flagpoles of the Cenotaph. 'Observers said as few as half of the crowd were students, with a rent-a-mob of anarchists and other thugs taking control',[4] it reported. The Metropolitan Police condemned the 'wanton vandalism' of the protest and said that its officers 'had to face a significant level of violence including fences, missiles and flares being thrown at them'.[5]

As the 21-year-old chief steward of the protest, I found myself on *BBC News* at around 10.00 am being confronted with the fact that Prince Charles and Camilla Parker-Bolls's Rolls Royce had been intercepted and brought to a standstill on Regents' Street by a mob of students while on its way to the Royal Variety Performance at the London Palladium. They rocked the car back and forth and, as the *Evening Standard* breathlessly revealed two days later, lightly prodded Camilla with a placard stick. Shouts of 'off with their heads' could be heard on the footage which quickly found its way onto Twitter. Would I condemn the violence of the protesters, the presenter demanded? With the battle lines drawn, there was only one answer I could give: 'no'.

A rebellion at the 'End of History'

The student movement of 2010 was a rebellion at the 'End of History'. Francis Fukuyama's 1989 essay, which was expanded into a book entitled *The End of History and The Last Man*, consolidated a triumphalist mood that had set in among many Western politicians and intellectuals following the fall of the Berlin Wall, advancing an argument that the world was moving unstoppably towards a state of equilibrium in which liberal democracy would be recognized as the end point of human development. Thinkers on the left were, in parallel, wrestling with the same reality: 'It seems to be easier for us today to imagine the thoroughgoing deterioration of the earth and of nature than the breakdown of late capitalism', Marxist theorist Fredric Jameson famously wrote in 1994; 'perhaps that is due to some weakness in our imaginations'.[6] Just two years before the student protests took place, in what would become a highly influential text among the new political generation that emerged in the 2010s, Mark Fisher went a step further, theorizing the idea that we were living in an era of 'capitalist realism' characterized by 'the widespread sense that not only is capitalism the only viable political and economic system, but also that it is now impossible even to *imagine* a coherent alternative to it'.[7]

This trend had soaked into every pore of mainstream Western culture – its films, art and public spaces, and in the political sphere an even narrower consensus had taken hold. The period since the collapse of the Soviet Union, which coincided with the decline of the labour movement following the defeat of the miners' strike, had seen a dramatic rightward shift in British politics. Thatcherism and the neoliberal economic model it pursued, once the radical outlier, had become a religion across the mainstream.

When it came to power in 1997, New Labour's fresh investment in public services acted for many progressives as compensation for its final break with the vestiges of social democracy. Tony Blair was open about the fact that he viewed Margaret Thatcher as an inspiration, and New Labour did things which the Tories had never dared to do in their eighteen years in office, deepening privatization in the NHS, transport and other public services. As if to confirm his status as a true believer in the End of History, Gordon Brown announced 'the end of boom and bust' and ensured that the City of London enjoyed rock-bottom levels of regulation. New Labour also, of course, introduced university tuition fees and pioneered the academization of schools.

Along with a consensus on policy came a narrative. With very few exceptions in parliament and the media, it was taken as gospel that private sector innovation was more efficient than the lumbering, bureaucratic public sector and that the only possible direction of travel was the deeper and deeper penetration of public services by private providers and user contributions. Unprecedented inequality was the price we had to pay for having a dynamic economy, and high corporate profits were synonymous with prosperity for everyone. Most journalists and centre-left politicians reproduced as fact a historical perspective that could have been lifted from a Conservative Party press release in the 1980s: Thatcher had saved Britain from economic ruin by destroying the power of the trade unions, and any notion of Labour presenting the electorate with an alternative point of view was brushed aside with reference to its humiliating defeat in the 1983 general election (and its left-wing manifesto in that year, famously dubbed 'the longest suicide note in history'), which was by now almost three decades ago. When Labour lost elections – in 2010 and in 2015 – it was widely understood within the mainstream commentariat that it did so because it was too left wing and had not sufficiently distanced itself from the trade unions and the modest remnants of its commitment to public investment and ownership.

This narrative was characterized not just by its ubiquity but by its aggressive tone. To place oneself outside of the consensus was to risk isolation and ridicule. This atmosphere was most suffocating in the United Kingdom and the United States, because of both their centrality to world capitalism and their voting systems, which prevented the radical left from gaining an electoral foothold outside of the main parties.

The old world clung on by its fingertips. Tony Benn, the 85-year-old veteran of the Labour left, toured the country making the same speech about the creation of the post-war welfare state. Seamas Milne, who had edited the *Guardian's Opinion* section for six years, was a prominent critic of the War on Terror but, like many left wingers of his generation, confined to the margins. In parliament, a handful of MPs – among them Jeremy Corbyn, John McDonnell and Diane Abbott – had outlasted Blair's attempts to purge the left from the Labour Party but in truth barely anyone would have recognized them on a university campus in the autumn of 2010, let alone in a school or college. Abbott was perhaps the most prominent, having just received around 7 per cent of the vote in the 2010 Labour leadership election. So far right had the party moved that by the time Gordon Brown left office, some of the most reliable critics of New Labour from the left – on the Iraq War, rapidly growing inequality and civil liberties – were people like Polly Toynbee, Roy Hattersley and Shirley Williams, who in the 1980s had either been stalwarts of the Labour Right or had split from the party altogether to create the Social Democratic Party.

Within the broadcast media, Paul Mason, then *Newsnight*'s economics editor, was one of the few journalists who consciously stood outside the prevailing consensus. Born at the tail end of the baby boomer generation, Mason was the product of the former strength of the British left. He was the son and grandson of Lancashire miners, and some of his earliest memories are of attending a miners' gala in Leigh: 'Almost everyone on that field, of which there were tens of thousands, was employed by the state, they lived in houses owned by the state and they consumed gas and electricity provided by the state at almost no cost', he reflects. 'Until about 1972', he says, 'you lived in a world in which things basically seemed OK. Progress happened. There was free school milk, free school meals, free dentistry.' Then, over the course of the 1970s, things changed. Mason has vivid memories of the three-day week, 'having to be let out of school because there were no street lights. There used to be an indoor market in Bolton where I went to school, and stupidly they kept it open – so it was an indoor market in complete darkness, and we used to run in in school uniforms and steal everything.'

He was heavily embedded in the northern soul music scene and by his mid-teens was attending all-nighters in the Wigan Casino ('you had to queue from midnight to 2.00 am in this boisterous, violent crowd which was full of weird Scottish hard men, and then people would dance till 8.00 am, lots of them speeded up to their eyeballs'). But seeing Ken Loach's early work being on the TV and growing up in Leigh, being political was a fact of life. 'It was the tail end of a period of radicalisation', he says, 'a kind of working class syndicalism – and it was everywhere in life. All my cousins were shop stewards.' One day, he was walking down the street with his girlfriend and fifteen police vans went screaming past him. 'I got home and on the radio and it said that the ANL [Anti-Nazi League] had been fighting the National Front in Bolton.' In the era of Rock Against Racism, Mason identified with the anti-fascist movement ('I never attended any meetings, but I went to demos and I had all the stickers – that kind of thing'), and between his experiences of growing up and his discovery of the *The Communist Manifesto* in his school library, he arrived at university in Sheffield already semi-politicized. Mason's second year coincided with the steel strike, one of the great early confrontations between Thatcher and the unions, and he was at the Hadfield pickets. 'I turned up at 5 am, having walked overnight to get there', he says, 'and the police form this wedge attack on the pickets, it's one of the first times ever the police were used in that way. But then Scargill turns up with an equally massive wedge of miners, and the next minute all these policemen are being carted away with their arms in slings or in ambulances.' Mason was arrested himself, though was released pretty immediately.

Right in the middle of the steel strike, Mason joined Workers' Power, one of the smaller Trotskyist organizations in circulation. 'They were the ones who seemed to me to respect intellectuality, they weren't a cult, they respected ideas', he says. He would go on to be a leading member of Workers' Power and would stay in the organization for two decades, though by the time he was recruited by the BBC after a period as deputy editor of *Computer Weekly*, he had grown disillusioned with Leninism. 'By that point I had left the left, though of course the left hadn't left me.' The consensus that ruled politics in Britain and across the Western world – and which had sunk deep into the psyche of the centre-left – regarded a background like Mason's as a silly, youthful dalliance with the politics of the past, but it was precisely his training in the radical left which enabled him to grasp what was happening in the aftermath of the financial crash. 'You have to remember', he says, 'that the BBC is full of people who say things like "the middle way is always best, the path of least resistance is the way to success". They all believed in the End of History. I was in the US covering the downturn and the Lehman Brothers crash happened while I was there. Every day you'd wake up saying to them "X is going to happen" and they'd come back to you and say "are you sure? It doesn't say that in the FT" – and by tea time it would have happened. The Marxists among us were basically always right.'

In the post-crash era, Mason was on the front line covering mass movements and revolutions as they interacted with the new economic realities and for the first time with social media. 'With the Green Revolution in Iran', he says, 'I noticed that Twitter, rather than just being able to report like Facebook did, could actually influence events.' Revolts, he observed, were becoming more networked, horizontal and less hierarchical. In the autumn and winter of 2010, he would be presented with a real-life example much closer to home.

The 2008 financial crash ought to have blunted the hubris of the political establishment. The UK handled the world in financial deregulation and dependence on the finance sector: by 2007, 35 per cent of all global trades took place in the City of London, making it by far the biggest trading centre in the world. When the entire system came tumbling down under the weight of its own greed and lack of rules, free-market orthodoxy was suddenly abandoned in favour of a government bailout package which almost doubled the UK's debt-to-GDP ratio.[8] This was a crisis of capitalism and of the state finances unseen since the Great Depression of 1929. It demonstrated in a spectacular way both that capitalism had not transcended boom and bust and that the political consensus that favoured giving capital increasingly unbridled freedom to make profit at the expense of all else was unsustainable and damaging to the rest of us.

And yet the political consensus that was created under the joint leadership of Margaret Thatcher and Tony Blair remained dominant in the late 2000s. Instead of breaking down, it mutated into a new consensus around the need for cuts to public spending to pay for the bailout. By the autumn of 2010, Labour, the Lib Dems and the Conservatives were all committed to deep austerity at slightly different paces, and no major party spoke seriously about a policy of public ownership or wealth redistribution. With the help of a compliant media and a Labour leadership seemingly unable to articulate an alternative, the Conservatives managed to turn a crisis that was so obviously the fault of the banking system into a narrative about profligate public spending under Labour. Bankers even managed to keep their bonuses, which shrank only slightly from £9 billion to £7 billion between 2008 and 2010.[9] As sections of the public began to feel that something was wrong, this naked injustice gave the student movement of 2010, and all of the movements that followed it, the window they needed for a counter-narrative. What is astonishing is that the new consensus persisted all the way until 2015. Any alternative – and certainly any political project of the radical left – remained a fringe curiosity.

It would take another seismic series of events, and the election of Jeremy Corbyn as Labour leader, to finally break the hold of Thatcherism and austerity over British politics, and if the generation of young Corbynistas seemed experienced at fighting and breaking a political consensus, it was because they had done it once already. The people who came of age in the 2010 student movement – and who were kettled and beaten in the Battle of Parliament Square – were born around the same time that the Berlin Wall fell. We grew up in an era in which a left-wing alternative to Toryism or Third Way centrism was regarded as a joke or an anachronism. Now, against the backdrop of a multifaceted crisis of the economy and politics, hundreds of thousands of students would fight toe to toe with the state and what they perceived as the entirety of the political establishment. It was, in so many ways, the moment that defined a generation – and it was a clarion call to other sections of society, to the unions and to previous generations of radicals who would form part of the even bigger events that followed. Movements against the Iraq War and profit-driven globalization had all come and gone and had played a crucial role in laying the foundations of what was to come. But in the autumn of 2010, Britain's streets witnessed the reassertion of class politics by a generation of people who were widely thought to be incapable of even thinking in those terms. Their very existence shattered the idea that no alternative existed.

The generalized nature of the government's austerity agenda in 2010 lent itself to the development of a movement much wider than just students and lecturers.

Following the formation of Conservative-Liberal Democrat government, Britain's first coalition government since the Second World War, twenty-three of its twenty-nine Cabinet members were millionaires.[10] In October, Chancellor George Osborne published a Comprehensive Spending Review which outlined the scale of the cuts. In an effort to eliminate the budget deficit in five years, around half a million public sector jobs were to be axed, part of an average cut of 19 per cent in each government department. The retirement age was to rise, and £7 billion of additional welfare cuts were outlined, much of which would hit the disabled and carers. Every aspect of life was to be squeezed. The NHS and schools were, to begin with, supposed to be ringfenced, partly as a result of Liberal Democrat bargaining and partly because David Cameron was keen to convince the public, in truly Orwellian style, that the Conservatives were 'the party of the NHS' – but these guarantees would prove worthless in the firestorm that was to follow.

Higher and further education was where the axe would fall hardest and first. In the dying days of the Gordon Brown government, Peter Mandelson had commissioned the former chief executive of BP, Lord Browne, to conduct a review of the existing higher education funding model which everyone – government, university managements and the National Union of Students (NUS) – agreed was unsustainable and regressive. Chaired by a loud advocate of market economics, aided by a panel dominated by business leaders and university managers, and taking place in an atmosphere in which all major parties accepted that cuts to public spending were necessary, the outcome seemed inevitable. The Review's recommendation, that universities be allowed to charge unlimited fees, was watered down by the Coalition to a mere tripling of the cap from £3,225 to £9,000, but the overall vision was not. Under the leadership of Universities Minister David Willetts, the Coalition proposed the fee rise as part of an open attempt to marketize the sector. Government funding was to be wiped out for the arts, humanities and social sciences, while teaching grants to institutions were cut by 80 per cent overall.

This was a wholesale privatization of universities' income streams and a huge shift in the burden of paying for education onto students and their families in the form of debt. Crucially for the student movement, this policy was announced at the same time as the abolition of Education Maintenance Allowance (EMA), a weekly payment of £30 per week to working class school and further education students. In 2010, it was being paid out to something like 647,000 teenagers, and in cities like Birmingham and Leicester, four-fifths of sixteen-year-olds were in receipt of it.[11] Along with high youth unemployment (around one in five 18–24 years olds were out of work in 2010, the highest rate on record[12]), these two policies would unite a vast coalition of university students, school students and unemployed youth.

James Meadway would go on to be John McDonnell's chief economic advisor during the Corbyn years. He was in 2010 a PhD student at SOAS and a prominent organizer in the movement. Writing at the time, he summed up the situation:

> having agreed to socialize the costs of the banking system in the last crisis, we have also implicitly agreed to take on the costs of the next crisis – and the next, and the one after that. But British capitalism simply isn't big or dynamic enough to afford both a financial sector of this bloated size and other public services. The state cannot fund both.
>
> So a question is posed: Do we fund the City of London, or do we fund public services? This Coalition of millionaires has unabashedly chosen the former. That compels it to squeeze as much spending out of the state as possible. That means, for higher education, a lurch towards outright privatisation – throwing universities back into the private sector, with all the consequences for access and inequality this creates.[13]

The whole package of education reforms was, quite straightforwardly, a betrayal of the Liberal Democrats' election promise to introduce free higher education and was seen as such. Each and every Lib Dem MP had signed a NUS pledge to 'vote against any increase in fees in the next parliament', and they had benefited from a huge youth and student vote as a result. On election night, as the Lib Dems received their biggest share of the vote since the Liberal-SDP alliance of 1983, camera crews filmed queues outside polling stations in Nick Clegg's Sheffield Hallam constituency where irate students were turned away as voting closed. His volte-face on the issue was something to behold, and within a few months of his arrival into the office of deputy prime minister, he was in the House of Commons describing the government policy as 'fair and progressive solution to a very difficult problem'. As part of the Coalition Agreement, Clegg had the option to abstain on the proposals but with the zeal of a convert threw himself into backing them.

Seven years later, Nick Clegg would lose his seat to Labour in the general election of 2017, as the students and graduates of Sheffield Hallam turned from Cleggmania to Corbynism. For now, the Coalition government, with the full support of the Lib Dem leadership, was set on pushing through a series of policies which would see Britain's universities 'transformed into a patchwork of academic supermarkets'[14] in which students took on mortgage-sized debts in order to study and many working class teenagers would lose their EMA. Up against them was a generation of students and young people renowned for their apathy, who had never known an alternative to the onward march of market economics.

Only the beginning

In response to the threat of the Browne Review and the first Conservative-led government in thirteen years, the NUS and the lecturers' union UCU pulled together to organize what would become a gigantic mobilization of students and education workers on 10 November 2020. Convoys of coaches carried students south from every corner of the country, and a series of feeder marches brought more from London campuses into the protest, acting as a rallying point for the student left and many of those who were inclined to civil disobedience. The bright autumn weather helped the turnout, and by the time the free education feeder march reached Trafalgar Square, the whole of Westminster was already gridlocked, awash with banners and placards, many of them home-made, and reverberating with the noise of a thousand overlapping chants and the background hum of hundreds of vuvuzelas, which had come into fashion after the South African World Cup that summer. The day's most popular chant, which would be sung out to the tune of 'Oh My Darling, Clementine' with varying degrees of playfulness and venom throughout the autumn, captured the simmering mood:

> Build a bonfire, build a bonfire
> Put the To-ories on the top
> Put the Lib Dems in the middle
> And we'll bu-urn the fucking lot

The NUS estimated that 52,000 had taken to the streets, making it the biggest student protest in more than a generation. Judging from aerial footage and the general difficulty in counting numbers on protests once they reach a certain size, there could well have been more, but the really crucial thing was how it ended. As the march crawled past parliament and towards the rally point like a slow-motion flood, it went past the Millbank Tower complex, home to Conservative Party headquarters. In a moment of collective inspiration that seemed to happen all at once, thousands of protesters swarmed into the courtyard of the complex and began massing outside the glass-fronted building at 30 Millbank, building a literal bonfire of placards. Music blared out from speakers, and the courtyard filled with an impossibly loud roar that made the windows shake. Eventually, the glass began to break.

As the crowds poured into the foyer and headed up the stairs, some Conservative Party workers barricaded the first and second floors, while others fled from a fire escape. The riot moved up through the building and onto the roof, systematically wrecking the offices it moved through, painting slogans on the wall and smashing computers and furniture. At one point, a TV was sent down to the foyer in the lift and hurled through one of the last remaining window panes. And then, from the roof, came the moment that could have ended the student movement before it began, as one protester dropped a fire extinguisher from the top of the building. From the ground, the crowd responded in unison with boos and a chant of 'stop throwing shit'; this was not wanton destruction but a carefully and collectively understood exercise in political mayhem.

The occupiers of Millbank had a message of their own, sent to journalists from the roof by text message: 'this is only the beginning of the resistance to the destruction of our education system and public services.'[15]

Outside, the mood was one of euphoria, panic and disbelief – depending on who you were. 'I remember being at Millbank and feeling both completely thrilled and terrified', says Ash Sarkar. 'You see the glass breaking, and you realise that what's happening here isn't just anger. There is a break between your generation and the institutions that confer political legitimacy. It was a feeling of operating outside the bounds of normal politics.'

Many left-wing student activists knew that building a mass movement would require a spectacle – a moment, however symbolic, which sent a signal of disobedience and revolt. But none of us had expected or organized anything on the scale of the Millbank riot, and all of our plans, cooked up in secretive meetings in seminar rooms in Bloomsbury in the weeks leading up to the protest, had failed. Whitehall was too crowded to make an occupation of the Treasury or the Department of Education work, and plans to lead a breakaway march were foiled as the organizers failed to wade through the dense crowd in time to meet each other. Another group staged a short-lived occupation of the Department for Business, Innovation and Skills (BIS) but was quickly isolated and evicted by riot police.[16]

As it turns out, the rank and file of the protest was far more militant – far more willing not only think the unthinkable but also to do the undoable – than all of the seasoned activists of the organized left put together. The signal they sent, both to the world and, more importantly, to young people and students across the country, was one of defiance, transgression and collective determination. This was the birth of a movement that would fight to win and break the rules if necessary, and in their own way everyone recognized it. David Cameron took a break from his trade mission in Beijing to call for the 'full force of the law' to be brought to bear against the rioters. And the march, initially scheduled to get an average showing in the press, was on every front page and news bulletin in the country.

After Jeremy Corbyn's election as Labour leader, Hattie Craig would become a Momentum activist and a core organizer for The World Transformed, the new Labour left's annual festival around Labour Party conference. In 2010, she was a sixth-form student from Northampton who had managed to get to London on a university coach, and as she and a group of friends reached Millbank they were stopped by an NUS steward. 'Trying to warn us off, she gestured along the route towards the rally point and said "that way is the demonstration; behind me is a riot"', remembers Craig. 'Well, we obviously wanted to go to the riot.'

Joe Ryle was a first-year student at Leeds University who had already been politicized by climate activism. 'I remember doing an interview with Sky News on the day Millbank got smashed up', he recalls, 'and we were all using that line – "this is only the beginning". That was a really strong message – that this movement's not going away, it's not just a one-off protest.' Within a year, he had dropped out of university and was campaigning full time against Heathrow expansion where he met the local MP, John McDonnell. Eventually, McDonnell would offer him a temporary job in parliament, and when McDonnell was appointed as shadow chancellor in 2015, Ryle was one of the first people called in by his office to manage press engagements. 'I remember thinking of the student protests, and I particularly remember thinking the day that Tory HQ got smashed up', he reflects, 'this is power. This is how you have power and have impact and get noticed.'

As well as providing the spark which set that autumn alight, Millbank also provided the generation of 2010 with its first practical lesson in the inadequacy of the left's formal institutions. First in line was the NUS. Since the mid-1990s, the internal politics had been dominated by the National Organisation of Labour Students (NOLS), often described as the 'shock troops' of New Labour, and it was from the periphery of NOLS that NUS's leadership was drawn. The NUS leadership's plan was to be a credible voice on the inside of the debate now taking place in Westminster, not to build a transformative social movement. The Millbank riot cut right across this strategy, and Aaron Porter, the union's president, responded accordingly. Going live on air in the aftermath of the protest, he condemned it as 'despicable'.

Porter's condemnation of Millbank was only the first in a series of moves which completely cut off the NUS from the student movement of 2010. The movement against austerity would suffer similar failures of leadership on the part of some trade unions, and Ed Miliband's Labour Party would never truly take up its cause. In time, those who took to the streets would come to the conclusion that they would have to transform their own institutions; in 2010, the mood was quite different.

In the absence of the NUS, the task of coordinating the movement would fall to less established grassroots organizations and to the network of campus occupations that sprung up in the weeks after Millbank which communicated regularly by Skype and social media. The National Campaign Against Fees and Cuts (NCAFC) was the most prominent alternative centre of coordination, set up in February 2010 to coordinate as a series of campus anti-cuts campaigns that had kicked off earlier in the year when some vice chancellors had responded eagerly to talk of cuts to the universities' budget under New Labour. It brought together a broad political alliance that included organized socialists, anarchists, young Green Party members, a tiny number of left-wing Labour members and a large number of unaligned left activists. Also present during the autumn was the Education Activist Network, in essence a 'front' – a campaigning organization set up and controlled by the Socialist Workers Party (SWP) – which held large conferences and top-table rallies in London, benefitting from an especially big base among academic staff and a disciplined cadre of students across a number of university campuses. The NUS's autonomous campaigns for Black and LGBT students also played a role in providing an alternative base of leadership.

In London, all of the strands of the movement would join forces to form the London Student Assembly. These assemblies, which would take place every Sunday at 4.00 pm in the University of London Union, would at the height of the movement attract hundreds of students from all over the city and would play a pivotal role in coordinating days of action and marches in the capital.

The truth, however, is that 2010 was a genuinely leaderless movement. As one of the co-founders of the NCAFC and a full-time student union officer at UCL, I sometimes found myself playing a spokesperson role around the protests, as did University of London Union president Clare Solomon, SWP organizer Mark Bergfeld and a number of prominent university occupiers. But despite the media's need to identify leaders, all of us were undeniably passengers in a much bigger sea of events that swept us along. On one level, the NCAFC had come into its own; its aim of providing a non-sectarian and democratic space, not dominated by any one group or committee, allowed it to become the default home for many new activists. Throughout the autumn of 2010, it existed more as a brand than as an organization. Inspired by the Millbank riot, students at universities and schools which had seen no political activity in many years, if ever, looked at the NCAFC's website for updates on the next day of action and reproduced its logo and contact details on badly designed leaflets as they prepared walkouts and occupations.

The backbone of the protests, the working class further education students who swarmed across the UK's city centres, had almost certainly never been to an organizing meeting. No organization could contain them, their anger or their energy, and no leadership could have held them back, even if it had wanted to. The idea of them following any leader or set of leaders, let alone a leader of the Labour Party, would have been met with derision. Young people were, as UCL Occupation resident Laurie Penny wrote bluntly in the *Guardian*, 'unlikely to pay even a penny to a vacillating, pro-business party to be "our voice".[17] History was being written not by political hacks or MPs but by a whirlwind of feet rushing through the cold autumn air, often with a mobile sound system providing a backing track to the task of dodging police lines. The most that those of us who wanted to coordinate the movement centrally could do was to name dates for days of action, prepare the minority of students we could reach and talk to the media.

The streets erupt

The first day of action after Millbank was called by a London meeting of the NCAFC in late October, attended by around thirty people, most of them from a handful of posh universities in Bloomsbury. In the room was Edward Maltby, a recent Cambridge graduate who had just moved to London to work as an organizer for the socialist group Workers' Liberty and had played a crucial role in setting up the NCAFC on what might have been his way out of student politics. That autumn, with his phone number on the organization's leaflets and website, his was the voice that greeted countless calls from excited and panicked groups of school students on the verge of walking out of class and university students contemplating starting a campus occupation. When the proposal to call for a national day of walkouts at some point after the NUS march was raised in the meeting, Maltby initially opposed it.

I just thought we would look ridiculous to call for a walkout, because not enough people would answer the call – bringing out tens of thousands of people was just not the kind of thing we can make happen. But the events at Millbank themselves were also unimaginable: if I'd been in a meeting before November 10th and someone had said 'I've got 100 people who are up for anything, and fancy getting arrested', I wouldn't have suggested they do what was done that day, because running a demolition and removals services for CCHQ was just not a part of the direct-action repertoire of our movement. All of a sudden, we entered this period, in Lenin's phrase the 'weeks in which decades happen', and it's just understood you won't get much sleep. I entered emergency mode and stayed there for over a month.

Every seasoned activist who has been present in a moment of mass awakening – whether in the student movement of 2010, the Egyptian revolution at Tahrir Square or the moment when Occupy Wall Street took flight – can describe this sensation. You spend half your life sweating and toiling, and issuing a call for something to happen, and then, suddenly, it does – and on a scale and with a force you could never quite have imagined. Eventually, the meeting voted to organize for a day of walkouts on 24 November, and this call would be taken up not only by Maltby but by all of the assorted networks and left groups that had continued to mobilize in NUS's absence.

The task of promoting the day of action online and in the media fell to Joana Ramiro, a 22-year-old Portuguese activist who had led an occupation of the London College of Communication the year before and had also been involved in setting up the NCAFC. In 2010, she was the organization's press officer and spent much of her time rushing between protests and occupations and her Soho apartment, where she would write up the day's events and issue statements condemning police tactics. In the run up to the 24 November, she started what was one of the first attempts to use viral social media content for political ends. 'At the time I didn't think much about it', she says. 'I suppose now you'd call it a meme – we asked people to take a selfie holding up a piece of paper that said "24th November – walk out" and post it on social media.' The selfies spread like wildfire across Facebook and Twitter.

On 24 November, Joana Ramiro faced a barrage of press phone calls, and, in an effort to estimate turnout, she sat in her living room frantically tallying up the numbers on dozens of different Facebook events. In the end, journalists did their own counting and found that something like 130,000 students were on the streets – the biggest day of student protest in British history. Town centres were shut down as the spectacle of student protest which had filled television screens two weeks previously landed in town centres everywhere. Two hundred students blocked traffic in Morcambe. Lime Street Station in Liverpool was blockaded. In Milton Keynes they marched on the Town Hall. Further education students sat down in the road in Winchester. Thousands more marched through pretty much every major city in the UK, some of them with a planned route and support from older activists and organized left groups, others with nothing more than a sudden sense of collective agency and a plan to cause disruption.

In London, a 'Carnival of Resistance' was organized, led by University of London Union president Clare Solomon and a growing network of activists across Bloomsbury. At the front of the Carnival as it set off was a hand-painted banner, designed to unite the march and prevent the various factions rushing to the front with their own banners. Its slogan, painted in graffiti style, was the same as the line that had resonated two weeks previously: 'this is only the beginning'. Only there was an 'n' missing, so it read, 'this is only the begineing'. Determined to reassert their authority after the occupation of Millbank, the police turned out in vast numbers and moved to kettle the London march. We eventually ended up trapped in Whitehall for many hours, as the police pushed the crowd away from parliament, first with batons and then with horse charges. At some point after 10.00 pm, with many having gone without access to food, water or toilets, the students were released. Many found their panicked parents waiting outside.

Meanwhile, campus occupations took off decisively. Royal Holloway was the first to occupy on the day, as students took over space in the Founder's Building. Plymouth went next and then Birmingham, whose activists went into the Aston Webb Building and warned, in a pre-prepared statement, that 'the government must understand that if they continue to destroy the livelihoods of the majority to benefit the rich and powerful minority, they will face increasingly widespread and radical action'.[18]

A host of others followed. In Leeds, Joe Ryle and a group of other organizers led a crowd of about two thousand people into occupation at the university armed with a sound system, despite efforts by police to block their way. At UCL, hundreds of students descended on the Jeremy Bentham Room, levering security out of the way with a bongo drum ensemble, where they would remain for the next fifteen days. Owen Jones had, alongside fellow occupier Jess Riches, spent the afternoon setting up the UCL Occupation's Twitter and Facebook accounts and its blog. With the new occupation looking for messages of support, he dropped a text message to his old boss, John McDonnell.

McDonnell arrived early in the evening, conveying apologies from Jeremy Corbyn, who had a prior engagement at a Palestine solidarity meeting. 'I just want to congratulate you on what you've done', he said:

> What's happening is that large numbers of students are saying 'we've had enough, and we're not willing to take it any more'. We fought over generations for the right of free education, and these bastards are going to take it off us. And what this is all about is ensuring they don't. You're having that effect – whatever they say, whatever Clegg says.
>
> If governments won't listen, and if politicians lie, there is no other way but to resort to the streets, no other way in which we can register our voice. And I wanted to say: well done. [...] And what you're doing isn't just amongst students. You've given courage and determination to trade unionists fighting for their jobs and others that are campaigning for justice in their own fields. I think you've sparked off a new generation of protest in this country, but also a new belief that people can assert their rights when politicians ignore them.[19]

As he finished speaking in the UCL's Jeremy Bentham Room, the occupiers erupted with applause, and he then left, apologizing for the fact that he had to return to parliament, or as he put it 'that place which William Morris wanted to turn into a place to store detritus'. Earlier in the day, McDonnell had joined the student protest in central London and intervened in Whitehall as the police kettle closed in, sitting down and linking arms with students in front of a row of police horses.

Speaking to McDonnell now, you get the sense of a man who has stood in front of so many police lines that he can barely remember the individual occurrences. His whole adult life – from trade union organizing, to being deputy leader of the radical Greater London Council in the 1980s, to keeping the flame alive through the Blair years – he had dedicated himself to the task of giving voice to mass movements and rank-and-file trade unionists and linking them to a wider political project. 'So in 2010 when it started kicking off', he says, 'it was just the natural place to be.' By and large, the students of 2010 did not view their revolt in party political terms. They did not look to parliament for allies or a strategy, and they certainly did not view Labour as an organization they might one day join. But it is not difficult to see how this generation of young, angry people who hated the political establishment and wanted to overturn the system in its entirety might one day regard John McDonnell as a leader. After all, that's what he wanted to do, too, and he told them so himself.

As the movement headed into its next day of action on 30 November, both the weather and the mood of the protesters intensified. More campuses were occupied, and coordination between disparate groups of students began to take shape as occupations, school walkout organizers and the organized left started talking to each other. In Birmingham, students from three different universities were in constant touch with each other after an organizer from Birmingham City University had shown up at the Birmingham University occupation with a band from the conservatoire who played for the students who were living in the Aston Webb Building. On 30 November, they would combine with hundreds of school students to pull off an occupation of City Hall.

In London, reacting to police kettling, the street protests switched to swarming around the centre of the city in as many different directions as possible, making disruption rather than the symbolism of a march on parliament the primary focus. With sleet and snow falling heavily around them, groups of a few hundred students and pupils jogged their way down the Mall, Oxford Street, the Barbican, Victoria and all over the square mile of the City of London.

In the 'cat and mouse' protest of 30 November, many of the demonstrators were living out their ambition to break free of the standard A to B march that had always dominated the tradition of British dissent. Many of the university students who played an organizing role in 2010 – me included – had been in their mid-teens as the Iraq War broke out and had themselves walked out of school and college to join the protests in their local towns and cities. Those protests grew and grew, until on 15 February 2003, London was home to a record-breaking march of two million people. But as well as being inspired by the experience of taking part, the biggest lesson that many of us had taken from that period was the impotence of polite dissent. No matter how big the protest, no matter how great the moral resolution of those present, we concluded, governments could ignore anything that did not disrupt. The property damage and direct action of the 2010 protests escalated in response to police tactics and was fundamentally driven by the failure of the democratic process to deliver on its promises, but it was also informed by the experience of the older generation of student protesters, who were haunted by the legacy of the anti-war movement and its failure. James Butler, an Oxford University student, summed up the mood eloquently on his blog in the immediate aftermath of the student movement:

> To break with the traditional model of dissent is also to find a freedom in one's targets; things without the bounds of 'traditional' and easily-neutralised protest.

The image of a red and black flag over Millbank, or the wave of innovative occupations, or a stick in the ribs of Camila: these things should send an uncompromising message that we're not acting out a puppet theatre politics, where we stick to the hollow ghost of real protest, which has been relied on to prop up the mythic pluralist bedrock of a sham 'democracy' for decades.[20]

Along with Aaron Bastani and Ash Sarkar who met in the UCL Occupation ('we just bickered', laughs Sarkar), James Butler would in the years that followed set up Novara Media, which would eventually become British left's most successful alternative media project.

The endgame

The moment for building a new kind of street movement was cut short, or rather put on hold, by that ultimate harbinger of conventional politics, the parliamentary timetable. On Thursday, 2 December, the government announced that it would push for a vote on tuition fees on 9 December, in exactly one week, and there was nothing for it but to throw everything at a march on parliament.

For days all over the country, there seemed to be an interminable number of mass meetings, the rooms packed and sweaty and the atmosphere full of adrenaline and mad ideas. A long debate at the London Student Assembly established a name for the final protest, 'Shut Down London', and these three words spread like a virus across the capital in the days before the protest – on leaflets and posters and on walls and bridges in spray paint and chalk. In the campus occupations, many took the slogan literally. Working groups were tasked with coming up with elaborate plans to shut down the rail network. Groups of co-conspirators talked breathlessly in university corridors about the possibility of organizing an oil slick, or the dumping of millions of ball bearings, across Euston Road and the M25 in order to stop the city functioning. I remember an argument at one of the UCL Occupation's twice-daily general assemblies about the idea of physically blockading Conservative MPs in their homes on the morning of the vote in the hope of slimming the government's likely majority. In what became a comical game of radical one-upmanship by political factions, one SWP organizer implored one of the London meetings 'to make this march a torchlit procession on Parliament, and burn the fucker down'. The room cheered him on, and the *Sky News* journalist who was covering the event seemed at a loss as to what to do: it was almost too mad to broadcast.

Eventually, all of the more hair-brained schemes were dismissed, deemed either unworkable or unethical, and the plan became about getting as many students to march as humanly possible – not an easy task given the hostility of NUS and some students' unions and the gruelling experience that many people had already had at the hands of the police. That experience, and the widespread sense that the frictions between the police and students were reaching a crescendo, led many activists to make special measures. Teenagers and freshers, many of whom had voted Lib Dem in May and had not been particularly exercised about politics until a few weeks previously, donned hard hats and bicycle helmets and clutched their flagpoles and placard sticks like amateurish infantry soldiers. Activists from older generations toured occupations and seminar rooms across the country offering workshops in first aid, legal observing and methods by which desperate crowds might stand a chance of breaking out of a kettle. Inspired by Italian students, who were at the same time fighting Berlusconi's education reforms, a collective of artists and students brought together the 'Book Block', formed out of protective human-sized replicas of famous book covers.[21]

On 9 December, the Book Block would play a crucial role in providing a protective barrier between the police and the less prepared sections of the march. Esoteric home-made placards and the banners of trade union branches, Marxist sects and fledgling community anti-cuts groups would be joined on the front lines by five-foot-tall colourful shields bearing the titles of *One Dimensional Man*, *The Coming Insurrection* and *Catch 22*. Adorno, Subcommandante Marcos and Derida all featured. So too did Joyce, Shelley, Dante, Beckett, Homer, Huxley, Dostoyevsky and, capturing the surreal spirit of the day, *Just William*.

The NUS had other ideas. Having refused to support much of the action thus far, its leadership organized its own 'vigil for education' round the corner from Parliament Square on Embankment. There it would amass a few hundred of the most conservative student union officers from around the country to listen to speeches from an open top bus. Either because of the weather forecast or because they fell foul of a risk assessment, candles were eschewed in favour of glow sticks, which, years later when I was a dissident member of the organization's national executive, would still clutter NUS's headquarters. In NUS's continued absence, the protest was formally called by NCAFC and others, and I had been appointed as its chief steward by the London Student Assembly, while others took on the task of speaking at the opening rally on Malet Street. The mood of the crowd and its impatience to march on parliament can be best illustrated by the fact that, as world-renowned poet and novelist Ben Okri took to the stage, a young protester hurled a football at him in an effort to cut the rally short.

The only protest route which we could get the police to agree was one which ended at the NUS's glowstick-lit vigil after marching down Horseguards Avenue. Officially, this meant that the march was supposed to enter Parliament Square but then immediately leave it, turning up Whitehall and round onto the Embankment. Unofficially, we knew that this was never going to happen. As the stewards at the front of the protest reached the Square, they peeled off to reveal row after row of Book Block shields and university occupiers, who tore down the six-foot-tall fences as students rushed into the Square and towards parliament. The only thing separating them from the MPs voting on the fee rise would be row after row of riot police, batons raised. And the horses, and if necessary the army. In fact, we had been bluntly informed by police during negotiations over the route of the march that if the crowd managed to get into parliamentary estate, armed police would be authorized to open fire.

Simon Hannah, a mature student at Westminster University, would become a prominent activist in Corbyn's Labour Party and the author of a number of books on the Poll Tax riots and the Labour left. On 9 December, he and I were the only two identifiable senior stewards at the front of the protest as the fences were being smashed down and found ourselves surrounded by police doing a two-man march up the rest of the agreed route. As official organizers, we had kept ourselves deliberately ignorant of any plans for direct action, but we knew that the march would not follow us. 'There was this wonderful moment', he recalls, 'when I realised "Michael, we're the chief steward and deputy chief steward, but no one here even knows that – we're just two guys in yellow bibs". We'd done our job and we'd reached Parliament Square, and leadership was just with the crowd.'

Returning to the protest some minutes later, having briefly visited the NUS's sparsely populated vigil and evaded our police escort, we gathered as many stewards as we could. We had evidently lost control of the situation, and being identifiable as a steward on a march that had gone off route would make anyone wearing hi-viz liable for arrest. And so, sending one last message over the radios, we took off our bibs and melted into the crowd.

Generation desperation

Many of the students who poured into Parliament Square on 9 December knew that they were marching into battle, though many of course did not. As they shivered in the kettle and felt the full force of the state collide with their fragile skulls and limbs, they did not know that their revolt would trigger a much wider social movement against austerity, and they certainly had no idea that it was part of a series of events that would one day transform politics from the inside. In retrospect, moments like 2010 can seem too easy, too filled with joy and hope and a sense of invincibility. In reality it was also full of dread and pain and pessimism – a sense that, far witnessing the rebirth of our world, we were witnessing the end of it.

If this book is a tale of a new left, exploding into existence long after radical politics was supposed to have become an anachronism, it is also in part the tale of a hard right turn within the ruling elite, a radicalization of the market ideologies pioneered in the 1980s undertaken as shock therapy in post-crash Britain. As the Coalition prepared its reforms of the NHS and cuts on an unprecedented scale, it seemed like there was no limit to how far they would go in dismantling the welfare state. Facing the onslaught that the Coalition was promising in universities and further education, we acted out of hope and belief, but also out of desperation.

The transformation of the higher education system into a marketized sector was the open aim of the Coalition government, and, like all truly transformational projects, it was aimed not at moving numbers around on a spreadsheet but at altering the soul of institutions and the consciousness of the people who populated them. In fact, raising tuition fees was not even an especially good way of raising money. As opponents of the policy warned, the government would still end up fronting the cash to loan to students, and, because of the scale of the debt being accrued, much of the money would never come back to it. By 2014 the amount that the government expected to never be paid back (a measure known as the RAB Charge) had reached 45 per cent.[22] What the reforms were really about was a mission to turn students, in almost every generation a bastion of radicalism and dissent, into consumers of education and compliant, competitive graduates weighed down by debt.

The nature of the enemy against which we were mobilizing brought about a seemingly odd set of alliances with the ivory tower of academia. Many universities were, at the same time as lobbying for higher fees, in the process of completing a managerial revolution in their internal governance, abolishing or disempowering bodies like academic boards and other committees which gave teaching and research staff power over institutions. Those who engaged closely with the governance of universities and opposed this process – and this was certainly my experience as a student union education officer at UCL – were often struck by the extent to which academics who were otherwise quite conservative were willing to show support for the students.

The existential nature of the battle over tuition fees and EMA in 2010, and the fact that it foreshadowed a much wider war over austerity, created the conditions for a political generation to emerge. Much was said at the time about the generational conflict underway, often in rather simplistic terms, and certainly not all of it from a left-wing perspective. In his seminal account of the leftward shift among millennials, *Generation Left*, Keir Milburn points out that right-wing American figures like Bruce Gibney and Steve Bannon had already presented a story about the baby boomer generation which 'rolls seamlessly from the perceived self-indulgence of the counterculture to the greedy selfishness of the early 2000s. They suggest familiar causes for this generational flaw: lax parenting and the affordances of then dominant media technologies.'[23] David Willetts had just released a book called *The Pinch*, in which he in many ways pioneered the argument that baby boomers, who had enjoyed a youth with full employment and state-funded education, were now enjoying an unsustainably prosperous existence at the expense of their children. The fact that he ended up leading the charge on a set of reforms widely decried as a betrayal of Britain's youth, all the while cheered on by Nick Clegg, who had staked his reputation on opposing this exact set of policies, is just one of the many ironies dealt out by the situation.

It is worth saying something at this point about the scale of both the movement and its audience. The number of people who were actively involved in the student movement of 2010 and the activist scene that proliferated from it is, in the grand scheme of things, quite small. Out of a movement which peaked, in terms of the numbers of people participating, on 24 November that year with 130,000 students taking to the streets, only a small minority attended organizing meetings or spent the night in the forty or so university occupations across the country. Being generous, we could say that at most 200,000 people attended a protest at some point in the months of November and December. Despite this, the student movement and the moment from which it sprang played a defining role in what happened after it, and not just because of the prominent role that many of the movement's protagonists would play during the Corbyn era and beyond.

Higher education had already expanded dramatically. In the late 1960s, around 10 per cent of the population went to university, and by the end of the 1980s that number was still less than 15 per cent. In 2010, participation rate stood at 45.8 per cent, and around two million people were in higher education. Although student politics was a minority pastime – as indeed it always has been – for every student who took part in an occupation or attended a protest, there were many more who witnessed the movement and supported it. Student activism was not just a means of setting a tone or providing a point of reference for others, it was a means of directly influencing a large proportion of the population.

Unserious politics

Just as the Coalition threatened to transform the education system and the welfare state, the student movement offered this generation a transformational experience of its own: not in the form of a political programme, which would take years to come together, but in the form of struggle and an expansion in the horizons of what seemed possible.

Along with the experience of police violence and the material injustice and hardship that went with austerity, this moment saw thousands of students living and organizing together in confined spaces across the country. As well as providing a source of leverage – a means of applying pressure by disrupting universities' functioning, in the same manner that striking workers do – the student occupations of 2010 were in themselves a crucible of radical politics. They were regularly visited with messages of solidarity from campus trade union representatives, local trades council chairs and the wider layer of community activists who were beginning to set up more general anti-austerity activities. Veterans of recent movements on the climate, the Iraq War and previous battles against tuition fees could mingle with the current generation, have arguments and spread ideas. Many occupations actively sought to be a space for learning, running their own seminar series involving academics.

For many, the experience was one of a sudden discovery of agency. Kelly Rogers had started at Birmingham University that year without any idea of what was about to happen. 'In a matter of months, I'd occupied a university building, I'd been to gigantic protests and I was part of a movement', she says. 'I was being empowered in a way that I couldn't have imagined possible a few weeks previously. To think that what you do matters, that you can get the attention of university managers, of the government, and that thousands of people just like you are having the same awakening all over the country in rooms just the one you were in. It got me hooked, and what I did in the years that followed was really shaped by the experience of that autumn.'

These spaces were, in Owen Hatherley's words, 'not just a critique of the singularly grotesque millionaires' austerity government, but also an attempt to imagine a new kind of everyday life'.[24] They were where many young activists encountered organized politics for the first time. Some occupations, especially those in which the SWP had a large presence, witnessed a constant tug of war between the organized left and the anti-hierarchical practices of those who had been involved in climate activism and other social movements. In the occupations of London, where the organized left was weaker, consensus decision-making was a religion, which meant that decisions were made over the course of long, highly involved general assemblies at which everyone's consent was sought for every outcome. The staple method of showing your opinion – wiggling your hands upwards in agreement or downwards in disagreement – lived on as a reflex among many of those present for years afterwards.

This movement was, like youth rebellions before it, irreverent and confrontational. Using a situationist aesthetic consciously borrowed from 1968, students turned up the dial marked 'havoc', covering campuses with surrealist graffiti, posters and, at UCL, giant papier mache statues of robots holding signs bearing the reassuring slogan 'this is actually happening'. This wild atmosphere was pushed centre stage as the press and celebrities descended on the central London occupations of SOAS and UCL, where BBC journalists showed up carrying bin bags of leftover nibbles from their office Christmas party.

From the hoodied youths of London dancing in the streets to the latest hits of London's grime scene to the playful, at times gratingly pretentious, performance of some of the university students, those taking part often presented themselves as a caricature of what 'serious politics' was not supposed to be. Their secret weapon was the fact that they didn't care about looking serious or mainstream – in fact many revelled in being its opposite. When song sheets were printed by the UCL occupiers to distribute among the protesters at the 9 December protest, many of the choir referred to themselves as 'The Choir Extinguishers' in honour of the fire extinguisher thrown from Millbank's roof.

But the real anthems of 2010 were not straightforward protest songs composed by well-spoken university students. Projected by mobile sound systems, a very different kind of beat rang out across the demonstrations as they spread out across London in the sleet and surged towards police lines. Tempa T's *Next Hype* was probably the most-played song of the autumn. Like the school and college students who danced to it, the grime scene was about to go on a journey that would see it travel from the angry, disenfranchised margins into the political mainstream. By 2017, the officially coordinated 'Grime for Corbyn' collective would be mobilizing a youthquake in a general election. In 2010, it was the music that came on when working class kids took over streets, its beat matching the confrontational spirit of a generation in revolt. 'It's not about the content, it's about the energy and aura', as Tempa T later said when he was told his music had become the iconic soundtrack to the protests.[25]

It was in large part the meeting of these two worlds – of grime music and raw anger, mixing with the world of left politics and the university campus – that gave the student movement its transformative quality. Their paths would cross again and again in the coming decade, in protests and riots and eventually at the ballot box. But one must not be too romantic about it. There was, even at the time, something obviously problematic about the fact that a street movement whose backbone was made up of working class, often Black and Asian, kids was being led and directed by a mostly white set of students at posh universities – people like me and others who populated the university occupations and spoke to the media. The school and college students who threw themselves into the front lines of the protests had by and large been given no training or preparation in terms of how to stay out of trouble when the police attacked or how to make sure they didn't get caught when the protests got out of hand. Some already established activists, and some of the university occupations, did attempt to distribute legal information on protests. But in the heat of the moment, with events developing all around us, the new student movement did not have the capacity to make sure the kids from Peckham and Tower Hamlets had proper legal support or were met outside the police station when they got released. Some would get convictions; others were scared off for life.

The establishment dreaming

Although it erupted in response to a series of specific policies – chief among them the tripling of fees and the abolition of EMA – it is important to remember that the student movement of 2010 was in fact a response to a much broader crisis of the establishment. The financial crash had created an atmosphere in which bankers and capitalist institutions were subject to popular anger and scorn, even if politicians' appetite to re-regulate the banking sector quickly evaporated. The logic of austerity, and the idea that public services and wages needed to suffer in order to prop up the interests of corporations and the weal, was called into question the moment it emerged.

UK Uncut, a protest movement even more decentralized than that of the students, operated by means of setting examples which could be replicated by others on days of action. On 23 October 2010, its founders – themselves veterans of the climate movement of the 2000s – provided an example by occupying the Oxford Street branch of Vodafone, a company which George Osborne had just let off a £6 billion tax bill roughly equal to the £7 billion of austerity being imposed on workers, services and benefit claimants. Quickly videoed and uploaded to social media, the actions spread like wildfire. By December, around seventy autonomous groups were occupying their local Vodafone, some of them populated by students from local university occupations. They turned the shop fronts into libraries and nurseries, theatrical embodiments of the services being lost in the name of giving Vodafone a tax break.

Opposition to austerity and the financial crash weren't the only things troubling the political elite. The 2009 parliamentary expenses scandal demonstrated what much of the public viewed as straightforward corruption on the part of the political class. Dozens of MPs right across the political spectrum had claimed taxpayers' money to, among other things, buy themselves houses, maintain antique chandeliers and elaborately decorate their gardens. In the same year, the *Guardian* revealed a significant set of developments in the News International phone hacking scandal, which implicated *News of the World* editor Andy Coulson, by now David Cameron's press secretary, in hiring private investigators to illegally hack phones. The police, too, were rocked by scandal from a number of directions; the death of Ian Tomlinson, a bystander who had died after being assaulted by riot police during a 2009 protest in the City of London, was a constant reference point during the autumn of 2010. When Nick Clegg announced that his grand promise on tuition fees was in fact worth nothing, this too became part of a much bigger story of deceit and a self-serving establishment.

The wholesale nature of the establishment crisis dovetailed with the almost anti-political tone of the first movements against austerity and gave the student revolt a simple, easily digestible moral economy: with democracy this broken, what other means do we have to make ourselves heard?

Like generations of elite politicians before them, the confidence of the Lib Dems and the rest of the Coalition in delivering such a harsh regime of austerity and ideologically driven reforms rested on a belief that the world of social movements and politics are somehow separate, that politics and Politics would never meet. Giving his Hugo Young Lecture on 23 November, right at the height of the student movement, Nick Clegg argued that the task of cutting the deficit 'provides an opportunity for the renewal of progressive politics'. Austerity was, he said, 'opening up a real divide in progressive politics, between old progressives, who emphasise the power of the central state, and new progressives, who focus on the power of citizens'.[26] He did not mean the citizens who were outside protesting.

Riding high in the polls and with talk of a bold new politics of cross-party collaboration and the 'Big Society', the Coalition government found themselves piloting a political and economic system that was both morally and literally bankrupt. Prisoners of their own consensus, which simply did not see insurgent left-wing ideas or mass street movements as serious aspects of modern politics – least of all ones which danced to Lethal Bizzle in the cold and liberally smashed windows – the Lib Dem leadership was blind to the fact that politics was changing right under its feet. Five years later, another set of establishment politicians and commentators – this time the centrist old guard of the Labour Party – would make the same mistake.

On 9 December 2010, as MPs voted through the tripling of tuition fees and tens of thousands of protesters stood in a freezing kettle, the *Evening Standard* was being distributed to millions of commuters across the city. Its front page that day carried a photo of a crowd of young protesters and the headline 'CLEGG: STUDENTS IN DREAM WORLD'. Given the events that were to follow, we might reasonably ask who was really dreaming and who was awake.

A generation without a history

Moments of economic and political crisis do not renew the left all on their own. Neither do they necessarily lay the foundations for a consolidation of progressive opinions and generational identities among young people. For most voters, especially those who had grown up in the economic boom of the very early twenty-first century, austerity was a hard concept to understand in the abstract – but it is inescapably the case that the vast majority of the public accepted it in the aftermath of the 2008 crash. There was also no historically inevitable sense in which young people should have been expected to oppose the established consensus. In 1983, with youth unemployment rocketing, Margaret Thatcher held a ten-point lead over Labour among voters ages eighteen to thirty-four,[1] and in the 2010 general election, the first after the financial crash, David Cameron enjoyed a smaller but nonetheless significant lead over Labour among voters in the same age range.[2]

And yet, in the political polarization that was to take hold and deepen throughout the 2010s, Britain's youth knew exactly which side they were on. By the end of the decade, age had emerged as indisputably the biggest demographic factor in how people voted and what their attitudes to politics were. Jeremy Corbyn's Labour Party beat the Tories by forty points among voters in their twenties in 2017. His campaign for the Labour leadership two years earlier had drawn much of its strength from a generation undergoing a political awakening, and the content of his programme gave a pretty clear idea about some of the origins of the new Labour left's young support base. The abolition of tuition fees was one of Corbyn's most prominent pledges. Writing in the introduction to Labour's 2019 Youth Manifesto, as yet another generation of young radicals was being spawned by the school climate strike movement, he reflected that it was 'hard not to be inspired by this socially conscious generation who, despite the injustices they face, have not been deterred and continue to demand change'.[3]

The 2010s witnessed the emergence of a generation whose political centre of gravity was decisively to the left of those which preceded it and which defined itself against both the neoliberal consensus of the political establishment and its austerity response to the financial crisis. Just as importantly, this generation – because of the unique conditions of its formation and its relationship to history – would approach politics in a qualitatively different way and would form a core part of the development of the new left of the 2010s.

The nature of the crisis and its impact on the material conditions of the millennial generation is crucial to explaining this left turn. While stock markets and house prices quickly recovered from the crash, wages and employment figures did not.[4] Youth unemployment hit record levels in the aftermath of the crash, but this was only a prelude to a much longer attack on young people's living standards. Between 2007 and 2015, median earnings in the UK fell by 10.4 per cent, the second worst drop in the developed world after Greece.[5] High property prices meant that by 2016, those ages sixty-five to seventy-four owned more wealth than everyone in the UK under forty-five.[6] A 27-year-old born in the late 1980s had a roughly one in four chance of owning their own home, compared to an almost fifty-fifty chance for those born just ten years earlier and a 63 per cent chance for those born in the early 1970s.[7] At the same time, the cost of renting rose sharply, especially in London, where the centralization of the economy meant that many young people were forced to move in order to compete for the available pool of jobs. In the workplace, too, the crisis hit the young hardest. By 2015, more than three-quarters of sixteen- to twenty-year-olds were on low pay,[8] and the status of many workers was undergoing a qualitative shift. The ubiquitous experience of young workers in the UK was not unemployment but precarious employment and intensified exploitation, often on a zero-hours contract.

This experience of the post-crash economy was international, a common thread that ran through the lives of young people across the world. In southern Europe, the crisis was much worse and the experience of youth unemployment and precarity even sharper. In Spain, youth unemployment reached 40 per cent by 2010 and more than half by 2014;[9] in Greece, it hit 60 per cent towards the middle of the decade.[10] In every case, the pattern was the same: young people found themselves the disproportionate victims of a wider process of economic stagnation, in which the gap between the rich and poor grew exponentially and exploitation and immiseration intensified.

This generation had other things in common too: their political awakening took place at the dawn of the social media age, at a time when the organized left had suffered major defeats in recent years and the politics of revolt sought a new lexicon and a new organizational model. There were, of course, vulgar expressions of generational resentment mixed in with the development of an insurgent political identity. But by and large, for the generation that turned left, generational politics was not an alternative to class politics but a vehicle for understanding it and a means of expressing it.[11]

Also international was the anaemic state of the establishment centre-left. In the UK, New Labour had pushed the marketization of public services and the deregulation of the financial sector even further than Thatcher. In Germany, Gerhard Schroeder, who in 1998 had co-authored a pamphlet with Tony Blair on the Third Way (or *Die Neue Mitte* in German), had pushed forward an analogous agenda of tax cuts and marketization. Bill Clinton's presidency made the politics of the New Democrats hegemonic, a shift which Barack Obama ultimately embraced. The French Socialist Party drifted decisively to the right after Lionel Jospin's leadership ended and was joined by the Dutch Labour Party and most of the centre-left across Europe. Pasok, once one of Europe's most successful social democratic parties, ended up the intermediaries of Greece's first bailout package, willingly implementing a devastating programme of austerity. As a new generation awakened hungry for political alternatives, they found the mainstream of politics populated by right-wing ideologues and centrist technocrats. Ed Miliband's Labour Party had begun a journey back towards social democracy but was still wedded to the shibboleths of austerity.

The beginning of what?

Neither the idea of a 'lost generation' nor the shared experiences of capitalist crisis and political stagnation can on their own explain the political radicalization that took place in the 2010s. The 2008 crash and the economic crisis that followed was a seismic event, but it was a passively experienced one, which could easily have played into a narrative of nostalgia and national betrayal. A right-wing populist response to the crisis – at its centre a resurgent nationalism and a scapegoating of foreigners – could just as easily have captured the mood of the young and in some places did so. In the second round of the 2017 French presidential election, for instance, Marine Le Pen won the support of almost half of 18- to 24-year-olds, with much of that support geographically concentrated. She did even better in 2022. Greece's neo-Nazi party, Golden Dawn, polled exceptionally well among young voters.

It was social movements that would grab the imagination of the young and dispossessed and create both the narratives and human material for bigger projects later in the decade. These were the moments of collective power in which the horizons of what seemed possible expanded exponentially, and which made the development of a new mass politics necessary and possible.[12] The generation that came of age during and after the 2008 crash not only turned left but also played a crucial role in creating radical left-wing political alternatives that rammed their way into mainstream politics, largely at the expense of establishment liberals and social democrats.

In Spain, it was the 15-M movement and the Indignados. In the United States, it was Occupy Wall Street and a series of movements from the revolt in Wisconsin to student occupations in California. In Greece, a country with a historically strong organized left, it was the escalation of mass dissent in response to the bailout package in early 2010. These movements were part of a global moment of revolt, which included movements in the Global South and, most prominently early on, the Arab Spring. In the UK, the crucial moment was the awakening of a movement that could galvanize an alliance between the dispossessed youngster, the 'graduate with no future',[13] the precarious worker, the service users and staff of the embattled public sector and what remained of the organized left; and all that began in the autumn of 2010 when the plate glass of Conservative Party headquarters at 30 Millbank was unceremoniously kicked in.

The sudden unfurling of a mass movement against tuition fees and education cuts – in spite of the fact that Britain's youth had known no alternative to neoliberalism, in spite of the lack of leadership from the NUS – had taken everyone by surprise, including the trade unions. With half a million public sector jobs marked for demolition by the Coalition government over the lifetime of the parliament, along with a major restructuring of the NHS and swingeing cuts to local government planned, the leaderships of the major unions knew that they would have to show some fight. Len McCluskey, the general secretary of Britain's largest trade union, Unite, summed up the mood at the end of the year: 'The magnificent students' movement needs urgently to find a wider echo if the government is to be stopped', he said.[14]

'I saw that movement against tuition fees as a game-changer', Mark Serwotka, general secretary of the civil servants' union PCS, tells me. 'It lit a touch-paper that spread into the trade union movement and gave us the opportunity to light up a much wider range of struggles.' By the end of the year, the Trades Union Congress had set the date for a national protest for 26 March 2011, and the unions had agreed to engage in collective talks about coordinated strike action over cuts to pensions.

Local campaigns to save services and jobs were also popping up across the country by the autumn. Around a month before the student movement began, Disabled People Against the Cuts (DPAC) had formed to fight back against cuts to disability benefits and services and would be one of the most prominent voices against austerity in the coming years. Earlier in 2010, work had begun on setting up an organization which might be able to give national voice to the various struggles that were springing up. John Rees was already a veteran of the British socialist movement, who saw the opportunity to create a broad campaigning coalition. 'All the way through Stop the War', he says, 'I found that the sensible thing was to ring up Tony Benn, and if he thought it was a good idea and put his name to it, quite a lot of people on the left would say "oh, Tony Benn thinks it's a good idea, so let's go".' Sure enough, on 4 August, a letter signed by Benn and around seventy others appeared in the *Guardian* attacking the 'malicious vandalism' by a 'government of millionaires' and pledged to build a new organization to coordinate the movement. Among the other signatories to Benn's letter were Jeremy Corbyn and John McDonnell, the general secretaries of trade unions representing civil servants, transport workers and journalists, a smattering of authors and actors and a number of prominent student activists including myself, economist James Meadway and University of London Union president Clare Solomon. They and around a thousand others met as the Coalition of Resistance on 27 November, the first national conference of the anti-austerity movement, in an atmosphere made electric by the massive student protests that had taken place that week.

The students undoubtedly made the anti-austerity movement grow bigger and faster and pushed official institutions of the labour movement into action, but we did not invent the concept of it. Moments like Millbank and the Battle of Parliament Square were important but were, as the student protesters frequently said themselves, 'only the beginning'. Looking back, they were the starting point for two distinct but deeply connected revolts. One, which is the subject of the next chapter, was the anti-austerity movement that cleared the way for Corbynism. While the student movement could be measured in its hundreds of thousands, that movement would be measured in its millions.

The other, whose ramifications would go far beyond any dispute over education funding policy, was the radical shift in the political identity of millennials and their transformation into what Keir Milburn pithily theorized as Generation Left.[15] The youth who were involved in the anti-austerity movement, whether from the outset in 2010 or later on, form a kind of activist core for Generation Left, and an important part of the story of the 2010s – both in terms of the formation of a new left politics and in terms of understanding events – is about these people: where they came from, what conditioned their thinking and where they ended up.

Not from nowhere

Viewed from a distance, or in the reports of pundits who did not see it coming, the youth revolt of the 2010s looked like it 'came from nowhere'. But like all explosive moments, it had organizational roots from which it grew.

Had it not been for an existing layer of expertise and strategic direction, the events that began the youth revolt may not have happened with such ferocity. Many of the core activists of the 2010 student movement had already had a taste of how to run a university occupation following a wave of protest that had hit campuses in early 2009 in response to Israel's invasion of the Gaza Strip. When the anti-fees movement erupted, it was enormously fortunate that the NCAFC already existed and could play a role in naming days of action and providing an organizational front, a brand, which was relatively informal and not dominated by any one clique or sect; but its existence was also not an accident. During Peter Mandelson's time in charge of the higher education sector, universities had seen their first round of austerity, and this had in turn witnessed a small uptick in militancy among both staff and students. At campuses like Westminster, UCL, the London College of Communication, Birmingham and Middlesex, departmental cuts had sparked sizeable protest movements before the autumn of 2010. At the University of Sussex on the outskirts of Brighton, six students were suspended after their involvement in a solidarity protest with a lecturer's strike. The NCAFC was the product of these embryonic campaigns, its formation an attempt to bring together and coordinate what was a very small but already growing movement.

In large part because of the hangover from End of History, it offends the sensibilities of most commentators to talk about the British far left – the array of intellectual traditions, socialist grouplets and acronyms that have historically given shape to much bigger campaigns and strikes – in a way that does not immediately bookend any analysis with a flippant remark about the People's Front of Judea or some metaphor about dinosaurs. And yet the truth is that without understanding the organized left and the relationship of the wider movement to it, you simply cannot speak with any clarity about the social movements that laid the ground for Corbynism. In the same way, so many mainstream journalists who had spent years laughing at the very idea of 21st -century Maoism or Trotskyism would show up in Athens in the summer of 2015 and simply be unable to report on what was happening inside the governing party Syriza, as it took centre stage in an era-defining crisis of the European project. Unable to seriously discuss the development of the organized left, they reduced the Greek debt crisis to a series of snippets about negotiating red lines and confrontations between Euro-functionaries and the leather-clad finance minister Yanis Varoufakis. Just so, the rise of Jeremy Corbyn is so often reduced to a story of dispossessed youth and disembodied nice ideas.

In truth, the story of Corbynism, and indeed the rise of Bernie Sanders, is also a story of major changes within the left, in how it operates and what its goals are. By the end of the 2010s, the organized far left in Britain would, despite the huge increase in people being exposed to left-wing ideas, be at its lowest ebb ever, as large numbers were sucked into a very different kind of left politics within the Labour Party. But in the early part of the decade, these groups were a much bigger deal.

This was an era in which the SWP claimed to have thousands of members and in workplaces and on campuses where it existed could mobilize a substantial number of people. The student network NCAFC – which found itself constantly under siege from the SWP, which regarded it as a competitor – came together as a network of all kinds of activists including many independents, but it would in all likelihood never have held together without the energetic participation of two much smaller Trotskyist groups, Workers' Liberty and Workers' Power. The Socialist Party, one half of the old Militant Tendency, had a substantial presence in the trade unions, and although they did not prioritize student politics, they were nonetheless the core of anti-cuts mobilizations on a couple of campuses. Socialist Action, the secretive sect that surrounded Ken Livingstone when he was London mayor, did not operate in the open but had substantial influence in the hierarchies of a number of unions and on the left wing of the NUS. Counterfire, which split from the SWP in 2010 (taking the Stop the War Coalition with it), was the driving force behind the Coalition of Resistance. Of all of the national-level spokespeople for the student movement of 2010 – setting aside those whose prominence came later – I was in a minority, and maybe a minority of one, in at no point joining a Trotskyist organization.

None of these groups can claim to have organized the anti-austerity movement – and have even less claim to have organized the often leaderless student movement – but their presence provided a patchy, low-level base layer of organization to the protests. They also, via contact between students and their older party comrades, provided a pre-existing connection between younger and older generations of activists. Trotskyism is a much more diverse field than is often credited – spanning all the way from dissenting, radical traditions much informed by the new left of the 1960s and 1970s all the way through to barely modified Stalinism – and the organizing cultures of these groups ranged accordingly from the relatively libertarian and open to the controlling and secretive. If you asked a member of Workers' Liberty what debates the organization was currently having internally, she would cheerily give you a list; a member of the SWP would remain silent out of party discipline; and a member of Socialist Action would generally deny their own group's existence and hastily change the subject.

The explosion of social movements after 2010 had other roots, too. UK Uncut was a perfectly pitched intervention into the news cycle, its playful occupations of Vodafone and Topshop from October onwards neatly cutting through the austerity narrative coming out of central government and turning up the heat on the issue of corporate tax avoidance. It was initiated by the veterans of the Climate Camp movement, which from 2006 onwards set about trying to shut down major power stations and sources of carbon emissions, often while pitching tents and living outside them. Its internal culture was the diametric opposite of many of the centralized socialist groups, with a preference for prefigurative politics and consensus decision-making. In many ways, UK Uncut's decentralized model, utilizing social media, represented its transposition into the world of campaigning around post-crash economics.

Climate Camp's direct action politics and opposition to formal internal hierarchy (its 'horizontalism') drew much of its intellectual heritage from the anarchist movement and anti-globalization movement and had a lasting influence on many of the young activists who came of age in the early 2010s. 'Even if you didn't buy the whole package of it', says NCAFC organizer Edward Maltby, 'we were all in some sense intellectual products of the aftermath of the Battle of Seattle, and its mythology of spectacular actions and leaderlessness'. This approach to activism came to dominate the internal life of many campus occupations in 2010, as veterans of the last generation of social movements educated and influenced a layer of students who were entirely new to activist politics, and its influence played a major role in making the student movement a transformative, untameable event.

The generation without a history

The real defining factor in the political development of the people who took part in this moment, however, was not their connection to recent social movements and industrial struggle but their distance from them; and if this generation of precariously employed, debt-laden young people complained of having no future, it also lacked a past.

Influential though the movements of the recent past were among a small layer of older activists, the vast bulk of those who were involved in the explosion of youth politics in the early part of the decade had had no political training and no collective memory of recent social movements. Outside of the very core of the organizations that tried to coordinate the movement, the number of students who were actually members of socialist groups was negligible. When tactics were debated within the anti-austerity movement, there was much talk about the movement against the Iraq War and the need for direct action in order to avoid a repeat of its polite, toothless A to B marches; and when MPs voted through cuts, privatization and tuition fee rises, the Poll Tax riots were summoned up as a moment in which 'what parliament does, the streets can undo'.

But among the newly politicized youth, and especially during the student protests, these analogies had little purchase outside the activist core, and in comparison to 2003 or 1991, the number of people who were a conscious part of the left or the labour movement was much lower. The student movement exploded at a moment in which the British left was historically weak; it was like a light that switched on after all the other lights had gone out, and the collective memory of the people who populated it was correspondingly weak.

In the thirty years prior to the 2010s, the left and the labour movement in Britain had experienced a series of catastrophic defeats. In 1979, trade union membership stood at more than 13 million, concentrated largely in the public sector and industry. This mass membership was the lifeblood of a strong, confident organized left, both inside Labour and beyond it. In many communities across Britain, the labour movement wasn't just where you went to organize strikes or distribute socialist literature, its existence was woven into social lives and identities. Britain was near the top of the European league table – or near the bottom, depending on your perspective – in terms of trade union militancy, and the strength of the unions had kept wages rising and the average standard of living rising with them. The Winter of Discontent of 1978–9, in which the scale of industrial action meant that the bins piled up in the streets, hospitals shut to non-emergency patients and bodies went unburied, was not, for many people, a particularly pleasant experience, but it also coincided with the moment when Britain would never be so equal again. The events of that winter were a symptom of the fact that, due to a systemic international crisis, the old post-war economic model was dying. In response, Jim Callaghan's Labour government had announced that it would abandon Keynesianism wholesale.[16] There were two broadly convincing responses to the crisis: one was an intensification of common ownership and economic democratization, one incarnation of which was the Alternative Economic Strategy put forward by Tony Benn, Stuart Holland and others on the Labour left, and the other was Margaret Thatcher's.

The Conservative governments of the 1980s tore down the social and economic system which had sustained rising living standards and the labour movement in a deliberate attempt to crush the power of the organized left. Mass unemployment was in part a consequence of the government's economic policy, but it was also a deliberate strategy to bring down union density. The miners' strike of 1984–5 was just the most decisive of a series of life-and-death battles between the government and workers in major industries, which Margaret Thatcher systematically shut down. The number of steelworkers in Britain halved in the first two years of her administration[17] following an unsuccessful series of strikes. More heroic failures followed, as printers' unions unsuccessfully fought major job losses and union busting by managers on Fleet Street.

Running simultaneously with the industrial disputes was the fight over local government, a historic stronghold of the Labour left which Thatcher marked for demolition. When the government severely limited the amount that councils could raise in local taxes – a policy known as rate capping – fifteen councils refused to comply. This, too, failed, leaving only Lambeth and Liverpool holding out until government auditors fined their councillors and barred them from office. The Greater London Council, run by Ken Livingstone and John McDonnell, was shut down in early 1986 and its building sold to a Japanese investor. It is now host to the London Aquarium and Shrek's Adventure World. The 1980s were a period of intense struggle and unrest, which informed the development of a generation of older left-wing activists who came of age in that decade, but it was a story of unmitigated defeat.

The combined effect of Thatcherism and Blairism was to marginalize socialist politics in Britain. Trade union membership as a proportion of the overall workforce plummeted from more than half in the early 1980s to less than a quarter thirty years later,[18] and rather than scrapping Thatcher's anti-union laws, Tony Blair boasted of the fact that the UK would retain 'the most restrictive on trade unions in the Western world'.[19] His move to scrap Clause IV, Labour's commitment to common ownership, precipitated an exodus of left-wing activists from the party. This did not precipitate a growth in the extra-parliamentary left: in the first seven years of the Blair government, the membership of Britain's Trotskyist organizations roughly halved to around 6,500.[20] It wasn't just in parliament or on the news that alternatives to neoliberal economics had been marginalized; the left's roots had been dug up and burned. On many levels, it had lost the ability to reproduce itself as a coherent tradition, relying on singular moments of mass protest – such as the Iraq War – which boosted its prominence but never really its relevance or its organizational strength. The result was that, in the 2010s, the generation that woke up, took to the streets and occupied Vodafone was uniquely detached from Britain's long history of mass dissent and rebellion.

The nightmare and the mirror

This lack of historical rootedness gave the social movements of the early 2010s a sense of intense creativity and a lack of inhibition. There was no organization that could have contained or controlled the protests or the energy and anger of those who were involved in them. During the Poll Tax movement of 1991, the movement had been coordinated by an official coalition dominated by the Militant Tendency, which went so far as to condemn riots in central London. For the large majority of those taking part in the student movement of 2010, who had barely come into contact with the organized left and were born around the same time as the Poll Tax movement took off, the boundaries of what seemed possible to achieve by protest and direct action were not set by historical precedent but by strength of feeling and the raw confrontation between themselves and the state. These factors were important in giving much of the anti-austerity movement its explosive quality and its often radical tactical edge. The storming of Millbank was, as much as anything, an act of collective imagination and one which was inspired not by a sense of history but by freedom from it.

A sense of freshness and an edgy aesthetic is of course nothing new for youth revolts. The mass revolts of 1968 and thereafter also carried with them a sense of reinventing the art of dissent for a new age and building a self-consciously new left by rejecting the political and organizational methods of older generations. As Russian tanks rolled into Prague, just as they had rolled into Budapest twelve years earlier, a generation of left activists looked to issue a rebuke not only to the conservatism and world views of their parents but also to the paternalist model of social democracy that dominated the post-war settlement and the Moscow-aligned sympathies of their older comrades. Like in the 2010s, deep changes in the economy produced divides in how different generations experienced the world of work and organized within it. Herbert Marcuse was one of the biggest intellectual figures of 1968 and a key thinker of the new left of that period. His book *One Dimensional Man*, like Mark Fisher's *Capitalist Realism*, was published just a few years before the revolt kicked off. In it, he argued that developments in post-war capitalism and the Cold War (the 'Welfare State and the Warfare State') had created a political situation characterized by 'a marked unification or convergence of opposites', as a result of which political parties had become 'ever more indistinguishable, even in the degree of hypocrisy and in the odour of the clichés'. For Marcuse, this situation has serious consequences for 'the very possibilities of social change where it embraces those strata on whose back the system progresses – that is, the very classes whose existence once embodied the opposition to the system as a whole'.[21]

Like the students of 2010, the 1968 revolt set out – in hope and in desperation – to destabilize a society in which the possibility for alternatives and radical change seemed to be closing down, as a technological rationality permeated every part of life to the point that it was becoming impossible to even critique the status quo in language that it had not co-opted and defined. Consumer choice and nominal political rights were, for Marcuse, playing their part in the development of a totalitarian equilibrium, 'a comfortable, smooth, reasonable, democratic unfreedom'.[22]

When Mark Fisher theorized capitalist realism in 2008, he was of course talking about a unique historical moment. Some years later, cultural theorist Jeremy Gilbert began to theorize the concept of the 'long 1990s', a period 'in which technological change is accompanied by cultural stasis', a product of a hegemonic bloc of Silicon Valley and finance capital. 'The people who really got exactly the world they wanted – with its precise balance of social liberalisation, political demobilisation, globalised production, homogenised cultural content, and universal dependency on consumer electronics', he argued, 'were Steve Jobs, Bill Gates and their cohorts'.[23]

'The concept was really a response to the fact that, when I started teaching Cultural Studies in around 1995, I confidently assumed that by the time I was middle aged, there would be all this new music happening that would be interesting but that I would struggle to understand', Gilbert says now. 'But that future just never arrived. It became the case for about twenty years that if you asked someone what new music there was, they would say dubstep. A child could be born and achieve the age of majority during the period in which, if you asked what new music there was, the answer would still be "grime".'

The contexts may have been very different, but at a deep level I think we can view Capitalist Realism and the Long 1990s as echoes of a recurring nightmare of the modern left – expressed also by Marcuse, and even by George Orwell, in his depiction of a stable totalitarian planet dominated by three giant warring superstates in *1984* – that, despite the fact that the world seemed to be in a state of constant technological revolution, the possibilities for real political alternatives and cultural creativity, and with them the human spirit itself, were all being squeezed, even to the point of being in terminal danger. The potency of this nightmare goes some way to explaining why the left of the 2010s defined itself against the neoliberal centre – who were the standard bearers of the End of History – while at times neglecting the task of building a movement against the insurgent nationalist right. The rise of an authoritarian far right might have a greater human cost, but at various moments in history the more immediate dystopia has been stasis: it holds out the possibility that we might be wrong.

Naturally, the movements that are built in response to these nightmares share many features and will be endlessly compared – but they are not the same. At almost any other point in recent history, an emerging youth revolt would emerge to find itself surrounded by a sizeable, mobilized existing left. The generation without a history emerged in 2010 to find itself in what seemed like a desert. Its partisans and intellectuals did not issue denunciations of the 'old left' as a means of urging their contemporaries to take up a new form of Marxism or to join a particular organization, as many of the leaders of 1968 youth revolts had done, but as a means of proclaiming the death of such politics altogether. 'What are seeing here', wrote Laurie Penny in the immediate aftermath of the student movement,

> is no less than a fundamental reimagining of the British left: an organic reworking which rejects the old deferential structures of union-led action and interminable infighting among indistinguishable splinter parties for something far more inclusive and fast-moving. These new groups are principled and theoretically well-versed, but have no truck with the narcissism of small differences that used to corrupt even the most well-meaning of leftwing movements.[24]

There is, undeniably, something of the End of History about this version of reality, an internalization of the idea that the organized left is an anachronistic joke. And yet there were even some Leninists who had reached some of these conclusions, albeit in a watered-down form. Until 2010, John Rees and Lindsay German were probably the most famous figures in the SWP, having led the movement against the Iraq War. That year, they split from it, in part to pursue the setting up of an anti-austerity organization modelled on Stop the War, which they accomplished in the form of the Coalition of Resistance and later the People's Assembly Against Austerity. But, explains Rees, there were deeper problems with the SWP. 'I don't think that revolutionary organisations should exist in exactly the same format over decades', he says. 'In the time that the SWP had existed, the Bolsheviks had been formed, gone through 1905, gone through 1917, and been liquidated by Stalin – in fact in probably half that time. The organisation [the SWP] had grown sclerotic, and actually physically aged. Its joints had seized and it had become less and less likely to respond to situations flexibly and imaginatively.'

For some on the left, this moment had been a long time coming. Paul Mason had been a Trotskyist for almost twenty years, but in the 1990s his outlook had begun to change. 'I can almost remember the moment at which this old world of proletarian manual workers and hierarchical Marxist political organisation was being superseded by something else', he says. 'It was on a demo in support of the Liverpool dockers' strike, it must have been 1996, and we were all there with our leather jackets and our newspapers, and suddenly all of these young people with flags from the anti-road movement and Reclaim the Streets showed up. And the dockers, far from seeing them as petit-bourgeois, were all taking spliffs off them.' For Mason, the experience cut against the orthodoxy of what he'd been taught. 'I'd grown up with this idea – and this was much more a part of Militant's politics than it was mine – that the working class wouldn't accept middle class radicalism based outside the workplace', he says, 'and I began to realise that this was bullshit.'

In the youth revolt of the early 2010s, the organized left was not trusted by most activists to coordinate things and in any case was not up to the job – but there were benefits even to this. The character of the movement was unsectarian and undoctrinaire. As Mason later reflected, this generation's debates were not 'fiery, male and about which kind of Marxism was right, what it meant to be subordinate to the proletariat',[25] as his experience of youth movements in the 1980s had been. In the student movement, he observed, 'Anybody who sounds like a career politician, anybody who attempts rhetoric, espouses an ideology or lets their emotions overtake them is greeted with visceral distaste.'[26] 'What really shocked me', he reflects now, 'was the level of what you might call intrinsic, almost innate for this generation, rhizomic consciousness. People were activated around horizontalist principles in a way that I'd only ever in climate camps or among very dedicated anarchists. It was an education for me that a new kind of person was around.' When Jeremy Corbyn ran for Labour leader in 2015 promising 'a new kind of politics', he was in part channelling this mood.

A lack of history, and lack of historical consciousness, runs right through the experience of the Millbank generation. 'Look at the big figures of previous generations of the New Left', says Jon Moses, a writer and academic who in 2010 played a role in organizing students at UCL. 'E. P. Thompson, Eric Hobsbawm, CLR James, Stuart Hall, Perry Anderson, Raymond Williams – they're all historians, or people grounded in history. But if you look at the intellectual milieu of 2010 and you're talking about Frederic Jameson, David Harvey, David Graeber, Mark Fisher – and Slavoj Zizek was big at the time too. All big thinkers, but none of them historians, they're cultural and social theorists.' Right down to the books it was reading and the ideas it was discussing, the generation of 2010 was stubbornly ungrounded in the past. Rather than having a collective memory, they affected a kind of collective amnesia.

Along with the creativity and the fresh aesthetic came limitations and pitfalls. Cut off from the past in its moment of creation, the generation without a history had to invent everything from first principles, and in so doing it was doomed to repeat the mistakes of the movements that had come before it. As the 2010 student movement developed without democratically accountable hierarchies or formal organization, it developed informal and unacknowledged hierarchies instead. The vast majority of those who took part in the protests had no voice in organizing them or deciding what would happen next. Lacking a properly hammered-out strategy and organizational centre, the movement was limited to calling days of action and being blown along with events and had no time or mechanism by which to prepare its rank and file for the inevitable setbacks that came in the form of parliamentary votes and police repression. Trade unions and students made common cause, but the level of engagement was shallow and it was slow to take place, in part because the student movement did not have a strong organic link with organized workers.

One of the defining features of the generation without a history was its strong, but in retrospect short-term, addiction to particular concepts and practices. 'In 2010 there was this naive freshness and a willingness to entertain new alignments and possibilities', says Jon Moses, 'but alongside that I think our generation had this kind of endlessly faddish quality.' The movement, and the people who came of age within it, had no coherent or singular theory of change, and so they blew with the wind.

Throughout the early 2010s, many of the new generation of left-wing activists zealously advocated direct action politics – disruption and property damage committed in the hope of creating a spectacle that could capture imaginations and impose a penalty on the tax-avoiding corporations whose shop fronts it vandalized. Throughout the anti-austerity movement, the Black Bloc – masked protesters, identically dressed in order to avoid being identified – were a feature of most protests and would regularly cause mayhem. From UK Uncut's peaceful sit-ins, to the tent cities in town squares, to the daring occupations of major public buildings, abandoning the official channels and causing a scene were central to the moment.

This development was the product of many things and was to an extent inherited from the climate and anti-globalization movements. But it was also the product of a moment in which any kind of formal political organization, from the Labour Party all the way down to the NUS, seemed to have failed and in which mainstream politics was so far away from offering concessions to the movement in the streets that one might just as well bring down the entire system or, failing that, upset its custodians. The moral outrage of newspaper editors and liberal pundits at the breaking of windows or occupation of shops belied a lack of understanding and a lack of willingness to understand what was really happening. Whether it came in the form of passively blocking traffic or energetically breaking into buildings, direct action served as a dramatic enactment of the failure of the democratic process that was taking place. Rather than having a political programme of their own, its adherents held up a mirror.

As the size of the anti-austerity movement waned and the prospects for victory seemed to hinge more and more on the outcome of the next election, a trickle of activists from the social movements did go into Labour in an attempt to push it away from its embrace of austerity. I joined the party in autumn 2012, inspired by the rather basic idea that there was a burning need to inject some radicalism into what was supposed to be the political wing of the workers' movement. As a social movement activist used to organizing pickets and protests, I quickly came to regard Labour's endless meetings and posturing as a waste of my time. In any case, I was in a tiny minority: the overwhelming bulk of activists who had come through the series of mobilizations in the first half of the decade were largely uninterested in Labour. The party's membership figures remained stagnant throughout the period, at just under 200,000.

The fashionable approaches to politics among the youth of the anti-austerity movement were the Labour left's diametric ideological opposite. By the time of the 2010 student movement, Seth Wheeler had already been an activist for some time, having come through the direct action movements of the 1990s, a path which led him into anarchist circles. Via the climate camp movement, he had a number of contacts in the London occupations, 'so we went down to occupations, just to participate and observe', he says. 'Orthodox political tendencies did go there with a mind to recruit people, but what was more than apparent very early on was that the occupations had adopted methodologies like consensus decision making from climate camp, with a general assembly as the sovereign meeting and then working groups comprised of interested people. I was immediately struck that a lot of these younger activists seemed to be able to cherry pick the best ideas of the different traditions as they saw it. A kind of makeshift anarchism became the dominant orientation of the movement.'

In the early part of the decade, calling oneself an anarchist was an activity common to young activists across the Western world, for whom the political mainstream contained no real alternatives to neoliberalism and who did not find a home in the more formalized left traditions.

I first met Ben Beach at a Stop the War Coalition conference at some point in 2009. I was running the Stop the War society at UCL, and he was introduced to me by Lindsey German, one of the figureheads of the organization, because he was about to start an architecture degree there. By this point, he had already been thoroughly politicized. 'Growing up in a working class single parent household I think gives you a certain predilection towards understanding things in material terms', he says, 'but the two big issues that first politicised me were the Iraq War and climate change.' In late 2008 and early 2009, Beach had been involved in protests against Israel's Operation Cast Lead in Gaza, where he had witnessed police violence that had radicalized him. The first group he encountered was the SWP, and he joined it on a whim. 'For the first few months everyone was mobilising for the Gaza protests and it was exciting', he says. 'I wanted to feel like I was doing something, and I was quite dedicated to flyering on the tube and that kinds of thing.' But very quickly, he became disaffected with the highly centralized, disciplinarian model of the SWP. 'I thought that some things about the way we were organising were illogical, and if you challenged that you were shut down and told off. But what really put me off was that no one seemed to have any friends outside of the party, it felt culty.'

Meanwhile, Beach was studying at Byam Shaw School of Art – now a part of Central Saint Martins – where he encountered a very different kind of politics. 'While I was there, there was an occupation against course cuts, which was a forerunner of what was to come – and a lot of the people there were involved in groups like climate camp.' His encounter with the much more open consensus decision-making model was formative, and he never looked back. When the 2010 student movement happened, Beach was right in the thick of it, first at Millbank and then in organizing the occupation at UCL. 'There was quite a high degree of nihilism in politics at that time', he says. 'It was a long shockwave in response to the 2008 financial crisis, aiming to be a total opposition to the status quo – and along with the status quo went a lot of the organisational forms on the left. There was a big sense of "why would we replaster a rotten structure, why would we try to resuscitate these parties and sects that were so obviously inadequate" – and that lasted for a long time.'

For people like Beach, anarchism – and later autonomism and libertarian communism – would become serious intellectual commitments and shaped their politics in a deep way. But for most, the label of anarchism became so popular because it acted as a kind of catch-all for the sentiments and attitudes that were prevalent within the generation without a history and bound up with the movements they came to inhabit. When examined in detail, many of its adherents had very little common ground. Convinced and well-read anarchists shared a label with people who preferred networks to organizations, and others who thought that social media would end hierarchy on the left, and others who were hostile to the idea of selling papers, and others who mistook consensus decision-making and horizontalism for a full world view, and others who had witnessed the behaviour of the police and concluded that the state they served ought to be smashed. Most had no particular strategy for the overthrow of anything or any particular idea of what the state was or what should happen to it. Horizontalism and an antipathy to traditional left politics was a defining feature not only of the student movement but also of many of the movements that came later. As Podemos leader Pablo Iglesias put it, movements such as 15M (and to this we could add the global wave of Occupy protests) 'crystalized a new culture of contestation that could not be grasped by the categories of left and right – something that the leaders of the existing left refused to acknowledge from the start'.[27]

And yet the ranks of Britain's anarchist movement were not swelled in the long run by the generation that came of age in the anti-austerity movement, because its penchant for anarchism was a fad, a product of its lack of roots and the historic defeats of the left since the early 1980s. The vast majority of those who called themselves anarchists would end up as foot soldiers for the Labour leadership after 2015; and what is remarkable about this fad, and the atmosphere in which it thrived, is that it is about as far as it is possible to be from Corbynism and the Labour left project that was to follow.

Utopia and fluidity

It is not that the brief flourishing of horizontalist and anarchist politics was empty. On the contrary, the wavy hands and anti-organizational politics of this generation were straining towards a new reality at the dawn of a new political era, one defined by new technology, unending crisis, the collapse of the neoliberal consensus and the limitations of the pre-existing left. They had begun to grasp these realities but lacked the ability to fully conceptualize and comprehend them, in part because they were inventing everything from first principles and were separated from the traditions and ideas which might have given them the conceptual tools to do so – tools which they so often dismissed as 'baggage'.

But to a great extent they did not comprehend the new world because no one could. The global revolt of the 'long 2011' – from British anti-austerity movement and Occupy to revolutions in Egypt and Tunisia – took place at the dawn of the social media age. It spawned a truly utopian sense of what technology might bring, both to the movements and to wider society.

Writing in the immediate aftermath of the 2010 student movement, Aaron Bastani – then a PhD student at Royal Holloway, now a prominent left-wing commentator and Novara Media editor – viewed the future of the movement through the prism of 'open source activism', borrowing a set of analogies from the emerging world of software development in the late 1990s.[28] On the losing side of history stood the Cathedral model of organization, in which the code is accessible to an exclusive set of software developers, analogous to the formal structures of NGOs, trade unions and the groups of the organized left. 'From Microsoft to Manchester United, and many of our recently failed financial institutions, it has shaped our public values, shared spaces, and the nature of social interaction.'[29] On the winning side was the Bazaar, open-sourced systems like Linux and Wikipedia, analogous to the horizontalist campaigns of UK Uncut, and the networked activist circles of the student movement. Paul Mason, too, looked at the revolts and revolutions taking place across the world and observed that 'a network can usually defeat a hierarchy'.[30]

Technology was not just a source of analogy to this idea; it was the crucial practical element which would allow networked activists to take on the state. According to its enthusiasts, blogging and social media allowed the networks to form and function because they were inherently horizontal. From riots in Athens to the streets of Cairo, they enabled dissent to coordinate quickly and without centralized organization. 'I can remember this really distinctly', Paul Mason remembers of his time reporting on the Libyan revolution, 'someone tweeting "we're being shot at a thousand yards, what kind of rifles are they using?" and someone else chipping in with "the British have supplied the Libyan army with this kind of rifle" – incredible levels of networked density in revolutionary situations.' The students of 2010 were conscious participants in this utopian moment, and their use of Twitter and Facebook was one of the most reported-on aspects of the movement. At UCL, the occupation counted a number of coders in its ranks, who developed an app called Sukey. The idea was that, by crowdsourcing information sent in by SMS, Sukey would be able to pinpoint the position of police lines and tell demonstrators where to go in order to avoid them. 'It didn't really work', recalls Jon Moses, 'but its existence kind of added to the techno-future atmosphere and our sense of being something new and exciting.'

These utopian visions were both true and a fad. They contained the energy, and to an extent the identity, of many who were involved in the movements and were a portent of the extent to which organizations like Momentum would rely on apps and social media to spread their message in spite of an overwhelmingly hostile press. 'Sure', wrote Paul Mason in 2011, 'you can try and insert spin and propaganda, but the instantly networked consciousness of millions of people will set it right: they act like white blood cells against infection so that ultimately truth, or something close to it, persists longer than disinformation.'[31] Earlier that year, Bastani argued that a system of informational abundance and the ability of people to 'organise without organisations' could mean that 'many established political organisations [. . .] may become obsolete, just like the old model of the "Cathedral" par excellence – the Encyclopaedia Britannica'. The nation state, he wrote, was another 'Cathedral', which could be replaced by 'a networked "cosmopolis" with globalized dynamics of communication and movement of persons, goods and capital'.[32]

A few years later, Bastani would be a prominent cheerleader for the Labour Party leadership, and the internet would be a darker place. Facebook looks a lot less horizontal now, and social media more generally would become increasingly corporate, as maximizing advertising revenue became a driving aim. The nation state, far from withering, would be strengthened and reinforced by a wave of right-wing populism which used social media as a tool to deceive and mislead voters. Jair Bolsonaro in Brazil and Narendra Modi in India would both be swept to power on the back of decentralized campaigns of misinformation spread by WhatsApp. The utopian visions of the early part of the decade inspired countless activists and a debate about the renewal of the left, but it is impossible to imagine them being written now in the era after Brexit, Trump and Cambridge Analytica. As the decade unfolded, the emerging new left would learn the hard way that technology was not just a tool for us but a terrain of struggle in its own right. 'In a way we were right', says Bastani now,

in the sense that the internet and digital technologies are so utterly disruptive. It was very precocious for people to say at the age of 26 or 27: 'this is going to be like the printing press', but I think that's probably accurate [. . .] There's the Trump moment, there's Brexit, but I do think it goes beyond that – #MeToo doesn't happen without WhatsApp, certain conspiracy theories don't happen without WhatsApp and back channels and Telegram. So in a way I still think there is still a great deal of horizontality in digital media [. . .] But horizontalism can also be very regressive and right wing and nativist. What we thought in 2011 is that it could only possibly be positive and progressive and that's not accurate.

The contradictions between the spirit of the decade's early social movements and the trajectory of those who took part in them would play out most obviously in the sphere of electoral politics. As the social movements waned, often without producing much in the way of institutional legacy – as we shall see in the next chapter – some of their veterans looked for a political project that could advance, or at least maintain, a critique of austerity. Between October 2014 and May 2015, the membership of the Green Party tripled to 60,000, making it the third biggest party in England. By late 2014, the Greens were polling second (to Labour) in voting intentions among 18- to 24-year-olds. The 'Green Surge', as the moment became known, was driven by a youth and student influx, with many of the veterans of 2010 joining up, among them Aaron Bastani and Andrew Dolan, who is now Momentum's national coordinator. 'I joined in the sense that I filled out a membership form', Dolan says, 'but there was no sense of a collective knuckling down to take over a party. It was more just that the Greens were pitching to the left of Labour, they were a small party and were theoretically easier to influence because of that, so let's all join.'

The Green Surge was on a tiny scale in comparison with what would come later in Labour, and it did not last long, but it did demonstrate the fact that many of the inhabitants of the social movements were yearning for an electoral project which could carry their cause forward. Many passed through it as a pitstop on a truly epic political journey. When Aaron Bastani arrived at the UCL Occupation in 2010, he had come fresh from volunteering for David Miliband's Labour leadership campaign ('only very marginally', he protests, 'and that was largely because a friend of mine was involved and because of some very basic stuff on policy: I wanted to be a civil servant or work in a thinktank'). At the height of the student protests he was helping to organize UK Uncut actions in central London and was a prominent figure within the movement arguing for direct action and decentralized forms of organizing, calling himself a libertarian communist. In 2014, he joined the Greens and a year later rejoined Labour from the left.

Andrew Dolan was drawn into political activity in the wake of the student movement. 'I was more of a pragmatist than a horizontalist', he says, 'in the sense of understanding the need for different types of organisation for different circumstances.' He was drawn into the orbit of *Red Pepper*, a magazine with roots in feminist movement and extra-parliamentary traditions, which made him an editor in 2013. He then spent two years in Plan C, an anti-capitalist group heavily influenced by autonomism and the libertarian communist tradition which attracted a number of social movement veterans. 'I gravitated towards them because they had a critical perspective on the state and electoral politics that drew on anarchism but wasn't anarchistic. It was fairly flexible ideologically, and it understood the need for different forms of organisation in different terrains of struggle.' Soon, the terrain of struggle would change beyond all recognition and so would the organizational form: in the coming years, Dolan would join first the Greens and then Labour and would find himself at the heart of the Corbyn project working as an advisor to Jon Trickett.

From one perspective, then, with the generation without a history surging from one set of big ideas to another, and from one political project to another, Corbynism wasn't a new thing at all but part of a wider pattern. It was just the next and final fad, a project whose gravitational pull was so great that it sucked in, and held onto, everything around it. The zeitgeist was not any particular ideology or concept but rather the very fluidity of those ideologies and concepts.

The dream from below

There is an undeniable sense in which the development of the left throughout the 2010s – and especially the development of the new youth movements, with their faddishness, energy and openness to new ideas – was driven by an internalization of the End of History and the context of an all-prevailing hyper-capitalist society. In a situation in which the mainstream centre-left simply did not offer an alternative, and in which the more radical organized left was regarded as a relic of previous decades, the new generation picked up other labels and tools which it used to dissent.

A kind of consumer logic was also essential to its intensely pragmatic approach to politics and went alongside a very different attitude to party politics and left institutions to that of previous generations of left activists. Previous generations who had gone into the Labour Party, throughout the 1970s and 1980s, had viewed their party membership as an antagonistic activity, a means of agitating and forming an internal opposition to the establishment-aligned leadership, married to a movement in the trade unions and wider society. To a great extent, the generations that followed viewed political parties as a brand which one supported when they aligned with one's values. For the overwhelming majority of left wingers who came of age in the early part of the decade, their disinterest in Labour and other parties was not down to some serious ideological aversion to electoral politics; it was because no credible electoral project existed which corresponded to their own values. When it came into being in the summer of 2015, they exercised their consumer choice and joined it.

But to reduce this generation's political development to a series of fads or consumer choices would be an underestimation of what these moods represented. The nightmare of historical stasis, and of endlessly intensifying exploitation and environmental collapse, also bred dreams. Like actual dreams, these alternatives were non-linear and defied clear definition. They spent a decade being formulated, torn up, rewritten and experimented with, as their protagonists first awakened to the injustices and democratic failures of the system and then, slowly, formulated a politics of their own. The dreams of this generation searched constantly for a vessel that was big enough to hold them, and none could: not the protest movement of 2010, not technological utopianism, not horizontalism and not the Green Surge either. Eventually, the dreams would come to rest in a project – Corbynism – that became, in its electoralism and machine politics, the opposite of much of what this generation had initially hoped for.

'Raymond Williams would have called it a structure of feeling', says Jon Moses. 'Instead of following a rigid political orthodoxy, we were sensing our way through a new atmosphere by instinct. That made the movement highly creative at times, but also accounted for its volatility. Williams uses a metaphor taken from chemistry, "of social experiences in solution". We were a solution with lots of possible interactions, which changed as the political context changed. We could explode into extra-parliamentary anarchy, we could be tamed and distilled by a social democratic project, or fizzle out into nothing.'

This generation did not have a coherent or specific ideology, but that does not mean it cannot be defined. On the contrary, both it and the social movements in which it engaged laid the ground for a transformative shift within the left. At its heart was a visceral antipathy towards the political establishment as a whole and an opposition to undertaking any form of politics which spoke that establishment's language or could be co-opted by them.

What all of the various strands of thinking within the social movements – whether horizontalism, anarchism (real or imagined) or the battered remains of the organized socialist left – had in common was a conception of politics that was fundamentally bottom-up. Although the social movements contained a great variety of different decision-making systems – from the unruly mass meeting to the top-table conference and the consensus decision-making assembly – they shared a central uniting logic: in order to be legitimate, a decision or position needed to have the support of the mass base of the movement, whether in the form of a vote (however token) or via the filtering processes and autonomous activities of the horizontal network. Whether the activities were strikes, the smashing of windows, the occupation of space or the blockading of train stations, it bordered not just on the revolutionary but the insurrectionary. The path to bringing about real social change ran through building power in the streets and power in workplaces. By creating and sustaining mass movements with the ability to resist and disrupt, we could hope to extract concessions out of the political system and one day overturn it entirely. These characteristics were at the heart of a new left which, if it could maintain its independence and find more solid organizational forms, had the potential to transform politics from the outside.

Corbynism owed its existence to the same set of social conditions that created the social movements of 2010, 2011 and thereafter. But it was, as we shall see, in so many ways their mirror image – a recognizable image but an inverted one nonetheless.

The end of the beginning

The year of 2010 ended, superficially at least, in a moment of defeat for the nascent anti-austerity movement. To all intents and purposes, and despite our protestations at the time that it might somehow keep going, the student movement died on 9 December, as MPs voted through the government's rise in tuition fees and the police unleashed hell on the protesters trapped in the freezing Square outside. But the explosion of social movements in the second half of 2010 – from the student protests and UK Uncut to the formation of DPAC and of a number of community anti-cuts groups – had transformed the political horizons of those who had taken part and many of those who had watched it all happen.

The generation without a history had now had its first major outing, as the student movement crystalized a narrative about generational injustice which would prove crucial in the decade that was to come. Until late 2010, generational inequality was already quite widely understood but largely on terms set by older generations in policy papers and newspaper columns. With few exceptions, the debate around the relative wealth of baby boomers and the poor prospects for millennials was presented without reference to the legacy of neoliberalism and without questioning the major policy which would flush the life chances of the next generation down the toilet: austerity and the wider structure of the economy.

The mass mobilization of young people, often accompanied by the sound of roaring crowds and breaking glass, didn't just bring their plight up the news agenda; it also brought about a qualitative shift in what that plight meant politically. All of a sudden, Britain's youth and students were not passive victims of austerity but active fighters of it. The political elite was forced to switch from ignoring them to condemning them, and it could no longer paint them as apathetic or apolitical. The media portrayal of a generation in revolt created a feedback loop, mirroring back the image to a mass youth audience and broadcasting the injustices of low pay, student debt and cuts.

As a matter of course, all mass movements juxtapose the existing ossified system to their own attempts to transform it by taking over spaces, making collective decisions and changing the atmosphere in workplaces, on campuses and in neighbourhoods. It was impossible to miss the fact that the movement against austerity was from the outset part of a crisis not just of the economic system, but of democracy. No matter how much the media and the political establishment tried to turn the coverage of the protests into a rolling condemnation of vandalism and violence, the students and youth who swarmed across Britain's cities had an inalienable claim to be the victims of a great democratic betrayal by the Liberal Democrats who had pocketed their votes and broken their promises. Broken windows were, in the end, just the other side of the equation of this democratic crisis and served to draw attention to the fact that the system had failed.

The Liberal Democrats' tuition fee betrayal was the thin, immediately comprehensible, end of the wedge when it came to the crisis of democracy triggered by the financial crisis and the policy of austerity. For many of those who either directly or indirectly experienced the protest movements, it would be the beginning of a moment that would lead them to question their faith in the institutions of the state and the economic interests they served. 'At times like these', wrote left-wing thinker David Graeber, 'any awakening of the democratic impulse can only be a revolutionary urge.'[33] This framing of the crisis in democratic terms was essential to the emergence of the wider movements yet to come, both in terms of creating legitimacy and popular support for resisting the policies of an elected government and in terms of starting a discussion about what a really democratic society might look like.

Until the protest movements began, austerity was a simple consensus, which rested on a narrative of profligate public spending and the infallibility of the neoliberal economic system. In the autumn of 2010, the students and UK Uncut bulldozed an alternative narrative – of greedy bankers, lying politicians and a broken democracy – into the mainstream.

The left turn of Britain's youth would take time to come to full fruition, and neither the anti-austerity politics nor the insurgent nature of the movements of 2010 were taken up by the Labour Party immediately. But they lingered in the air and in the minds of millions. As the blood dried and the dust settled, the decade was only just about to begin.

The wave breaks

It is hard to overstate the impact of austerity on British society in the 2010s, and the variety of its effects make it hard to paint an adequate picture in raw statistics. One window onto the social crisis can be found in macroeconomic data. Despite containing no recession, the decade was one of the slowest for economic growth since the Second World War, second only to the 2000s, which contained the financial crash.[1] By 2020, real-terms wages were still lower than in 2008, and of thirty-five OECD countries the UK had very nearly the worst rate of growth in productivity per hour worked.[2] Over the course of the decade, unsecured personal debt – so excluding mortgages – increased by almost half to an average of £14,540 per household.[3]

Some statistics are more visceral. In seven years from 2010 to 2017, the proportion of out-of-work disabled people attempting suicide more than doubled from 21 per cent to 43 per cent.[4] In 2014, the Trussell Trust reported that it was delivering food parcels to 913,138 people, a sevenfold increase in three years. In 2010, the Trust ran food banks in 29 local authority areas; four years later, it was operating in 251.[5] The number of families being officially accepted as homeless by local authorities in England, likely to be a substantial underestimate of overall homelessness, rose by 36 per cent to 54,430 per year in the first five years of the decade.[6] In the first seven years of the decade, the number of evictions taking place through the courts (so again, likely a dramatic underestimate of overall evictions) rose by 56 per cent to 169 every day.[7] Shelter estimated that 135,000 children would be homeless at Christmas in 2019, and one in every twenty-four children in London was living in temporary accommodation that year.[8]

Then there is public health. Not only did the 2010s witness a rise in infant mortality unseen for a hundred years, it also witnessed an almost unprecedented stagnation in life expectancy, and this stagnation was driven by widening health inequalities.[9] Between 2012–14 and 2015–17, female life expectancy fell by 100 days in the most deprived 10 per cent of areas in England, while rising by 84 days in the least deprived ones.[10] In the ten years between 2008 and 2018, the number of antidepressant prescriptions doubled – meaning that almost one in five adults was taking them[11] – and this pattern was strongest in the most deprived areas of England. Blackpool, Sunderland and East Lindsey (in Skegness) were top of the league.[12]

This grim reality was not an act of god, or an automatic consequence of the financial crash, but the result of a conscious series of policies undertaken by the Coalition government. The programme of austerity spearheaded by George Osborne would, he predicted in 2010, cost around half a million public sector jobs over the course of the first five years, and this led to major cuts to frontline services. There was a 21 per cent fall in the number of firefighters in England over the decade, for instance,[13] and a chronic shortage of nurses. Those that remained faced an endless string of below-inflation pay rises and real-terms wage cuts so that within a few years millions of public sector workers were thousands of pounds a year worse off. At the same time, the government mounted a propaganda war against what Nick Clegg described as the 'unfair' and 'gold-plated' pension schemes enjoyed by public sector workers and set up a review led by Lord Hutton to recommend reform. The Coalition's reforms to public sector pensions – which included scrapping final salary elements of the schemes, raising the retirement age, increasing employee contributions and switching to a lower rate of inflation adjustment – gave the trade union movement its main grievance for coordinated strike action in 2011.

The Coalition aimed much of its firepower at benefit claimants, with freezes and cuts to the rates of jobseekers' allowance and the vast majority of working-age benefits. The Coalition introduced a cap on the amount that any family could receive in benefit and over the course of the first five years of the decade brought that cap downwards. Child benefit was limited to the oldest two children, leaving larger families with major falls in income. A number of grants for pregnant women and new mothers were abolished. Housing benefit was scrapped entirely for those under the age of twenty-one, and a new policy – the Bedroom Tax – meant that housing benefit was reduced substantially for any social tenant who had a spare room or allowed their children to have their own rooms. Towards the end of its time in office, the Coalition government swung the axe at the tax credit system set up by Labour, limiting the number of children who could receive child tax credit to two. It also drastically curtailed access to tax credits by changing the thresholds at which claimants became ineligible, costing many of the most hard-up families thousands of pounds a year. At the same time, VAT was put up to 20 per cent, its highest ever rate, making basic goods more expensive.

The biggest cuts were reserved for those who were disabled or unable to work because of illness. Incapacity Benefit was already due to be phased out and replaced by the Employment and Support Allowance (ESA), but rather than just being migrated onto the new benefit, recipients were pushed through 'work capability' assessments, which a large proportion of them failed. Similarly, when Disability Living Allowance (DLA) was replaced with the Personal Independence Payment (PIP), the eligibility criteria changed, removing the benefit from hundreds of thousands of people.[14] The assessments were carried out by a patchwork of private companies, including Atos and Capita. Mark Serwotka, general secretary of the civil servants' union PCS, was blunt about his view that the assessments were 'designed to harass vulnerable people and take their benefits away rather than provide support and guidance'.[15] Then, in 2015, the Independent Living Fund was abolished. By 2018, £5 billion a year had been cut from disability benefits alone.[16]

It should be noted that a small number of the Coalition's benefit reforms, and to a much greater extent the rhetoric used to justify them, had been pioneered in government by New Labour. They were rather proud of their record of being tough on 'benefit cheats' and 'scroungers', who found themselves on the receiving end of an organized tabloid campaign. Benefit sanctions – the withdrawal of benefits, often for such crimes as showing up ten minutes late for an appointment – were already growing before the Coalition entered office. In 2009, just under half a million sanctions were imposed on Jobseeker's Allowance claimants. That number doubled in the first few years of the Coalition, with almost a million sanctions applied in 2013, each meaning on average a loss of eight weeks of income.[17] The increasingly punitive nature of the benefits regime, and the sudden loss of income it brought, was a major driver of food bank use throughout the decade.[18]

The services that many of the most vulnerable people relied on were also decimated. Youth services were shut down entirely in many areas of the country and suffered a 70 per cent cut over the course of the decade.[19] Sure Start, a programme set up under New Labour to provide childcare, education and support to young families, especially in disadvantaged areas, was cut by two-thirds, and up to a thousand Sure Start centres had been closed by 2018.[20] Around a third of the NHS's mental health beds disappeared, and between 2013 and 2018, the nurse-to-patient ratio in mental health rose from 29 to 1 to 39 to 1.[21] With an ageing population, spending on adult social care would have needed to rise consistently in order to stand still in terms of provision, but in the first five years of the decade it fell by 17 per cent.[22] Meanwhile, cuts to legal aid meant that whole areas of law – including divorce, employment, benefits and housing – were now off-limits to anyone who could not pay their way, and that only a very small percentage of the population qualified for it at all, even in criminal cases. As a growing number of people struggled to make ends meet, and banks and landlords moved to evict or repossess, taking legal action to prevent homelessness was simply not an option for many tenants and homeowners.

The Coalition also pursued a number of policies aimed less at saving money and more at deepening the penetration of the public sector by market forces. In privatizing Royal Mail in 2013, Vince Cable saw through a project that had for at least twenty years been the ambition of Tory ministers. But it was the government's NHS reforms that would go further than anyone had thus far thought possible. Having repeatedly promised 'no more top-down reorganisations' of the health service – in large part as a response to New Labour's quite unpopular moves to introduce foundation hospitals and public–private partnerships – David Cameron went on to launch the biggest top-down reorganization in the NHS's history.

The NHS White Paper, published in July 2010 just two months after the coalition entered office and spearheaded by Health Secretary Andrew Lansley, laid out the reforms. They included the abolition of primary care trusts and strategic health authorities and their replacement by a system of NHS commissioning. In other words, the reforms opened the door to a situation in which the state would be reduced from a provider of healthcare to just a purchaser of it. Following threats of a Lib Dem rebellion, the Coalition paused the legislation for around a year to undertake a 'listening exercise', but it eventually passed with their support and became law in March 2012. For the first time since the establishment of the NHS in 1948, the Secretary of State for Health would no longer have a statutory duty to provide comprehensive free healthcare. As Allyson Pollock, professor of public health at Newcastle University, wrote in 2014, 'The Act effectively reduces the NHS to a funding stream and a logo. Behind the logo, corporations bid for health contracts in a regulated market.'[23] If the welfare state felt like it was being mortally wounded, that was because it was.

One of the strange aspects of this period was that austerity did not lead to a long-term rise in unemployment. After surging following the 2008 crash to a peak of 8.5 per cent in late 2011, unemployment dropped sharply to around 5 per cent by the middle of the decade and 3.8 per cent by its end – its lowest point since the 1970s, despite the loss of over a million public sector jobs over the decade.

Youth unemployment, high at the time of the 2010 student movement, also dropped away. This fact surprised much of the emerging anti-austerity movement and the organized left, who had expected to be running a campaign against joblessness (the SWP even called its main campaign of this era 'Right to Work' in anticipation of a fight over mass unemployment). Instead of a direct loss of jobs, workers faced an attack on the quality and stability of their employment. As real-terms wages fell, many more workers found themselves in a hand-to-mouth existence. By 2020, there were more than a million people employed on zero-hours contracts, an almost sixfold increase in 2010,[24] and bogus self-employment accounted for many more. The experience of millions of workers underwent a qualitative shift, marked by precarity and intensified exploitation. This shift happened overwhelmingly in workplaces in which the big unions had little or no membership density, and, as we shall see, they did not rise to the challenge of organizing in them, instead focussing their efforts on the public sector.

The Coalition government did not believe in austerity for everyone, though. Alongside the first tranche of cuts, it cut the top rate of income tax. It also cut the main rate of corporation tax from 28 to 20 per cent over the course of its time in office, giving Britain one of the lowest rates in Europe, and was repeatedly criticized for striking sweetheart deals which let companies like Vodafone off billions of pounds in tax. By the time the Coalition left office, the wealth of the richest 1,000 families in Britain had doubled to £547 billion. The surge in the Liberal Democrat vote in 2010 came in large part from centre-left voters, many of them young and progressive, who had cheered on Vince Cable as he slammed the 'foolish, greedy, irresponsible behaviour' of 'Britain's financial aristocracy' and joked that 'they are lucky the British have no guillotines in stock'.[25] The reality of the Lib Dems in government could barely have been more different to what was promised.

From these conditions, the radical left sprang back from irrelevance, taking centre stage in British politics for the first time since the 1980s. It erupted as a response to an attempt to abolish what remained of the welfare state and an assault on the living standards and security of a majority of the population. It was aided by the existence of an enemy, in the form of the Coalition government, that was overwhelmingly composed of millionaires and which handed out tax breaks to big business and the rich at the same time as cutting public services to the bone. Following the tripling of tuition fees, it was also a government whose junior partner, the Liberal Democrats, had barefacedly broken a crucial election promise and which simply did not match the expectations of those who had voted for them.

And yet the return of a left-wing alternative in British politics did not come from a simple juxtaposition, or from a passively experienced sense of injustice, but from a series of confrontations between movements and the state, and between unions and employers, which breathed life back into the left and brought hundreds of thousands of people into political activity and into contact with new ideas. The way in which the left regrew – culminating in an electoral project within the Labour Party – owes its existence not only to the movements themselves but also to the fact that they were defeated. As the rank and file of the new left fought and lost, they were exploring, almost as if by process of elimination, the possibilities for a revival.

Understanding the terrain

Looking back on the effects of austerity over the course of the decade, the depth and breadth of the cuts and social damage can seem like a wall of noise. But the catastrophe that occurred, and to a great extent is still occurring, in British society and in its public services did not happen all at once. The cuts and the structural reforms to the public sector came as a series of government announcements and votes on legislation and were then implemented over the course of months and years. The movement against austerity faced a battle on multiple fronts immediately after the election of the Coalition. In the first wave of measures, all of them announced in 2010, came cuts to local government, the higher education reforms, the cuts to welfare, the attack on public sector pensions and pay, and the NHS White Paper – and the initial wave of opposition to austerity was inevitably structured around these.

In order to understand the resistance to cuts and the development of the left, it is necessary to understand the disaggregated nature of what occurred, for austerity was not simply a policy but a whole string of cuts, reforms, restructurings and wage freezes. Although it was made to happen by central government, it was implemented by a whole series of other bodies – by quangos, agencies and above all by local government. Shifting responsibility onto local councils was a conscious strategy of the Coalition government. It deliberately legislated to transfer statutory duties to local authorities, for instance on public health, at the same time as cutting their budgets by around 40 per cent between 2010 and 2015 (and by more than half in some areas). It also made it impossible to raise council tax by more than 2 per cent without holding a local referendum. In many Labour-run areas, this dynamic created an explosive showdown between local communities and councillors. Unlike in the 1980s, there was no strategy of disobedience or defiance by Labour councils, and many of them were blamed by their communities for implementing Tory cuts.

The outsourcing of blame was only one effect of this strategy, however. The other crucial thing it did was to take away a whole series of national flashpoints which otherwise could have provided anti-cuts campaigners and unions with a moment to mobilize, in much the same way that the students had been able to mobilize around the 9 December parliamentary vote on tuition fees in 2010. In previous eras, movements had been able to coalesce much more easily around single moments of mass protest, direct action or industrial action. The Poll Tax, for instance, was a single policy, and there was a simple and effective set of actions that any individual could take in order to oppose it: refuse to pay the tax and perhaps come on a protest. Before the tightening of trade union laws under Margaret Thatcher, unions could engage in secondary action in solidarity with other workers and could strike against a government policy in general, rather than only within the terms of a narrowly defined trade despite.

In the early years of the 2010s, the government could pass cuts at a stroke in the knowledge that a large chunk of them would be implemented in a piecemeal and uneven fashion so that there was no national moment at which local library services were decimated, or Sure Start centres closed, around which opposition could mobilize in a united fashion. Because of the anti-union legislation, trade unions could not legally strike on a national level over cuts which were technically speaking local. They, and the wider campaigns, had to fight inch by inch against a programme of cuts which was, as far as the government was concerned, a cohesive programme.

And so, just as austerity was not a single policy, the anti-austerity movement was not a single movement. Instead, it consisted of five distinct strands. First, there were the local anti-cuts groups and grassroots campaigns, which sprung up in response to cuts and organized under a plethora of different banners, fighting a plethora of different battles in local communities. Second, there was the continuing push in higher education, where students and staff continued, in spite of their diminished numbers and parliamentary defeats in 2010, to mobilize. Third, there were the mass protests, consisting primarily of large set-piece marches which gave cover to a smaller group of activists who engaged in disruptive direct action and otherwise caused mayhem. Fourth, there was the industrial action over pensions and pay, which shut down swathes of the public sector. Fifth, there was the Occupy movement and its offshoots, which symbolically took over the area outside the London Stock Exchange with a tent city and spread across the country. Alongside these, there were the riots of the summer of 2011, which, although not a social movement in a formal sense, held up a mirror to a society in breakdown. These strands were obviously connected in various ways but at the time functioned separately from one another and often lacked coordination. Each on their own would have been a large but passing event in the life of the country. Taken together, they constituted a mass movement which, even in defeat, transformed the political atmosphere in the UK.

All of these strands – the campaigns, the protests, the strikes and the camps – drew strength from the movements that had preceded them and from an international wave of protests of which Britain was only one part. And all were active roughly simultaneously, peaking relatively early on. Over the course of 2011, they would build and combine to ensure that the movement went into the November of that year like a coiled spring.

The grassroots builds

At the base of the anti-austerity movement was a colossal network of local groups and community campaigns. The Coalition might not always have acted in line with each and every one of its manifesto promises, but its agenda in broad brush strokes was perfectly open and easy to understand and triggered the usual set of responses among the organized left. Tony Benn's open letter, co-signed by around seventy other notable politicians, activists and trade unionists, was followed by a Downing Street rally organized by the newly established Coalition of Resistance, working in coalition with Camden Trades Council, which coincided with George Osborne's autumn statement on 20 October 2010.

As the chancellor set out his austerity programme, the resistance set out its stall. Jeremy Corbyn, the left-wing backbencher for Islington North, warned,

> What the IMF has done in the Global South for the past three decades is now being done in Europe: to Greece, to Spain, to Portugal, to Ireland, to France, and now today here in Britain . . . We are here to make the argument that a decent civilised society taxes those who are rich enough to pay to provide resources and services for everyone on the principle of universal health, universal benefits and a universally decent society. Join every campaign, fight all the cuts (except those in the armed forces, where we'd like to see a few more cuts and no more nuclear weapons) . . .[26]

'Today it's important that we give the clearest message possible to the millionaires who live down there on Downing Street'[27], said Mark Serwotka, the general secretary of the civil service union PCS. 'We didn't cause the crisis, their mates caused the crisis.' Grasping the scale of the attacks that were about to land and the scale of the movement that might be required to stop them, he called on the unions to take industrial action together and to build links with 'the students, the pensioners, the unemployed'. 'Now is the time', he implored from the stage, 'in every town in every city to plan together, to get people together, organise marches, organise protests.'

Across the country, while students plotted and the founders of UK Uncut identified their targets, community activists and trade unionists had already begun to come together to form local campaigns and alliances to oppose the cuts. As early as autumn 2010, a hubbub of dissent and anger proliferated, led by the new anti-cuts campaigns. As Lewisham's Labour-run Council met to discuss plans to scrap £60 million of local services on 23 November, an alliance of Goldsmiths students and local trade unionists tried to storm the chamber, resulting in several arrests. Local industrial disputes – for instance, the Birmingham bin strike, which started in December – also proliferated, giving a sharper sense of disruption to go alongside the protests.

Many drew on the existing infrastructure of the left and the labour movement. Local Trades Councils – central hubs to which all trade unions in a given area send a delegate – were in many places moribund after decades of declining union membership. Camden was no exception, but there, the energetic chair of the Trades Council, George Binette, used the structure to call the march on Downing Street on 20 October. Out of the back of the demonstration, Camden United Against the Cuts developed into a broad coalition of local union branches, working alongside a handful of Labour activists and a large number of ordinary local residents. It held regular mass meetings and engaged in a fair bit of rowdy protest around strikes and council meetings. On 28 February 2011, as Camden Council was meeting to pass its budget (and pass on the government's austerity programme), hundreds of demonstrators blocked traffic on Euston Road.

In Lambeth, it was the local Unison branch which would be the organizational core for the anti-cuts campaign, though, says local Unison activist Dan Jeffery, 'it quickly got a lot bigger than that'. Lambeth Save Our Services (or Lambeth SOS) was set up in the autumn of 2010 following a series of open meetings. Like many local groups, it found itself with an influx of supporters from all walks of life. 'Sometimes when you set up a campaign, you end up bringing together the people you already know', says Ruth Cashman, Lambeth Unison's branch secretary, 'but this time there really was a surge of people who were just very pissed off about the Coalition government, including a fair few younger people.' The group produced a Lambeth Newsletter and distributed propaganda. Its protests got gradually larger, building up to a demonstration several hundred strong on 23 February 2011 to coincide with the budget-setting meeting of Lambeth Council. 'Only a very limited number of people were allowed in to watch the councillors debate, and the frustration just built', says Jeffery, 'and relatively spontaneously the crowd just went in and occupied the Town Hall.' The council administration fled the scene and reconvened in another room, leaving the protesters to hold an assembly in the Council Chamber. 'We had streams of people joining as the word got out – including a lot of students', recalls Cashman. 'It was one of the first protests I'd been on when social media played a role in broadcasting what was happening in real time.'

A similar pattern could be seen across the country. On February 2011, the same day that Camden United Against the Cuts was blocking Euston Road, around a thousand people marched on Birmingham Town Hall as the council prepared to set its budget. The protest was organized by Birmingham Against the Cuts, another coalition which brought together a wide array of campaigns and groups. In the crowd were contingents from the Save Birmingham Youth Services campaign, the Social Work Action Group, Friends of Moseley Baths, the Campaign to Retain Our School Service, and the Alliance Against Birmingham Academies. UK Uncut shut down a branch of Barclays bank as the protest marched past. By spring 2011, pretty much every town and city had a local anti-cuts group: a mishmash of activists organizing meetings, stalls, protests and more ambitious action like Town Hall occupations, gravitating around local council budget-setting meetings, strikes and national calls to action like the national demonstration scheduled for 26 March.

By and large, the local groups were broad, non-sectarian and action-oriented. Because they developed organically, rather than being created by a central campaign or party structure, they created a home for everyone: local trade union branches worked with local branches of Green Party, newly created single-issue networks, residents' associations, local Labour Party branches that were willing to make a stand and multiple different socialist grouplets. They were genuinely grassroots campaigns, lacking both the inhibitions and the spellchecking abilities of more professionalized organizations: Ruth Cashman recalls how, in early 2011, Lambeth SOS printed tens of thousands of leaflets calling for 'coordinated streaking'.

The proliferation of campaigns was not just area by area but issue by issue as well. One of the earliest, and most high profile, was DPAC, which formed following a protest outside Tory Party conference in 2010. In the following months and years, it would spread across the country, with dozens of local chapters. 'I went to the founding conference and spoke', remembers John McDonnell. 'There must have been about 60 or 70 of us, and for the first time we had a really strong disability movement.' Led by disabled people, DPAC spearheaded campaigns against welfare changes and service cuts, targeting Atos, the company responsible for the 'work capability assessments' which were stripping many thousands of their right to benefits. Other campaigns also rose to prominence and had fresh life breathed into them by the government's agenda. Keep Our NHS Public was formed in 2005 and now came into its own as a hub for opposition against the Health and Social Care Bill, coordinating protests alongside the health unions and recruiting thousands of new people into campaigns against localized cuts to the NHS.

Attempts to coordinate the movement on a national level began with the creation of the Coalition of Resistance, which held its founding conference at the end of November 2010. Attended by around a thousand activists including representatives of many of the new anti-cuts campaigns, the conference was addressed by union leaders including the newly elected Unite general secretary Len McCluskey, who quoted Engels and gave a tub-thumping call to arms.

The upsurge in social struggle and the gravity of the situation did not create organizational unity, however. The Coalition of Resistance was not controlled by any single faction or party but had been initiated by Counterfire, a socialist group which had split from the SWP in 2010. The SWP itself decided to focus on building Right to Work, its own national network, whose conference took place in January 2011. Also taking place in January was the national conference of the National Shop Stewards Network, at which the Socialist Party used its majority to create yet another national anti-cuts organization.

These divisions inevitably grew as time wore on and more sharp political questions were posed. In Birmingham, Communities Against the Cuts formed as a split from Birmingham Stop the Cuts over a disagreement about running candidates against Labour in the local elections. Gradually, the national divisions also began to be played out on a local level, as the SWP instructed its members to set up their own local Right to Work groups. At no point during the height of the anti-austerity movement was there a united national organization which brought all of the anti-cuts campaigns under one banner. With the voice of the grassroots fragmented, the movement relied on the unions and their timetable of strikes and marches for the nationwide moments around which everyone could mobilize.

Looking back, it is remarkable that the organized left succeeded in dividing the movement in spite of a clear unifying goal (stopping the cuts), a shared strategy (of mass social and industrial struggle) and an overwhelming appetite for a united organization at the grassroots. To understand why this happened, you have to understand the political method of some of the groups involved. The SWP and the Socialist Party were genuinely committed to the project of opposing austerity and rebuilding the left, but they were also concerned with building their own organizations. Their approach to organizing campaigns, which drew on an especially sectarian brand of Leninism, was coloured by a desire to enlarge and empower themselves and an unwillingness to prioritize broad organizations over which they did not have tight control. In the end, this inflexibility would prove their undoing. The mass base of the new movement had little time for sectarian politics and in the end would look elsewhere for a moment of political revival. For many of the young recent veterans of the student movement, who were gravitating towards anarchism and direct action politics, the way things played out seemed to vindicate the horizontalist and anti-organizational politics that was taking root.

Despite these problems, the nexus of the organized left and the local anti-cuts groups was the engine of the anti-austerity movement. For all the wrangling on a national level, most local activists just got on with it, either navigating or ignoring the forest of acronyms and arguments going on overhead. 'The thing that stayed with me from that time', says Ruth Cashman, 'is the fact that it was very possible to hold something together that would be united in action despite some big political differences on things like the Labour Party.' What the local groups built was in many places a durable source of mobilization rooted in local communities and visible within them which, crucially, was not reliant on a central national leadership for permission or political orientation. The pickets and occupations of Town Halls, the strike solidarity protests, the coaches organized for the big London demonstrations, the marches to the local hospital and the outpouring of meetings and cultural events: all had the effect not just of making a scene or stopping the odd cut but also of normalizing opposition to austerity and of recruiting many thousands to the cause.

Not everyone who got involved in the movement behind Jeremy Corbyn was a twenty-something precariously employed graduate or a teenager determined to fight climate change. Many were returners to politics after decades out of action, and many others were recently radicalized opponents of austerity. When, in 2015, the left once again sprung into life in towns and cities across the country – this time with the aim of getting Corbyn elected as Labour leader – many of its organizers had come of age in the previous five years. Many of the networks they used were the reanimated remnants of the local anti-cuts groups, whose support base had flooded into the Labour Party.

The students march on

The student movement of 2010 was defeated on 9 December when MPs voted to triple tuition fees. Its lack of central organization meant that it had no means of preparing the mass of young people whom it had brought into political activity for the fact that fees would be raised or the fact that a longer-term strategy would be needed. It had no cohesive or enduring radical political programme to go alongside its radical tactics. In the course of one month of intense struggle, the students had mobilized in unprecedented numbers, come to new conclusions about the world and built friendships and political connections that would last years; but they had also been kettled and assaulted by the police, disciplined by their school and university managements and, as far as many were concerned, abjectly defeated. The indelible mark of having realized their agency in the heat of a mass movement would remain, and many would come back to politics but not immediately and not to repeat the events of that autumn.

Those of us at the core of the student mobilizations underestimated this attrition, however, and continued to organize as if the movement would emerge from its Christmas hiatus in high spirits. The London Student Assembly and the NCAFC called further days of action for 29 January and then on 24 February, planting red flags into the ground in the hope that the usual mob of uniformed school kids and angry twenty-somethings would run at them. They didn't. At the two separate protests on 29 January – one in London called by the student left, one in Manchester called by the NUS – turnout went down to the low thousands. 24 February saw just a few hundred protesters march in London, though a few campus protests did occur elsewhere, and by spring the London Student Assembly had stopped meeting altogether.

Just because the rhythm of the autumn had stopped beating didn't mean that the student movement was dead. Activist groups had begun to form from the remnants of the campus occupations and organizing networks of 2010 and on many campuses only properly got going in 2011. At the University of Kent, they'd stayed in occupation over Christmas and New Year, and at some campuses, like Birmingham and Hull, they began 2011 by reoccupying. On 1 February, students at the University of Glasgow occupied a largely disused building, founding the Free Hetherington occupation. Lasting until the end of August that year, it was probably the longest-running student occupation in British history.

But for most of those still mobilizing, the immediate battle had moved on from being a purely student affair. The growing number of anti-cuts groups gave students a means of getting involved in politics in the community beyond campus and a window onto the wider movement against austerity. The defeated movement of 2010 had triggered a much bigger wave of protest with whose fate it was now intimately bound up.

As the wider movement prepared for its first national protest on 26 March and its first major strike action in the summer, higher education was once again the first sector where it started to kick off. The lecturers' union UCU called a series of strikes over pensions from 17 March, peaking on 24 March, two days before the TUC-organized march in London. On the day, as picket lines massed outside universities across England, another wave of campus occupations took root, many of them aimed at shutting down the administrative functions of the universities for the duration of the strike. At UCL, students stormed the registry and held it for almost a week. Students from Goldsmiths College took over Deptford Town Hall. Other occupations started in Newcastle, SOAS and a number of other campuses, and the strength of the picket lines gave heart to trade unionists in other sectors preparing to ballot. For the entire academic year, or at least the period up until exams, many university campuses had been in a solid state of ferment. Those who had been part of the action would go into the 26 March national demonstration, and the months beyond it, not as fresh-faced new recruits but as tooled-up veterans with a penchant for direct action.

With spring and the exam season came a lull in proceedings but not an end to developments. In the NUS, the movement had its revenge as Aaron Porter, whose refusal to back the protests had made him infamous among many activists, decided not to run for re-election and became the first NUS president since the 1970s not to serve two terms. He had already been physically chased through the streets by his members, once in Manchester and once in Glasgow. The NUS's conference, which took place in April, did see a minor shift leftwards among the leadership but not one significant enough to see the union take up leadership of the movement against the government's programme of cuts and privatization in the sector. Mark Bergfeld, the left's candidate for NUS president, was soundly beaten, and a proposal to call a national demonstration was voted down on leadership recommendation, meaning that the task of organizing one would once again fall to the NCAFC.

In June 2011, the government announced the higher education white paper, its vision for a marketized higher education system in a world of sky-high tuition fees. For-profit providers would increasingly be allowed to operate, and institutions would be allowed to go bankrupt as the logic of the market permeated deeper and deeper into the sector. The NCAFC, also in June, had for the first time developed national structures and a network of affiliated local campus groups, and we used this new-found sense of central organization to name the date for a national protest for 9 November. In the run up to the protest we would build links with a whole new set of movements, a network of electricians on wildcat strike and an occupation of a very different kind which had set up camp outside the London Stock Exchange. Either the students would win alongside the communities resisting cuts and the public sector workers balloting for strike action or we would all lose together.

The banners unfurl

The anti-austerity movement first marched together on 26 March 2011. Officially organized by the TUC, this protest became the focal point for every strand of the left, every campaign or direct action group and every concerned citizen whose local library was being cut. National unions, local branches and community campaign groups put on more than 600 coaches and chartered dozens of trains to bring protesters to London. Estimates put the numbers on the protest at around half a million, making it the biggest since the Iraq War.

The protest was organized under the banner of 'March for the Alternative: Jobs, Growth, Justice', a loosely worded title under which everyone could write their own content. For the leadership of some of the trade unions, 'the alternative' was a slightly less bad deal on pensions than the one currently being proposed by the Coalition. For other unions, and probably the bulk of those on the protest, it was stopping all the cuts. For the Labour leadership, it was slightly fewer cuts delivered slightly later. For the newly awakened radical edge of the movement, many of them anarchists and horizontalists brought into activity by the student movement and UK Uncut, the alternative was something altogether more radical and anti-capitalist.

This collision of worlds and motivations is a common feature to all great protest movements, and the diversity of politics was mirrored in a diversity of tactics, in what became a tale of two marches. In the official protest, the massed ranks of organized labour trudged through central London, their spirits high and their mood calm but determined, towards the rally in Hyde Park. Neighbours marched together and whole workplaces marched side by side behind union branch banners, some attending their first-ever protest. As the university feeder march arrived from Bloomsbury conveying many thousands of angry, chanting students, the contrast was stark. 'I remember all these older trade unionists looking at us like we were from another planet', says Simon Hannah. 'There was a genuine sense of warmth towards the students in the wider crowd, but you also got this sense that many workers didn't feel that they'd ever be in a struggle as militant as we were in.' As we crawled round Embankment, I remember being told off by an elderly woman for absent-mindedly swearing over the megaphone.

If she had been at Oxford Circus, she might have been even more disapproving. There, with the roads jammed full of youths, arts collectives and the activist scenes of London, people were preparing to burn a gigantic Trojan Horse in the middle of the street, a symbol of the Liberal Democrats' betrayal on tuition fees. The horse had been wheeled to the scene of its incineration from Kennington, travelling with the tens of thousands-strong south London feeder march organized by Lambeth SOS, which had broken police lines to get over Westminster Bridge ('it's not often you get anarchists, a giant wooden horse and mainstream Labour MPs on the same demo', remarks Ruth Cashman).

The crowd at Oxford Circus had gathered for much more than just an A to B march. Just as the student movement of 2010 had set aside the passive protest model in favour of a more disruptive model, many at the sharp end of austerity were already willing to take direct action. Some of the more organized activists in the crowd carried maps and leaflets urging others to 'kick off for the alternative' and 'occupy for the alternative'. UK Uncut's callout was for demonstrators to peacefully protest tax-avoiding companies like Topshop and Boots as well as Whittington Investments, the company which owned Fortnum & Mason. Others went a lot further. Thousands ran amok down Oxford Street, Piccadilly and across central London. Dozens of tax-avoiding shop fronts were done in, some with paint and some with bricks, as were many banks, branches of McDonalds and the Ritz. For a number of hours, the police lost control of much of central London.

Having taken over the streets, the Black Bloc and the thousands who simply milled around while the mayhem took place were consciously creating an echo of the revolutionary atmosphere being experienced in Egypt and across the Arab world. Student organizers, including myself, had earlier in the week issued a call to 'turn Trafalgar Square into Tahrir Square', hoping to hold the space and to make it a focal point and organizing hub for the movement in the coming period. Jeremy Corbyn and John McDonnell endorsed the call, putting their names to a statement which called on protesters to

> stay in Trafalgar square for 24 hours to discuss how we can beat this government and to send a message across the globe that we stand with the people of Egypt, Libya, Wisconsin and with all those fighting for equality, freedom and justice. We want to turn Trafalgar square into a place of people's power where we assert our alternative to cuts and austerity and make it a day that this Government won't forget.[28]

In the end, it came to nothing. Most of those committed to occupying the square were drawn north into Piccadilly, where much of the action was happening, and riot police eventually surged into Trafalgar Square, batons raised.

At the official rally in Hyde Park, a surreal event of a different kind was taking place, as Ed Miliband delivered his speech. Clearly, he viewed the demonstrators as 'his people', to whom he owed his presence, but was heckled by large parts of the crowd when he clarified that 'there is a need for difficult choices, and some cuts'. The most remarkable and telling lines came in the form of a grand allusion to history:

> We come in the tradition of movements that have marched in peaceful but
>   powerful protest for justice, fairness and political change.
> The suffragettes who fought for votes for women and won.
> The civil rights movement in America that fought against racism and won.
> The anti apartheid movement that fought the horror of that system and won.[29]

Miliband had attended the protest in the hope of offering solidarity, but his speech cemented mistrust in the minds of many opponents of austerity (which, after all, was a policy he did not oppose). Then, as mobs of protesters tore across central London setting fire to giant wooden horses and smashing windows, he pointedly called for 'peaceful but powerful protest' and, as his historical examples, cited the suffragettes (who engaged in a bombing and arson campaign), the US civil rights movement (whose full history goes well beyond the pacifism of Martin Luther King) and the struggle against apartheid (in which the ANC and uMkhonto we Sizwe waged an armed struggle against the South African state). The anti-austerity movement did not just mainstream alternative narratives and raise the expectations of millions, it also simultaneously showcased the inadequacies and contortions of the existing Labour Party establishment.

Back in Piccadilly, things did not end well. That afternoon hundreds of people, including many of UK Uncut's key activists, had walked into Fortnum & Mason and hung some banners up. The police, having lost control of the streets for some hours, moved in against a group whose protest was, by all accounts, polite and peaceful. The protesters were first trapped in the building and then told they were being released but were in fact arrested outside and taken to police stations. There, many had their clothes and phones confiscated and were released the next day dressed in police-issue boiler suits with no phone on the outer edges of London. A total of 138 were later charged with offences, and many convicted, in a mass prosecution which UK Uncut described as a deliberate attempt to forcibly disband the campaign group. UK Uncut's vitality and fearlessness would never be quite the same again.

Nonetheless, the March for the Alternative provided the occasion for the anti-austerity movement to come together, a moment when all of its strands saw and began to comprehend one another. The mass of protesters and sense of energy was publicly juxtaposed with the inadequacies of the political representation that the movement could rely on. But big marches, and even large-scale direct action, was no substitute for a movement in workplaces. In the end, it was always going to be down the unions to show the government what real disruption looked like.

The workers crank into action

The great leftward shift in the leadership of the Labour Party which took place with the election of Jeremy Corbyn in 2015 had, to a certain extent, already happened in many trade unions. During the Blair era, as the prospects for the left looked increasingly bleak in the world of politics, a slew of left wingers were elected to lead the unions. In 2011, the civil servants' union PCS was led by Mark Serwotka, who had been expelled from the Labour Party in the late 1990s for his membership of the group Socialist Organiser; his former comrades, now operating under the name Workers' Liberty, had helped me and others set up the NCAFC in 2010. In 2000, he had been a rank-and-file organizer when he very reluctantly put his name forward to be the far left's candidate for general secretary. He assumed that his candidacy was a no hoper, but, he says, 'it absolutely caught a mood – talking about strike action over pay and pensions, how badly we were being done over by New Labour. There was a real sense that the unions now needed to be the real opposition to the Blair government, which was very pro-market and pro-privatisation.'

Sertwotka's victory was the start of a trend, and soon he would be joined by many other left union leaders. Together, they would be known as 'the awkward

squad', and they would outlast Blair and Brown by some way. By the time the
Coalition came to power, the Communication Workers Union (CWU) was led
by left-winger Billy Hayes, who was elected in 2002. Jeremy Dear was leading the
National Union of Journalists (NUJ). The general secretary of the Fire Brigades
Union (FBU) was Matt Wrack, elected in 2005, who had been in Militant in
the 1980s and had lost none of his enthusiasm for socialist transformation or
his firebrand oratory skills. Bob Crow, an outspoken communist, was general
secretary of transport union RMT. The National Union of Teachers (NUT) was
led by Christine Blower, who had run as a candidate for the Socialist Alliance
in the 2000 London Assembly elections and would later be elevated to the
House of Lords by Jeremy Corbyn. By the end of 2011, Manuel Cortes had
been elected leader of the Transport Salaried Staffs Association (TSSA), whose
Euston headquarters would later host Momentum's offices and both of Corbyn's
leadership campaigns.

Perhaps most significantly, the election in 2010 of Len McCluskey as the
general secretary of Unite meant that the country's largest union was led from
the left. Andrew Murray, a long-time member of the Communist Party of Britain,
was swiftly appointed as his chief of staff. 'After the defeats of the 80s, there was
a consolidated view of social partnership led by the TUC which in the end was
embraced by almost all unions', remembers Murray:

> The union leaders who'd been there in 1997, including those with a leftwing
> history, were very concerned not to rock the boat. But a few years into New
> Labour, people began to realise that the boat wasn't really going anywhere for
> them anyway . . . [The shift] was driven by frustration with New Labour – the
> failure to remove the anti-union laws that had been put in place by Thatcher,
> the absence of a radical domestic agenda, and also somewhat by the movement
> against the Iraq War. It affected all the unions to some degree of another – you
> had this accumulation of unions trying to do something different to stand up to
> Blair and Brown.

As we shall see, the political clarity and anti-New Labour sentiment of the new
wave of left union leaderships did not always translate into industrial strength
or a sure-fire willingness to maintain and escalate strike action. What it did
mean was that when George Osborne announced the bulldozing of the welfare
state, the trade union movement knew exactly which side it was on and what
was at stake. There was no serious argument within it, as there was in Labour,
about whether or not to oppose austerity or if some cuts might be necessary.
The message broadcast from the likes of Len McCluskey from the moment that

the Coalition entered office was that all the cuts should be fought and that strike action was inevitable. When the student movement exploded in the autumn of 2010, he, Mark Serwotka and other union leaders seized on it as an opportunity to accelerate the development of a broad alliance of resistance across society and began, slowly, to prepare their own members for battle.

The unions were also, at least superficially, relatively united in their main strategy. There were a plethora of local and sector-specific disputes throughout the initial period of austerity, for instance in the fire service and on the transport network, but the big weapon that the trade union movement could deploy was the prospect of coordinated strike action. Legal restrictions meant that workers could not take action against the general policy of the government but could strike over the same thing, or even over different things, at the same time. Discussions over coordinated strike action over the government's public sector pensions proposals began in January 2011, hosted by the TUC.

Some unions mobilized faster than others. On 30 June, civil servants in the PCS, the lecturers' union UCU and the two main teaching unions, NUT and ATL, initiated the first day of coordinated action. As workers walked out of work across the country, something like 11,000 schools were affected, as were job centres, courts, prisons and central government departments. Despite the fact that many students were on summer break, some universities saw lively pickets with a heavy student presence. Just as significant as the strikes themselves were the protests, which for the first time since the student movement took on a nationwide dimension. Tens of thousands marched in London, but also hundreds in Truro and Cambridge, and thousands in Manchester, Birmingham and other major cities. J30, as the day was known, became a focal point for the wider movement, too, with UK Uncut calling a range of local actions and local anti-cuts groups mobilizing the wider community. Activists inspired by the *indignados* movement in Spain organized 'J30 assemblies' in some cities, bringing together the wider community to plan solidarity pickets, protests and even parties around the strikes.

Once again, the Labour leadership's intervention into the situation was not welcomed by the movement. In a BBC interview, Ed Miliband said that 'parents and the public have been let down by both sides' and condemned the strikes, saying that they were 'wrong at a time when negotiations are ongoing'. He urged 'both sides to put aside the rhetoric, get round the negotiating table and stop this from happening again'. Asked several different questions by the interviewer, he repeated these lines verbatim five times. The robotic nature of the interview made it infamous for many years to come.

The position of the Labour leadership was not the only issue that the movement would have to address following J30, however. While there was significant disruption to schools and some of the public sector, it was limited to a single day. Aside from sending a signal to the government that workers were willing to take action, its main effects were its mobilization of demonstrations and rallies and its ability to bring the struggle of public sector workers into town centres across the country. Ultimately, one-day strikes would always be an act of protest rather than an act of resistance and simply did not have the disruptive force to make the government reconsider its programme. On the day, Francis Maude, the government's paymaster general, appeared on BBC quite calmly to deliver his talking points. 'People are living longer, we know that', he said, unaware that life expectancy was beginning to stall, 'and so it's perfectly reasonable for people to expect to work a bit longer before they start drawing their pension.' As the unions warmed up and the wider movement continued to grow, J30 provided a focus, but in the coming period something bigger would be needed.

As the autumn drew nearer, it became clear that the cavalry would, at last, arrive. Unison, by far the biggest public sector union, balloted a million members in early October, and the other big unions, Unite and the GMB, also finally pressed the button. They were joined by a patchwork of smaller unions across the public sector. It had taken a full year from the smashing of the glass at Millbank Tower for the labour movement to finally gear up for a battle over austerity, not just by waving placards but by creating disruption on such a scale that the government simply could not ignore it.

The strikes, eventually set for 30 November and touted as a 'public sector general strike', would be the biggest single day of industrial action in more than a generation. For Dan Jeffery, like so many in the rank and file of the trade union movement, the hope was that the day would 'let the genie out of the bottle and mean that the strikes would then escalate'. To succeed, it would need to be the beginning of a concerted period of action which would, they hoped, evolve into something much more serious. 'We hoped that after starting something, the trade unions wouldn't be able to just call the whole thing off. If there was concerted action by the movement, the government might fold', he says.

John Moloney is now the deputy general secretary of PCS. In 2011, he was a shop steward in representing civil servants in the Department of Transport and remembers the fighting mood ahead of 30 November:

> There was real optimism. I've been in lots of disputes when you loyally go on strike but you think 'jeez, this is going to go nowhere', but we didn't feel like that

in the run up to November. We felt that although this was a one day strike, the next thing that would be called would be a much wider strike – whether for a week or two weeks, or rolling strikes by different unions or selective action. Given the sheer range of unions and the mood, everybody believed – at least activists that I knew – that the next stage was a deepening and a marked acceleration of the dispute, and we assumed this would happen very rapidly.

The tents are pitched

Protest camps were not invented in 2011, but it was in that year and in the heart of many of the world's cities that the tactic perhaps reached its zenith. In Spain, a gigantic anti-austerity street movement, which began on 15 May, had resulted in several thousand people taking and holding public spaces – such as the Puerta del Sol in Madrid and Barcelona's Plaça Catalunya – and living there in tents. The residents of the squares and plazas held gigantic public assemblies in the open air to organize themselves and set their demands. Similar scenes could be witnessed in Athens and Thessaloniki in the following weeks. Tent cities had already appeared during the Arab Spring earlier in the year, notably in Tahrir Square where the camp had played a crucial role in a movement not of protest but of revolution, providing a hub for the resistance and an ongoing spectacle of popular dissent.

In the early autumn, what would become the Occupy movement began in earnest. Inspired by events in Madrid, Cairo and elsewhere, a network of anarchists and anti-globalization movement veterans in New York latched onto a call initially circulated by the anti-capitalist magazine *Adbusters* to set up a camp on Wall Street. Rather than predetermining the demands of the action, the organizers of the initial Occupy Wall Street call made the act of occupying, and the holding of the assembly, the main message, giving the protest an open-ended, self-made quality. As David Graeber, one of the initial organizers, later wrote:

> [. . .] our entire vision was based on a kind of faith that democracy was contagious. Or at least, the kind of leaderless direct democracy we had spent so much care and effort on developing. The moment people were exposed to it, to watch a group of people actually listen to each other, and come up to an intelligent decision, collectively [. . .] it tended to change their perception over what was politically possible.[30]

The Occupy Wall Street protest took root in Zuccotti Park on 17 September, hoping that 'the assembly could be a model that would spread until there was an assembly in every neighbourhood in New York, on every block, in every workplace.[31] It would go much further than that: within a few months, hundreds of urban protest camps were underway all over the world. These protests shared a common idea that the system was broken and had a shared slogan originating from the New York organizers ('we are the 99%'), but all held their own assemblies and, if they issued demands at all, they came up with them themselves.

The movement reached Britain on 15 October, on an international day of action called to mark five months since the beginning of the 15-M movement in Spain. When a hastily organized demonstration was denied access to Paternoster Square, the home of the London Stock Exchange, thousands of protesters held an assembly on the steps of neighbouring St Paul's Cathedral. As usual, John McDonnell came along, having heard about the plan while taking part in a protest against the government's NHS reforms on Westminster Bridge the previous weekend. 'Funnily enough, I got there a bit late', he remembers. 'So when I got there there was a ring of police officers all around them and I couldn't get through, so I was on the other side of the police lines making sure that people got represented if they were arrested.'

Eventually, the situation calmed down, and before long the protesters had put tents up. Hundreds of people were now living on the concrete Square, erecting banners and holding events and assemblies. The protest camp quickly gelled as a constantly evolving community, discussing its political output and its practical living arrangements collectively. It drew in supporters and curious bystanders, who were made cups of tea and shown around, and it quickly became a hub of organizing and alternative media. In less than two weeks, a newspaper called the *Occupied London Times* was being published, and copycat actions were taking place the length and breadth of the country.

Compared to the rest of the anti-austerity movement, Occupy operated on an altogether different wavelength. Anti-cuts groups ran events, did protests, raised demands on their local councillors and then went home again. Unions balloted, negotiated and went on strike. Even the more radical elements of the labour movement saw the struggle underway in terms of amassing leverage against the government in the form of disruption in workplaces and on the streets. The tent cities and the general assemblies offered something altogether more idealistic: a space in which ordinary people could, right here and now, explore alternatives to the current system, both in terms of discussing the issues and in terms of being part of a community run by direct democracy in the heart of London and other major cities. The slogans and politics raised by Occupy – in London, the first assembly called for 'an alternative' to the 'undemocratic and unjust' 'current system' – were at once both vague and compelling. In strict terms they could mean almost anything, but in spirit they pointed to something much more radical than demanding an end to cuts or the continuation of a final salary pension scheme.

We had seen aspects of this kind of movement before, of course. The student movement of 2010 had also contained an element of prefigurative politics, with its campus occupations providing a space for newly politicized young activists to reimagine what life could be like as well as how a new politics might be practised. In their direct action methods, their anti-authoritarian attitudes and their roots in the anti-globalization movement, Occupy and the student movement shared some of the same lineage. David Graeber, who was a lecturer at Goldsmiths College in London when he was not in New York, was deeply embedded in the student activist scene, and he had in fact spent much of the autumn of 2010 touring university occupations. In the tent cities that were spreading across the world, just as in the occupations that took root after Millbank, participants engaged in consensus decision-making rather than the usual model of voting which dominated political organization more generally. The wavy hands and other obscure gestures used in the process would now be learned by countless new people who joined the camps and assemblies: single mums whose benefits had been cut, teenagers in school uniform, old timers returning to active politics for the first time since the 1980s, even the odd curious and liberal-minded banker. All went in search of something new, driven by a common feeling, and pursued it well away from conventional party politics.

Although Occupy shared a common lineage with the anti-globalization movement and climate camps of the 1990s and 2000s, its approach to politics marked a clear evolution towards something bigger and broader. Jeremy Gilbert was busy having his first kids in 2011 but had been heavily involved in the movements around the European Social Forum in previous decades, and he paid attention as the moment unfolded. 'It was immediately apparent that Occupy was very different from the direct action politics that took place around the Millennium', he says. 'There wasn't the same anti-intellectualism and it was less about creating a cultural enclave to feel at home in. It was a real break when they started talking about 99% – it marked a shift towards the idea of wanting to build a mass movement, even if it was just an aspiration.'

The Occupy protests were disruptive in their own way. As they took root in the heart of the city and spread to other towns and cities across the UK, they sometimes closed roads; and occasionally there was a confrontation with police. But the really disruptive effect they had was on the news cycle and the wider public narrative. While the rest of the movement tended to speak in defensive terms, opposing cuts and government policy, Occupy pointed the finger directly at the banks. As part of an international wave of protest which provided broadcast journalists with unlimited vox pops and a striking visual backdrop to the economic crisis (a giant pink banner bearing the slogan 'capitalism is crisis' was ever-present in reports), it remained constantly in the news. The national media was fixated on the tents outside St Paul's and on a persistent saga within the Church of England which saw both the Dean and the Canon of the Cathedral resign in protest at plans to evict the camp. Local media across the country was also full of reports of Occupy protests from Bath to Norwich, from Thanet to Glasgow.

As well as dominating the airwaves, these camps acted as a point of confluence for the anti-austerity movement, a physical space in which activists from its different strands mixed. Occupy was characterized by its philosophical distance from the organized left, and yet the steps of St Paul's Cathedral in late 2011 were probably the closest thing I have ever experienced to the London left having a common social scene. Drifting down to the camp after meetings or lectures, I would run into almost every stripe of socialist, motley crews of anarchists, old friends and new acquaintances, who would usually want to share a beer on the steps while discussing the state of the movement and half-participating in the ongoing daily assembly. In Wisconsin, Ian's Pizza joint had famously kept protesters fed while they occupied the state legislature in late 2010; in London, it was an army of off-duty patisserie workers and supermarket staff armed with sacks full of recently out-of-date bakery items and volunteers from who-knows-where bringing in home-cooked vats of hot food.

There were, of course, big weaknesses to the kind of political model that Occupy operated. Horizontalism and consensus decision-making worked well in groups which were ideologically homogenous. In what was effectively a constant ongoing public meeting, it was a recipe for confusion and was prone to making the focus of the camp demoralizingly self-referential. Without a strategy to cause disruption or resist government policy directly, it was limited to an amorphous role in changing the narrative about the economic crisis.

Nonetheless, with a wider movement building all around it, Occupy presented another front in the battle against austerity and captured the public mood in a way that the conventional left and the labour movement never could on their own. One of the people who understood this fact was John McDonnell, who two days after the protest started laid down an Early Day Motion in parliament which declared 'support for and solidarity with Occupy LSX' and demanded 'an end to global tax injustice and a democratic system that represents corporations instead of people.[32] So too did Jeremy Corbyn, who visited the camp the same day. As we moved into November, it really was kicking off everywhere.

Red November

In the early evening of Sunday 9 October, in a sweaty overheated hall inside the University of London Union, a vote is taking place. The meeting is an open assembly, called by the NCAFC, to plan its national demonstration scheduled for 9 November, the first major student mobilization since the autumn of 2010. After what seems like an interminable debate (and with the start time of the meeting pushed back to accommodate attendees making their way up from a blockade of Westminster Bridge against the government's NHS reforms), the room finally divides to decide the route of the march. On one side is an alliance of left-wing student union officers and a few small Trotskyist groups, who argue that we should march on parliament; that is, after all, the real target of our demands. On the other is a weird coalition of anarchists and oddballs, supported by a relatively small delegation from the SWP, who argue that we should march on the City of London to join up with the Occupy movement and turn our fire on the banks. In an unlikely moment of interfactional unity, I find myself on the same side as the SWP. As the hands go up it becomes clear that our side has won easily, and I and a small team are struck off to negotiate a march on the city with the police.

There are many metrics by which one can measure protests. The numbers we mobilized for 9 November, somewhere between ten and fifteen thousand, were more than respectable for a student march on a cold Wednesday afternoon, especially given the lack of support we had from the NUS. The press attention it received was widespread and relatively positive. The symbolism of the route, marching from the student district of Bloomsbury, down the Strand, and up to the city, was striking, taking us past banks and a series of private education companies which stood to profit from the marketization of the university sector. We rallied in Moorgate, near the heart of London's financial district.

But in hindsight, it was the policing of the protest that really demonstrated the scale of what was at stake. Determined not to allow any prospect of direct action taking place, the Metropolitan Police deployed four thousand officers, sealing the march in a walking kettle from beginning to end. Plain-clothes police operated snatch squads in the crowd, targeting those perceived to be troublemakers. Legal conditions were imposed, making it an offence for anyone to stray off the agreed route, and, just to make sure, roads around the march were either fenced off or jammed full of police horses and vans. Those who did diverge from the route – like the Occupy protesters who tried to set up camp in Trafalgar Square – were summarily roughed up and arrested. Most dramatically, two days before the march was set to take place, the Met let it be known that, for the first time ever on the British mainland, they were planning to use rubber bullets if things kicked off, an announcement which made many students rethink their intention to attend. It also sent threatening letters to hundreds of anti-cuts activists who had been arrested at anti-austerity protests in the course of the previous year.

In part, this 'total policing', as the Met called it, was a response to the rioting that had hit England's cities over the summer, which had broken out after the police shooting of Mark Duggan in north London. On 6 August, a crowd marched on Tottenham police station. The protest was peaceful and demanded nothing more than an audience with a senior police officer, but later that day, chaos broke out. Police cars were attacked and so were shops, buses and the local post office. From Sunday, 7 August, widespread rioting and looting broke out across working class areas of London and over the next few days spread to Birmingham, Manchester, Liverpool, Bristol and other locations across the country. The police fully lost control of parts of some cities, and the level of violence and destruction was extreme: a number of people died in the course of the riots, warehouses and shop fronts burned down and whole neighbourhoods shut down and boarded up.

The riots were not a protest in the conventional sense, but it would be wholly wrong to deny their status as a political event. They had their roots in the police killing of an unarmed Black man and the collective reaction of a group of people whose anger at the condition of their lives and their treatment by the police spilled over. More deeply, the riots reflected a society in crisis: by and large, they took off in poor areas with high unemployment which had experienced swingeing cuts to youth centres and other local services. Some of those participating were there to loot consumer goods which they could never hope to purchase legally. Others were there to express generalized rage at the world they lived in and the system that governed it. There were a number of reported cases of crowds attacking corporate chains while leaving local shops alone.

According to at least one veteran of the autumn of 2010, there was also a direct, though completely informal, connection between the riots and the student movement. 'I went down to the riots a fair few times, though I didn't do any actual rioting', she says, 'and it felt like the tactics were taken from the student movement. There was a sophisticated understanding of police and public order tactics.' The activist, who showed up at the Pembrey Estate in Hackney, went as part of a group of anarchists, who, she says, were not regarded as out of place in the crowd. 'We'd explain to people who we were, that we were anarchists and so on, and the response – very often from people who looked and sounded exactly the same as the kids we'd met on the protests in 2010 – was "yeah, we know who *you* are". The atmosphere, too, was reminiscent. 'It had that sense of liberated territory – a lot like parliament square on the day of the fees vote – people were sharing beer that had been looted from shops, hanging around and joking, people of all ages, united in opposition to the cops.' Although the riots did draw some sympathetic attention from activists of the 2010 generation, these activists were in a minority. In a media atmosphere dominated by rolling condemnations of property damage, there was relatively little engagement from the organized left, and still less from the leadership of the labour movement, in the crowds themselves.

Ash Sarkar was both a left-wing activist and a lifelong Londoner who had roots in neighbourhoods that rose up. 'These were the communities who were having the life squeezed out of them by austerity', she says. 'They were communities that were over policed, over surveilled and under supported, and also places that were experiencing gentrification and corrosion of the social fabric and support networks that sustain deprived and minoritised communities. The left at the time tried to engage with it in a limited way, but in terms of understanding where it was coming from and thinking of them as political agents, the left didn't grapple with it. It was almost like the riots were operating at a frequency people couldn't hear.'

If the roots of the riots were political, the response to them was even more so: David Cameron recalled parliament amid a wild moral panic. The court system was empowered to sit through the night to process the prosecutions and meat out punishment. More than half of 3,051 defendants whose cases reached court within a year were under twenty, and they received an average sentence of 16.8 months – four and a half times the normal sentence.[33] This response was undoubtedly racialized and targeted at marginalized communities with few champions in the tabloid press. While the demographics of who took part in the riots was diverse and complex, those being hauled in front of the courts in the middle of the night to be handed substantial custodial sentences were very disproportionately Black, mixed race or Asian. Of the children (ages ten to seventeen) prosecuted, 64 per cent came from the most deprived 20 per cent of areas, while only 3 per cent came from the richest 20 per cent.[34]

Behind the riots lay the story of a deep social and moral crisis, which was now impossible to conceal. The political establishment met the situation not with self-reflection but with steel, force and indignation. And so when they interacted with the student march on 9 November, the police knew they were dealing with a different kind of event, but they feared that our movement might be made of the same flammable material as the riots that had just spread across London.

There was, however, a bigger reason why the state was so concerned with clamping down on the students. November 2011 marks the moment at which the anti-austerity movement not only marched together, as it had done already in the spring, but became a force that might be capable of producing a more serious challenge to the political equilibrium. Over the course of a year, more and more public spaces and neighbourhoods were physically taken over by rioters and occupiers. Now, on the eve of the big strike, there was a real sense that the movement might be enough to force the government to retreat. At the time many of us talked, in retrospect rather idealistically, about bringing the government down entirely; the Coalition relied, after all, on the fragile consent of backbench Liberal Democrat MPs. The student march of 9 November was a good symbol for this sense of everything coming together. It marched on the city in a conscious homage to Occupy. Its biggest funder was the PCS, whose modest £4,000 donation was the most money the NCAFC had ever seen, as left-wing trade unions rallied round their allies. On the day, the protest symbolically coincided with a strike by thousands of electricians against cuts to pay and deskilling organized by Unite, many of whom joined the march around Blackfriars.

In the following weeks, things escalated. Following the initial wave of Occupy protests in late October, more followed in November: Plymouth, Cardiff, Exeter, Leeds, Liverpool and many other cities now also had full-time protest camps in their town centres. On 18 November, protesters 'repossessed' an abandoned office block owned by UBS on Sun Street in the City of London. 'Whilst over 9,000 families were kicked out of their homes in the last three months for failing to keep up mortgage payments – mostly due to the recession caused by the banks', the occupiers told the press, 'UBS and others financial giants are sitting on massive abandoned properties.'[35] The occupation, which called itself the 'Bank of Ideas', would remain open for a number of months, hosting radical lectures at the heart of the City of London. The student movement, too, kicked off again in a distant echo of the previous year. By the end of the month, St Andrews, Birmingham, Edinburgh, Cambridge, Aberdeen, UWE, UEA, York, Warwick, Goldsmiths and others had been occupied. On 23 November, a day of action called by NCAFC coincided with NUS Scotland's national protest against tuition fees in Edinburgh. On the same day, students from across London took over 53 Gordon Square and renamed it the 'Bloomsbury Social Centre'.

The event towards which all of these actions were building was, in terms of the numbers participating, the biggest single day of strike action since the general strike of 1926. On 30 November 2011, a grand total of twenty-nine unions called on their members to walk out of work over pensions, and something like two million workers answered the call. Almost 70 per cent of schools were shut entirely and many more severely affected. Courts, passport offices and job centres closed or were disrupted. The Port of Dover was picketed and the Mersey Tunnels shut down. Skeleton staff teams operated in hospitals and clinics. It was not just the depth of the strike that was remarkable but also its breadth. The Prison Officers' Association called its members out. So too did the Association of Educational Psychologists, the Chartered Society of Physiotherapy and the Society of Radiographers. The Headteachers' unions also struck, and for only the second time in its history, the First Division Association called senior civil servants out. When David Cameron took to the airwaves to claim that the day had been a 'damp squib', the BBC reported that he had to do without the press officer who usually dealt with public sector strikes, because he was himself on strike. The level of disruption caused by the strikes prompted BBC presenter Jeremy Clarkson to say that if he had his way with the strikers, he would 'take them outside and execute them in front of their families', prompting Unison to call for him to be sacked.[36]

Hundreds of thousands of workers marched on the strike day – fifty thousand in London alone and twenty thousand each in Birmingham, Bristol and Manchester. The nationwide proliferation of rallies and protests was impossible to keep track of, and strikers were joined in the streets, and sometimes on their picket lines, by a much broader section of society that opposed the cuts.

The strike hadn't just disrupted services. It had also built the confidence of those who had taken part and given millions of people a taste of what the labour movement and political activism could achieve. As those who had taken part headed home, it felt for all the world like 30 November was the start of something, not the end of it. If it was, we thought, then 2012 really might be the year that the government was forced to retreat.

What you don't understand, Mark

It was not to be. Unbeknownst to most of the union members on picket lines, moves were already underway which would end the pensions dispute and cut short the renaissance of industrial militancy. Weeks prior to the strike, after months of fruitless back and forth, the government made it known that it was willing to offer a few piecemeal concessions on its pensions proposals, including on the security of pensions for employees whose jobs moved from the public to the private sector. The government was clear, however, that no new money was on the table. In effect, the only negotiations it was willing to entertain were over the distribution of the pain.[37]

As Christmas approached, the unity of the unions broke down. Unison (by far the biggest public sector union) and the GMB were both keen to cut a deal, and so rather than waging a united campaign to stop all cuts to pensions, each sector – the NHS, local government, the civil service and teaching – cut deals separately. On 19 December, TUC general secretary Brendan Barber appeared in front of the news cameras outside Congress House to praise 'a new atmosphere in the negotiations' following the strikes. He reported that in two sectors, the NHS and local government, a deal had been reached in principle, though in teaching and the civil service negotiations continued.

The negotiations delivered the odd concession around the edges, making the overall system slightly more progressive, but the bottom line was that, following the ratification of the deals by various union committees in early January, the vast majority of public sector employees would face an increase in their contributions (on top of the pay freeze they were already suffering), a later retirement age and a worse pension at the end. For some workers, the final deal was a worse outcome than the initial proposal they had struck against. Even worse than the long-term hit was the demoralizing defeat to which the movement had been subjected. Many workers thought they were on the cusp of achieving something extraordinary but had been unceremoniously taken out of the fight by their leadership. 'If you take people up that hill, and you give people a glimpse of their potential power, and then you come down it', says PCS general secretary Mark Serwotka, 'that sets the scene for more defeats.' Jon Rogers, a dissident left-wing member of the Unison NEC, agrees: 'If we'd carried on, going onwards and upwards, we could have got a better settlement, and we could have come out of that with workers prepared for future battles to come on a local level', he says. 'As much as they tried to market it as a good deal, everyone knew it wasn't.'

Unite did not go along with the new deals, but most of its membership was in the private sector and was therefore not in the dispute anyway. And so with Unison, the GMB and other unions gone, a smaller alliance led by the PCS and NUT continued the fight into 2012. Early January saw a flurry of attempts to cohere a new fighting spirit, with the various national-level anti-cuts coalitions holding competing conferences addressed by PCS general secretary Mark Serwotka and John McDonnell. Joint strike action by civil servants and teachers could, even without the other unions, have provided one prong of a viable strategy to defeat the government and could have had a seriously disruptive impact on the wider economy. 'We still thought it was winnable, even if we only ended up getting some more concessions – but we knew that it wasn't going to be a blitzkrieg, it was going to be a real slog', says PCS activist John Moloney. What he and other activists feared was that the unions would continue to engage in large symbolic one-day strikes rather than longer or more targeted action, and these fears proved justified. 'The one day strikes appeared like little blips, where we did something massive, but then things went back to normal.' Ultimately, despite further days of strike action in the spring, the new coalition of teachers and civil servants failed to muster enough disruptive power to seriously challenge the government, and by the middle of 2012 it was clear that the pensions dispute was dead.

When London played host to the Olympic games, a shiny showcasing of Britishness presided over by Tory mayor Boris Johnson and sponsored by Coca Cola, McDonalds and Atos, some found solace in the opening ceremony, with its troupe of dancing nurses and pointed use of the NHS logo – though that did not stop the passing of the Health and Social Care Bill in September. Protest was effectively banned in parts of the capital using special laws, and much of the east of the city began to resemble a militarized zone. The athlete's village had been built over the top of the Clays Lane estate, demolished some years previously, and the legacy of the games would lead to a long fight over gentrification and further council estate demolitions. As David Beckham relayed the Olympic flame up the Thames by speedboat, it seemed like we were experiencing another dystopian high point in capitalist realism. 'The function of the Hunger Games', wrote Mark Fisher on his influential blog *K-Punk*, 'is to suppress antagonism, via spectacle and terror. In the same way, London 2012 – preceded and accompanied by the authoritarian lockdown and militarisation of the city – are being held up as the antidote to all discontent.'[38]

The divisions in the unions were philosophical as well as tactical. For many of the left-led unions, the pensions strikes were a strike against austerity. For others, they were an effort to gain marginal concessions on members' pensions and a token effort at that. At the time, Mark Serwotka was scathing about some of his fellow union leaders who were, he said, 'infected with a deep-seated fatalism'[39] following decades of defeat after the election of Margaret Thatcher. His public statements were based on his experiences of the dispute, in which he frequently clashed behind closed doors with the more moderate union leaders. 'It was very clear from the outset that some unions were there reluctantly, and they were intent on cutting a deal as soon as possible', he says now. 'You would very regularly hear people say things like "we've got to let people let off some steam". Many of them wanted out right from the get-go.' In a remarkable moment of clarity, while in heated conversations with a colleague at the very top of the trade union movement, Sertowka was told: 'what you don't understand, Mark, is that since the miners' strike you cannot win through industrial means.'

'There's an approach to leadership in trade unions', says Unison activist Jon Rogers, 'which is all about holding up a mirror to apathy and demoralisation among your own membership, and people who get into that habit over a lifetime – they forget that sometimes if you hold a mirror up you can't see demoralisation and weakness, they've got to the point where they *know* there's demoralisation and weakness.' At the highest levels of the trade union movement, there existed a kind of defeatist realism; the moderate union leaders had drunk from the same well as so many centre-left politicians. They still believed in the End of History, even as history was coming to life all around them.

Others saw a familiar pattern of top-down union bureaucracies simply not being up for a fight. 'Some people get exhilarated by big industrial actions', one senior trade unionist told me, 'but some union leaders (though not all of them) get terrified. They wonder "where on earth is this going to end up, how are we going to bring this under control?"' Ruth Cashman, the Lambeth Unison activist, puts it more bluntly: 'Theoretically speaking, I suppose none of it surprised me. The inspiring struggle of my local community happened just the way you read about in books, and so did the trade union leaders selling it out.'

At the grassroots of the trade union movement, reps generally reported a high degree of confidence and willingness to take further action, but the state of the labour movement made this impossible to achieve. Despite high levels of participation by members in strike action, many union branches had fallen into disrepair during the long downturn in union militancy after the 1980s, and some struggled to hold quorate meetings. There were practically no democratic mechanisms by which the rank-and-file union members could force their leaders to reconsider the compromise in a meaningful way.

Even more fatally, there was no rank-and-file network, either in Unison or in the other unions, that could agitate to keep the strikes going. Throughout the heyday of the British labour movement, right up until its collapse in the 1980s, there existed independent networks of shop stewards and activists who could organize campaigns of industrial action 'from below' in the absence of a willing national leadership. In 2012, following the collapse of the pensions dispute, some local branches of Unison did bring out members on the same day as the ongoing PCS and NUT strikes, but there weren't enough willing branches to keep the action going or escalate it. 'We had the mood', says Cashman, 'but we just didn't have the organisation.' Overcentralization and a lack of grassroots organization were problems which would haunt the left and the labour movement in both halves of the decade.

Going through the motions

The defeat of the trade union movement was contagious. Throughout 2011, the whole anti-austerity movement had relied on the unions to provide the focal points for its mobilization, whether in the form of marches or days of coordinated strike action. Without them, the anti-cuts groups could plod along at a local level, but nationally there was still no united coalition that could take over leadership of the movement. In late January, Occupy was evicted from outside St Paul's, as was the Bank of Ideas, and the tents had already evaporated in many other parts of the country. On the very same weekend, hundreds of student activists gathered in Liverpool for the NCAFC's annual conference, a meeting which witnessed such displays of division and sectarian intrigue that entire coachloads of activists simply abandoned it.

The movement marched on, but it did so in defeat. The TUC's 'A Future that Works' march on 20 October 2012 drew just over 100,000 people, around a fifth of the number who took to the streets a year and a half earlier. Speaking at the rally, Ed Miliband doubled down on his refusal to oppose austerity. 'It's right that we level with people that there will still be hard choices', he said, promising to make 'different but fairer choices including on pay and jobs'. The boos, which in 2011 had been a background irritant, were deafening. By this point, the Shadow Chancellor Ed Balls had already made it clear in an interview with the *Guardian* that 'my starting point is, I am afraid, we are going to have to keep all these cuts'[40] and that Labour fully supported the government's policy of public sector pay restraint.

A month later, the NUS organized a march entitled 'Educate, Employ, Empower' which, organized on a budget many times that of the NCAFC march the previous year, drew around the same number of people. In an unconsciously tragic re-enactment of history, it marched them from Westminster to Kennington Park in the pouring rain, the same route that had been taken by the Chartists in

1848, but in reverse. The new NUS president, Liam Burns, acrobatically dodged eggs thrown at him from the crowd, and the rally had to be abandoned after the stage was stormed by an angry mob of students. The following three years were full of campaigns and strikes here and there, but from 2012 onwards, after the highs of the previous year, the central task of mobilizing a movement that could defeat austerity felt like trying to reanimate a corpse.

That is not to say that nothing important or worthwhile happened after the end of the pensions dispute – far from it. The grassroots of the movement continued to evolve and to spawn an array of campaigns which challenged power and changed the public mood in a variety of ways. Sisters Uncut, a feminist direct action collective using the horizontal methods of UK Uncut, emerged in 2014 in response to cuts to domestic violence services and rose to international prominence when it disrupted the opening night of the film *Suffragette* in 2015. Docs Not Cops, also formed in 2014, sat at the intersection between an ongoing and sizable campaign around NHS reforms and the campaign against the government's new 'Hostile Environment' immigration policy, which pushed medical professionals, as well as landlords, to act as agents of border enforcement. The accelerating housing crisis which gripped many cities, along the criminalization of squatting, spawned a variety of responses. Focus E15 was established in 2013 by a group of mums who, when given notice of eviction from their hostel after budget cuts in the London Borough of Newham, occupied the nearby empty Carpenter's Estate. Anti-gentrification campaigns and networks of radical housing activists took root in many cities and laid the ground for the growth of community unions like ACORN later in the decade.

The student movement also continued to kick off sporadically, with smaller waves of campus occupations and local protests taking place in opposition to the course cuts and restructurings that arose out of the government's higher education reforms. In the spring of 2012, it scored its only national-level victory when Vince Cable announced the shelving of the Higher Education Bill and watered down plans to privatize student debt. The NCAFC continued to coordinate the student left, with an increasingly anaemic network of campus activist groups and a national student protest almost every year between 2011 and 2017. And, slowly but surely, NUS was pushed to the left, in 2014 finally adopting support for free higher education, a policy it had not supported since its takeover by acolytes of New Labour in 1996.

Gradually, however, the student movement went into decline, and an intensification of repression was a key factor in this. At Birmingham University, activists had waged an escalating campaign around living wage, bursaries and cuts. 'We were a tight-knit group and we were good at what we did', reflects Kelly Rogers, one of the key activists with Birmingham Defend Education. 'We built a broad political coalition, we had a very democratic set up, and we had a programme of hard-hitting direct action campaigns which became increasingly ambitious.' But when the NCAFC organized a national demonstration on the campus in January 2014, police kettled hundreds of us on a freezing rooftop and arrested anyone who refused to give their name and address. Rogers was among them, and after being strip-searched and held for twenty-nine hours (illegally, as it turned out[41]) she found herself suspended from university and banned from congregating in groups of more than ten. 'It was a genuine shock, I think, and while the activist group was determined to fight back, it was also clear that we had crossed a new threshold and that people were genuinely scared.'

Despite no charges ever being brought, Rogers would remain suspended for a full year, along with another student, and Birmingham University managers made no secret of their desire to have some activists permanently expelled. At Warwick University in December 2014, the police were called in and attacked occupiers with pepper spray. The previous year, the Metropolitan Police had aggressively evicted an occupation at the University of London. In response to the escalation of police brutality on campus protests, a nationwide 'Cops off Campus' movement took form (in London, thousands marched on the Old Bailey, where the inquest into Mark Duggan's shooting was ongoing) but its flourishing was not as long-lasting as the demoralizing effects of the repression that sparked it.

As austerity was slowly rolled out in the following years, anti-cuts groups and trade union branches did what they could. George Binette talks of his sense of collective achievement when in 2012 Camden Unison organized a strike of traffic wardens who had been outsourced to the private sector, winning them a living wage and a couple of other concessions. 'It was a strong dispute, quite militant and transcended some ethnic and religious divisions', he says. 'And it showed that in the context of a pretty disastrous period for trade unionism, there could still be small victories won.' In Lambeth, the local college was host to a long-running industrial dispute, and the Ritzy Cinema in Brixton witnessed a high-profile living wage battle by a young, precarious workforce. The mobilization of the anti-austerity movement left behind a sense of collective power and a network of support which gave campaigners confidence. In the years that followed, Ruth Cashman would lead wildcat strikes and a series of occupations across the borough's libraries. Pockets of resistance and heroic stands by local campaigners and workers could be witnessed across the country long after any hope of stopping austerity had passed.

On a national level, the focus was gone. The formation of the People's Assembly Against Austerity in 2013 – whose founding conference drew thousands of people to Methodist Central Hall to hear speeches from Tony Benn, and also Owen Jones who had by now come to prominence – finally meant that the movement had a national anti-cuts coalition that was indisputably its official centre. Many of us had issues with what we saw as the People Assembly's lack of internal democracy, but almost all of the strands of the anti-austerity movement related to it and answered its calls for protests and days of action. And yet it was simply unable to resuscitate the movement via force of will or centralized diktat. 'You can't undo the fact that the movement had already happened', laments John Rees, one of its key organizers. 'You can't just go back and say "let's go back and do that in a more centralised and effective way". You're living in the aftermath of a set of movements which had already detonated.' After all, many of the cuts had simply already happened. It was like setting up the Stop the War Coalition months after Baghdad had been bombed and the occupation had started.

Some unions only just got going as the wider movement went into decline. In early 2013, cleaning staff at the University of London were on a high after winning their campaign for living wage. Jason Moyer-Lee, who had moved to London from the United States in 2009 in order to do a PhD in economics at the School of Oriental and African Studies, found himself in the thick of the campaign and had helped to recruit more than a hundred outsourced Latin American workers to Unison in the course of the dispute. The branch he had recruited them to, however, had until recently been dominated by British nine-to-five employees, and Unison seemed reluctant to continue organizing its new members. After what Moyer-Lee describes as 'an abysmal experience' with the union in which its London Regional Office was perceived to have presided over irregularities in the branch elections, the cleaners left to join the recently created Independent Workers of Great Britain (IWGB). With the IWGB, they and other university staff organized a militant, colourful campaign for sick pay, holiday pay and pensions (three things – or Tres Cosas as the campaign was called in Spanish). They struck and struck again and organized demonstrations and pickets outside major university events. Students (myself included) ran into Senate House dressed in beach attire playing the Beach Boys out of portable CD players. By the end of the year, the new union branch had won its first victory.

The IWGB was the model for a new kind of trade unionism, which prioritized recruiting precarious and low-paid workers, many of them migrants.

It organized unapologetically militant strikes and campaigns of protest which often produced quick results. Its ability to do so resulted from its freedom – not only from the organizational bureaucracy of the bigger unions but also from the legacy of historic defeats. 'A lot of us didn't come from a strong trade union background, and I think that's definitely been a strength', says Moyer-Lee. 'It's helped us approach trade unionism as a means to an end, not an ideological pursuit – we're focused on results and winning stuff, rather than being bogged down in the negativity and pessimism that's accumulated over the past three decades.' Within a few years, Moyer-Lee would become the union's general secretary, and the IWGB would be organizing Uber drivers, foster care workers and couriers, among others. Other unions, like the United Voices of the World, would also grow and deploy a similar model of campaigning. Though small – the IWGB's membership increased tenfold to just over five thousand by the end of the decade – these unions pointed the way to a means of organizing in the outsourced, precarious economy that eluded their larger siblings.

It was a different story in the mainstream of the trade union movement. In the summer of 2014, public sector unions once again struck in a coordinated fashion, this time over pay – but the result was never in doubt. 'Having already been through the defeat of the pensions dispute, and more local defeats since then, people tried to gee themselves up – but it was really tough', says Jon Rogers. In the end, Unison accepted a pay offer that was straightforwardly worse than the one it had gone on strike against; all that activists could do was pass motions of censure against the leadership at a special conference months later ('it was an enjoyable day', says Rogers, 'but things like that don't win you the class struggle'). Meanwhile, the People's Assembly called regular national protests, which were well-attended but passive in nature. Speaking at the long rallies that took place at the end of the marches, trade union general like Len McCluskey secretaries would regularly issue tub-thumping calls for a general strike, or for strike action that defied the anti-union laws, but with the movement defeated, this was all just rhetoric. The radical edge, the direct action and the disruptive potential of the earlier years were gone.

To push austerity back, the movement needed to escalate and innovate, but its institutions remained addicted to the one-day strike and the A to B march, if indeed they were willing to do anything at all. These methods might have been an important starting point, but on their own they were impotent and everyone – the government, trade union members and anti-cuts activists – knew it. Neither the new People's Assembly nor even the left-led unions seemed to be capable of breaking with them, and so we spent years going through the motions.

The disorganized left

By the time of the general election in 2015, millions of people in the UK had lived through an era-defining struggle against austerity. Millions of workers had taken strike action, many of them on multiple occasions. Hundreds of thousands of people had repeatedly marched through central London. Tens of thousands had taken part in direct action, hurled a paint bomb at a police line or smashed through the front of glass-fronted buildings. Countless more had stood outside their Town Hall chanting slogans or handed out leaflets in the rain. And, of course, the movement was more than the sum of its parts, because for every person who participated, there were many more who looked on with sympathy or began to question how they were being governed. After the abject defeat of the labour movement in the 1980s and the rise of New Labour, these movements were a moment of mass politicization and radicalization on a scale not seen in decades. The hegemony of the neoliberal consensus was broken at a deep, sociological level, even if it persisted in the political mainstream for some years. In the end, the resistance lost – but, as is so often the case, the really crucial question was not just whether the mass movement failed, but *how* it did so.

The defeat of the anti-austerity movement was above all a story of the institutional failure on the left. In 2010, the NUS abandoned the biggest student movement in British history: its leadership openly urged students not to participate in the protests and did not, in principle, disagree with tuition fees in some form. In 2011, the leadership of the trade union movement squandered one of its greatest opportunities to re-energize its rank and file and push the government back, cutting short the pensions dispute just as it had mobilized millions of workers. In 2012 and beyond, an assortment of left-led unions, most prominently the PCS and NUT, continued the fight but failed to break free from the model of symbolic one-day strikes. From 2013, the People's Assembly Against Austerity brought the remains of the movement together but was unable to muster anything more than well-attended top-table rallies and passive, formulaic marches. Throughout the period, Labour councils – that in the 1980s had joined the resistance against Thatcherism – lacked any kind of collective strategy and had quietly implemented the Coalition's programme of cuts, brushing aside pleas and protests from the communities they represented.

It was the position of the Labour Party's national leadership, however, that was most striking. Ed Miliband had been elected as Labour leader as the leftish alternative to his brother David. He had pointedly stated during his campaign that he believed the Iraq War had been a mistake and enjoyed the support of the big majority of trade union members. But, for a politician who had come of age as a political adviser to New Labour, taking on the political establishment and opposing austerity was simply not within the realm of the possible. He and his even more hawkish Shadow Chancellor Ed Balls had flirted with a more oppositional economic policy in the first year of the Coalition but from 2012 onwards made it clear that they would, in the name of electoral credibility, broadly toe George Osborne's line. Miliband would often behave as if he wanted to be the tribune of a mass movement, appearing on stages at demonstrations and at TUC conference, but the words that came out of his mouth made him a figure less of fun, disappointment and even hate in crowds he addressed. As millions went through a moment of political awakening and looked for someone to represent them, Labour actively condemned their strikes and in broad terms supported austerity.

With Labour absent (outside the antics of oddball backbenchers like Jeremy Corbyn and John McDonnell) the anti-austerity movement had no meaningful political expression, and this had serious consequences for its prospects for success. No matter how big and disruptive the movement had been, the fact that the Coalition had a majority and a clear sense of what it wanted to achieve meant that many cuts and marketizing reforms would simply have happened. However much we might have focussed on revolutionary rhetoric and direct action tactics, the long-term prospects for the movement rested on the possibility of a future government reversing the cuts and reforms of the current one. It was therefore essential for the momentum of the strikes and protests that, as the years wore on, the movement could see its demands reflected in the political mainstream – and so Labour's acquiescence to austerity had a terminal impact on morale. It also had a severely negative impact on the resolve of many of its official leaders. 'Often there's a view', explains Andrew Murray, 'that unions take their views into the Labour Party, but actually it's two-way traffic. In effect, once a Labour leadership has taken a position, that then finds expression in sections of union officialdom.' The unions were united in opposing the cuts in principle, but a contrary position from Labour had a chilling effect on their unity and collective willingness to fight.

The institutions of the far-left witnessed, if anything, an even deeper crisis. From some time in the 1980s to the middle of the 2010s, the most significant organized forces on the British left were the Socialist Party (the artist formerly known as the Militant Tendency) and the SWP. They were small in numerical terms, boasting around 2,000 and 6,000 members, respectively, and had far fewer active members than that[42] but played a crucial role at the core of local anti-cuts groups and in the wider labour movement, even if their methods were often frustrating and off-putting. It is not a coincidence that the most militant unions during the pensions dispute – the PCS, NUT and UCU, which were the first to start striking and the last to stop – were all unions in which the organized socialist left had a large degree of influence, either because they closely supported the leadership or because they controlled a significant number of branches. And yet despite the upsurge in social movements and industrial struggle, the Trotskyist left barely recruited anyone. The urge that groups like the SWP and SP had to build themselves, often at the expense of the wider movement, often jarred with the unsectarian mood of the movement around them. For the crucial first two years after the election of the Coalition, this way of doing politics had ensured that the movement had no united national anti-cuts coalition. And so they were out-organized and eclipsed, first in the student movement by the sprawling and ill-disciplined coalition of the NCAFC and then in the wider anti-austerity movement by the much broader, more mainstream People's Assembly Against Austerity. As the tide rose around the old sects, they barely floated.

The unfashionableness of Leninist politics was just the start of their problems, however. In the period immediately after the pensions dispute, stagnation turned into meltdown as the SWP leadership was accused of covering up accusations of rape against a senior party member (who was known in party documents as 'Comrade Delta'). The accusations were found 'not proven' by the party's Disputes Committee, which was in part composed of friends of the accused and which asked the complainants a number of inappropriate questions about their sexual history and drinking habits. When the matter came to a head at the party's conference in January 2013, the leadership circled the wagons around both the findings of the report and their comrade in the leadership and began to expel opponents and purge dissenters from the Central Committee. But the controversy proved too much to contain. Following the calling of a special conference in March, at which the opposition was decisively defeated, an exodus began. It is impossible to tell how many of the SWP's activists quit the party, but it is certainly the case that the vast majority of its young members and students left, along with a number of its leading intellectuals, including Richard Seymour and China Mieville. The comedian Mark Steel, a former SWP member of twenty-eight years' standing, lamented the behaviour of party loyalists who would 'say or do anything, defend any act no matter how appalling, to protect one of their "leaders", in a manner approaching that of a cult.'[43] For years after the Comrade Delta crisis, the SWP would always be a shadow of its former self and was so toxic that many on the left refused even to work alongside it in broad campaigns.

Unable to find a true home in either Labour or the orbit of the organized far left, the movement lacked not only a political expression but also any form of collective political strategy. The flourishing of the politics of anarchism and horizontalism was an attempt to make a virtue of this deficiency, but it created problems of its own. The student movement, UK Uncut, Occupy and other projects witnessed a grand attempt to renew and transform the left and to find new ways to organize and network a movement without centralized leadership. But these movements produced barely any organizational or ideological legacy. 'It's partly because there was a fetish made of organisational forms, which was a big strategic mistake', explains Aaron Bastani, who in 2010 and 2011 was a horizontalist. 'The Leninists were effectively right about that – I mean they were wrong, because the organisations they were building were generally terrible – but there was a fetish made of leaderlessness which was incorrect.'

By early 2015, the upsurge of social movements and the mass political awakening that had gone with it felt like it had hit a dead end. Campaigns, on housing, for instance, and industrial struggles on pay, continued in pockets, but the inescapable fact was that everything we had tried hadn't worked. The institutions of the organized left – the unions, the Labour Party and the sects – had failed. So too had the networked endeavours of UK Uncut, the student movement and the briefly flourishing anarchist scene. The movements had created the human material for a much bigger rejuvenation, but the organizations through which the mass of people had become politicized – the community anti-cuts groups, the organized left and the grassroots campaigns – had by the middle of the decade almost all fallen apart or declined into inactivity. What existed was a situation that demanded an answer – a credible project that could embody the sentiment of the movements that had emerged – and a disorganized soup of left-wing people looking for one.

If movements sharpened the weapon, Jeremy Corbyn was not the first one to try to pick it up. The Green Party enjoyed a surge in membership in the run up to the 2015 general election. North of the border, the SNP and pro-independence groupings to their left like the Radical Independence Convention and the Scottish Greens were capturing the radical mood. Other attempts were more surreal. Stand-up comedian Russell Brand became an overnight media sensation when, in an interview with the BBC's Newsnight programme in October 2013, he nonchalantly called for a revolution and encouraged people not to vote. Brand later went back on his opposition to voting, and the political programme he espoused was one of moderate social democratic redistribution, but the episode seemed to illustrate the widespread desperation for someone, anyone, in the public sphere to reflect an aesthetically radical, anti-establishment politics.

Night

After the highs of 2010 and the wider rebellion that followed it, the following years were a time of depression and disappointment for many of us. No matter how inspiring the campaigns, no matter how burning and blatant the injustice being fought, nothing seemed to be able to hold back the evaporation of public services and the penetration of market logic into every area of life and public space. In the student movement, and this experience was by no means unique, we experienced a constant barrage of police intrusion and victimization by university managements, to the point that some activists were simply pummelled into inactivity.

I spent the period immediately following the decline of the anti-austerity movement, from 2012 to 2014, as the elected president of the University of London Union, a body which represented just over a hundred thousand students across the capital. Its building on Malet Street was the starting point for every student march, and it served as a hub and meeting space not just for the student movement but the whole of the left in London. In my time, the union had played a role in supporting a variety of new initiatives and protest movements on housing, policing and course cuts as well as supporting the cleaners' strike by the new IWGB union. But in what was a sign of the changing landscape in higher education, the University of London management announced that from 2014 the union would be derecognized and its building and services taken over by the university. The policy was fought with protests and occupations that were often brutally policed, but we lost. After almost a hundred years in existence, I would be its last ever president.

For many of the people who became active in the anti-austerity movement, the first half of the decade was full of hope and excitement, but it was not without hardship or sacrifice. To organize and give life to the mass movements, activists had faced jail, lost their jobs, ended up in hospital and shivered in police kettles. They had, by and large, spent most of the first five of the decade years being battered and defeated as cuts, estate demolitions and tuition fee rises simply went through despite public opposition. But they had fought on in the hope of changing the narrative and winning in the long run, despite being abandoned by Labour and much of the official trade union movement. Their reward in May 2015 was a majority Conservative government which won on a platform of entrenched austerity and clamping down on the right to strike. The rise of the UK Independence Party signalled an even grimmer reality: that an insurgent nationalist right could also break through in an era of rising anti-establishment sentiment, presenting a narrative which blamed foreigners and migrants for the hardships being endured by much of the electorate. Its high vote share meant that the parties of the right – the Tories, UKIP and the Northern Irish unionists – won a majority of the popular vote for the first time since the Second World War.

On the day that the University of London Union was shut down in the summer of 2014, we set up a plan to occupy the building, bringing together a selection of seasoned occupiers from university campuses like Birmingham and a handful of keen volunteers from London's squatting scene. Despite initially taking control of the building, the plan quickly descended into farce as one of the participants began having a breakdown and hurling objects around. It was an ignominious end. A few days later, I returned to the steps of the building and bumped into Ed Maltby, my old comrade with whom I had set up the NCAFC some four and a half years earlier. We soon found ourselves in the pub, and at some point that evening he said something which stuck with me. He said,

> Look, I suppose my analysis is this: over the past few years loads of young people have been brought into activity. They've made mistakes and they've been exposed to some crap ideas – but they're political beings who don't like capitalism very much and in principle they're up for a fight. Either all of those people are going to become radicals and activists in the labour movement, or we're just fucked aren't we.

It is always darkest right before the dawn.

Part II

2015–20

4

The riptide

The story of the British left in the 2010s can be viewed as the confluence of two surreal moments. The first took place on 10 November 2010, when a mob of students and unemployed youth smashed the plate glass front of Conservative Party headquarters at Millbank and occupied the roof. The crowd that had assembled that morning – drawn from a generation that had known no alternative to the onward march of market economics – had been expected to march politely, make some noise and then go home and wait for tuition fees to be tripled. And yet somehow, quite spontaneously, they sent a message of defiance and transgression, kickstarting a mass anti-austerity movement for which they were merely the warm-up act, a movement that would spread into every town and city in Britain, mobilizing millions of people and remoulding the terrain under the feet of the political establishment.

In the heat of these movements, a new left had begun to take form – radical in its tactics, often horizontally organized, suspicious of leaders and built 'from below' by social and industrial struggle – but it would have no time to cohere itself. A surreal moment on an altogether different scale was about to occur.

On 12 September 2015, Jeremy Corbyn was elected leader of the Labour Party. A political outsider who had been a backbench rebel for more than three decades, Corbyn's prospects of victory were initially rated at 200 to 1 by bookies. In the wake of Labour's gruelling defeat at the general election in May, it was a consensus among the other candidates that even Ed Miliband's very tentative moves away from New Labour had been a mistake, and that the party's electoral future lay in shifting rightwards again. Corbyn had only made it onto the ballot as an afterthought, following a campaign of grassroots pressure and a sense among a layer of otherwise unsympathetic Labour MPs that the left ought to have a candidate in the race, if only so that they could be soundly defeated.

But deep within society, and most importantly within the support base of the Labour Party, something had changed. Whereas the political mainstream had responded to the financial crisis by developing a consensus that enshrined deep cuts to wages and services, millions of people had reached the opposite conclusion, and had over the course of the first half of the 2010s stood up and fought back, articulating the beginnings of an alternative. The pro-market consensus which had been established by Margaret Thatcher in the 1980s had finally come to an end. It wasn't just that new members had flooded into Labour in order to vote for Corbyn; he led from very early in the campaign among the existing Labour membership. Everything about the man – his radical politics, his sincerity, his lack of polish and conventional oratorical skills – struck a chord with the anti-establishment mood generated by the movements of the preceding years. This was a fact that Corbyn pro-actively recognized when he addressed a crowd in Parliament Square at a People's Assembly Against Austerity protest just five days after he made it onto the ballot paper:

> This anti-austerity movement is a movement. This is absolutely not about ambitious individuals. This is about a social movement of all of us that can change our society into something good rather than something that is cruel and divided. You all know the way forward.[1]

As the summer rolled on, Jeremy Corbyn found himself surfing a wave, his leadership campaign inundated with volunteers and his events mobbed. In the course of less than three months, he went from being a token tribune of nice ideas to being the Leader of the Opposition, elected with a 59.5 per cent of the vote. Labour's membership had roughly doubled to 388,000. The media, the parliamentary Labour Party and the wider political establishment experienced a mixture of shock, panic and disbelief.

There was, on the surface, a great deal of symmetry between the two moments of 2010 and 2015. They had common roots in the conditions that produced them: declining wages, worsening inequality and insecurity; a sense of generational betrayal and youth identity that bolstered rather than weakening class politics; and a crisis of the democratic system. Both were impossible until they happened, confounded their opponents and seemed to many observers as if they 'came from nowhere'. Both were moments at which the boundaries of what seemed possible or achievable broke open: first came the prospect of a political awakening and a movement of mass resistance long after history was supposed to have ended, then came the equally impossible penetration of a left-wing alternative into the heart of mainstream politics. In both, ideas and dreams which had been written off as dead ends were thrust centre stage and examined anew. People, organizations and whole demographics that had been marginal suddenly acquired relevance and respect.

Below the surface, however, the moments could barely have been more different. When the glass of number 30 Millbank was shattered – and documents, flags and fire extinguishers were brandished from its roof – the message received was one of anger finding a form, a silenced generation rejecting the modes of acceptable dissent in favour of something more genuinely disruptive. Though the movement was born in a dispute over tuition fees – and its successor movements continued to fight on many individual issues such as pensions, gentrification and welfare cuts – it quickly developed a systemic critique of neoliberalism, the state and its own formal leaders. For the mass movement against austerity, politicians were people to be wary of – people who, at best, might be pushed and cajoled into supporting strikes, protests and progressive policies. Unlike in previous generations of social struggle in the 1970s and 1980s, these movements had no serious orientation towards party politics. While their disruptive power and breadth of mobilization was sizeable, their political demands were marginal and their parliamentary tribunes doubly so. Tony Benn was regarded as a menace and a threat by the British establishment throughout the 1980s; between 2010 and 2015, John McDonnell, Jeremy Corbyn and Diane Abbott were regarded as relics of a bygone age.

On 12 September 2015, a suited Jeremy Corbyn rose to give his acceptance speech after being elected Labour leader. To reach the podium, he had wielded the same sense of disenfranchisement, the same anti-establishment sentiment and the same critique of Thatcherism and Blairism that had animated the movements that had gone before him. It wasn't just the policies put forward by his campaign that reflected the demands raised by social movements: the whole manner of it, right down to the slogans – which promised 'a new kind of politics', 'people-powered politics' and 'straight-talking, honest politics' – were rooted in years, and in fact decades, of struggle and hope and disappointment. But at the moment the result was read out that day, a new political project – Corbynism – was born, and its logic was very different to what had come before it. Suddenly, Corbyn was not just a tribune of wider movements: he was the leader of the Labour Party and – inescapably and in spite of his own instincts – the author of a new chapter in the history of the British left. Having spent decades railing against the leadership of the Labour Party – and its record of privatization, military adventurism and deregulation – he now sought from the podium to reclaim the mantle of 'a party that is about justice and democracy, about the great traditions we walk in. Those that founded our party and our movement, those that stood up for human rights and justice . . .'

The process that swept hundreds of thousands of students, young people, public sector workers, benefit claimants and pensioners into the Labour Party in 2015 was not, as we shall see, a new one. Every cycle of social upheaval in modern times in Britain has been subject to the same tidal system which has drawn generation after generation into the Labour Party and then spat it back out again. Corbynism undoubtedly represents the most extreme version of this phenomenon, however. As the social movements began to ebb in the run up to the 2015 election, there was already a natural but very modest influx of new recruits on the Labour left, but the presence of Jeremy Corbyn's victory in the summer of that year had the effect of turning the social movements on their heads.

Suddenly, politics became about trying to win elections and take control of a political party. The vast majority of the new recruits had no collective understanding of the task at hand beyond supporting the new leadership. In an era in which the existing traditions of the organized left had first stagnated and then collapsed, they had no collective organization either, nor even a space in which they could discuss and develop a strategy beyond cheerleading. Eventually, in the form of Momentum, a collective organization would be established – and its existence and the quality of its internal life would to a great extent determine the fate of this new Labour left.

Saving social democracy from itself

The birth of Corbynism was a resurrection in more ways than one. For those who had been brought into politics in the previous five years, it was a chance to win by the ballot box even after the social movements seemed to have failed. For the long-suffering existing Labour left, it was a vindication of the seemingly fruitless decades they had spent in the party and a chance to push forward the programme first advanced by Tony Benn and the Campaign for Labour Party Democracy before the defeat of the left in the 1980s.

But perhaps the biggest beneficiary was the Labour Party itself. The 2010s are rightly understood as a period of desolation for Europe's social democratic parties. As the effects of the financial crash became felt, the centre-left across the continent joined the consensus behind austerity measures. We have already seen how Ed Miliband's Labour Party supported the broad principle of cutting public sector pay and public services, even while he attended marches and rallies against them. In France, socialist president Francois Hollande abandoned much of the anti-austerity platform on which he was elected in order to implement a raft of corporate tax cuts, austerity measures and labour market regulations, a direction of travel which was intensified following the launch of the Pacte de Responsabilité in early 2014.[2] The German SPD spent most of the 2010s as the junior coalition partner in government with Angela Merkel, presiding over belt-tightening at home and very harsh austerity in the European periphery. Pasok, the party of the Greek centre-left, was responsible for implementing a package of measures so harsh that it precipitated a catastrophic fall in GDP and a humanitarian crisis, with widespread destitution and suicide rates jumping sharply. The Dutch Labour Party, which entered government as a junior partner in 2012, dutifully oversaw pay freezes and tens of billions of Euros' worth of cuts, and the Dutch government was among the biggest advocates of fiscal discipline at a European level.

While the centre-left in government acquiesced to austerity, often enthusiastically, it found itself on the wrong side of emerging movements demanding an alternative to rampant social injustice and inequality. The energies of a new generation of left activists went into other electoral projects: in Spain, the Indignados built Podemos; in Greece, the movements vested their hopes in Syriza; in France, the Front de Gauche was built from a mixture of left-wing splits from the Parti Socialiste and a beefed-up activist left. The centre-left paid for its acquiescence with organizational and electoral oblivion. Between 2014 and 2020, the Parti Socialiste lost something like 75 per cent of its members. Having won the 2012 presidential election, it plummeted to fifth place with 6.36 per cent in 2017. The German SPD experienced a less dramatic but nonetheless steady decline in membership and in 2017 recorded its lowest share of the vote since 1933. In the same year, the Dutch Labour Party scored 5.7 per cent of the vote and lost just under three-quarters of its seats in the House of Representatives. In 2009, George Papandreou had led Pasok into government with 44 per cent of the vote; by 2015 the party had lost 90 per cent of its voters and polled seventh. In many countries, the primary beneficiaries of the collapse of the centre-left were not more radical parties but insurgent far-right ones: Geert Wilders in Holland, Alternativ fuer Deutschland in Germany and Rassemblement National in France.

Corbynism successfully insulated the Labour Party against this process by taking it over. Unlike in the rest of Europe, the British left's great renewal took place within a mainstream social democratic party, and the result was that Labour underwent a dynamic rebirth. Not only did the party membership double in the course of the 2015 leadership campaign to 388,000, it continued to grow for some time afterwards. In 2017, the year that its sister parties in France, Germany and Holland faced collapse, Labour's membership peaked at 575,000, making it the biggest political party in the European Union. Its annual income jumped from £39.6 million in 2014 to £57.3 million in 2020.

While the rest of Europe's social democratic parties saw their activist base dwindle, Labour's general election campaigns in 2017 and 2019 were arguably its biggest campaigns in living memory. Much of the mobilization was done not by the central party but by Momentum, the new Labour left's organizational vehicle which had, as we will see, dedicated itself almost entirely to electioneering. In 2019, its digital tools – My Campaign Map, which had been known as My Nearest Marginal in 2017 – allowed 170,000 activists to identify where they would be most useful and go there. A single one of its irreverent 2017 election videos – which featured a small child asking her Conservative-voting father, 'Dad, do you hate me?' – reached 12.7 million Facebook users, one in every three users in the UK. In the course of the 2019 election, its videos amassed 106 million views, and half of the UK Facebook users had watched at least one of them.[3]

Mass mobilization and a re-energization of the Labour Party were only possible because of the ideas and politics of the new Labour left. Corbynism took form in an era of polarization, in which the old technocratic order seemed to have run out of ideas and answers. Its love affair with deregulated capitalism and big finance failed as the economic order collapsed in 2008. Austerity and the erosion of the welfare state had brought insecurity and suffering and a mistrust of both the political establishment and the integrity of the political system in which they swam. Corbynism brought the Labour Party a series of tools to navigate this world, not least an insurgent bottom-up strategy and an anti-establishment tone, embodied by the ultimate outsider candidate for prime minister. It also enshrined a policy platform which broke free from the constraints of the centrist triangulation of previous years and was objectively popular. Taxing the wealthy more, nationalizing rail and utilities and introducing rent controls – to name only a few policies – all carried overwhelming support in the general population and were supported by around half of Conservative Party voters.[4] Between the 2015 and 2017 general elections, Labour's vote share increased by 9.6 per cent – the biggest increase since 1945.

When Jeremy Corbyn's Labour Party went down to defeat in December 2019, it was not because of the policies in the party's manifesto, which remained overwhelmingly popular or because of the gigantic army of canvassers who had been mobilized by them. The real reasons were deeper. Some, like the overwhelming hostility of the media and the long-term trends among older socially conservative voters, were beyond the new Labour left's control. Others – such as the failure to take a clear position on the question of Brexit and the culture of controlling managerialism at the heart of the project – were not.

According to the rubric of professional politics, issues like Brexit, the popularity (and unpopularity) of leaders and economic policy are discrete and separate fields which can be successfully managed by skilled tacticians. Only very rarely is the connection made between these front-facing issues and the seemingly backroom matters of the Corbyn project's internal culture and democracy, its orientation towards social struggle and the democratization of the Labour Party as a whole. From the perspective of a mass movement, however, it is obvious that all of these are intimately connected. As we shall see in the next chapter, the limitations of the Corbyn project and its failures on policy questions like Brexit stemmed primarily from the widening gap between its claim to be a grassroots mass movement and its real existence as a bunkered-down and increasingly conventional leadership of a conventional political party.

The left captured the leadership of the Labour at a moment in which the party was historically indisposed to socialist politics and as detached from social movements and striking workers as it had ever been. Much has been written about the uncooperative nature of the existing apparatus of the party at its headquarters at Southside, but the truth is that the problems ran much deeper than staffing. Throughout its history, the party had been designed to be structurally resistant to left-wing ideas and sudden radical changes, and the era of New Labour had turbocharged this and hollowed out what little internal democracy the party had. Party conference was a stage-managed rally that barely discussed motions from local parties and trade unions. Perhaps worst of all, though, was the orientation of the party towards smooth, professionalized politics which by 2015 jarred with the increasingly anti-establishment sentiment among many voters. Alongside a dramatic shift to the right had come a deepening of the Labour Party establishment's perspective on who ought to have agency (the party leadership) and how politics ought to be done (by seeming respectable and triangulating towards existing public opinion). To the extent that members mattered at all, they did so for the purposes of cheering along and doorknocking every few years.

It was never going to be enough, then, for the Corbyn project to give Labour the tools (in the form of members, ideas and insurgency) it needed to win. In order to make the left's return to the political mainstream lasting, and safeguard the legacy of the movements and campaigns that had created the conditions for Corbynism over the course of decades, the new Labour left would have to qualitatively transform Labour, democratize it and change its internal culture. In order to understand that challenge, we must first look at who the new Labour left was, where they came from and what they were trying to achieve.

Into the party

At the heart of the Corbyn surge in 2015 were the veterans of the social movements that had just taken place and which had to a great extent had ended in failure. By the time that the new Labour left took shape, tuition fees had been tripled, public sector pensions restructured and local council services decimated. Many thousands of public sector jobs had been lost and the welfare system had, especially as far as disabled people were concerned, been cut beyond all recognition. In one way or another – whether by striking at work, marching through Britain's cities, sitting down in Vodafone and Topshop, occupying their university, smashing windows or squatting buildings marked for demolition – millions of people had participated in the resistance against austerity. They had experienced first-hand a catastrophic failure of political leadership from the official institutions of the left: the pensions strikes of 2011, which were the backbone of the wider movement, had been sold short by trade union leaders; and the Labour Party under Ed Miliband had repeatedly condemned strike action and had doubled down on its support for austerity.

The failures of the first half of the decade created a receptive, almost desperate audience for the experiment within the Labour Party that followed it. Corbynism made sense to the veterans of the social movements of 2010 to 2015 not just because Jeremy Corbyn and John McDonnell were long-time allies of these movements, but because it represented the missing part of the jigsaw puzzle: an organizational project into which a newly politicized mass of people could direct their energies. Had it taken shape a few years previously, the new Labour left might have acted as the much-needed political expression of the mass movement that was taking place, with the parliamentary and extra-parliamentary projects growing in tandem with each other, just as the rise of Bennism and the Labour left in the late 1970s and early 1980s had coincided with a period of major industrial and social unrest.

As it happened, the resurgence of the Labour left in the 2010s would take on a quite different character – and would mean very different things to the different sets of people that comprised its supporter base. For many of those who had come into Labour from social movements, Corbynism represented an opportunity to institutionalize the legacy of those movements before they dissipated entirely and before those who had participated in them fell permanently into demoralized inactivity. It was clear from the outset that our prospects for electoral victory were remote: we faced a hostile media and a hostile parliamentary Labour Party and had inherited an electoral base that had been in retreat since 1997, especially among its traditional voters in towns in the North and Midlands. In Scotland, where Labour had lost forty of its forty-one MPs just before Corbyn became leader, the picture was even bleaker.

Corbyn *could* become prime minister, and we all had to behave as if this might happen, but deep down – at least before the intoxication of the 2017 general election – most politically experienced Corbynites knew that what really mattered was what came after him, and that was not just about succession planning. The road to rebuilding the left ran through rebuilding its strength from the ground up – and we had only begun to scratch the surface of this task in the five years prior to Corbyn's election. While it was exciting to see the leadership of a major political party finally bury the austerity consensus that had prevailed in mainstream politics since the financial crash, what was more exciting was the sudden mobilization of hundreds of thousands of people, who might be turned from passive cheering crowds into a new generation of organizers in workplaces and communities. For those who shared this analysis, including me, the aim had to be to use Corbynism to build wider movements rather than the other way around.

Deborah Hermanns was too young to be at Millbank and watched the student protest of 2010 and the riots of the summer of 2011 on news bulletins on her parents' television as a teenager in Berlin. But in 2011 she started an undergraduate degree at the University of Birmingham, where she soon met activists who had been involved in the tumult of the previous year. 'I guess mine was a very typical student story', she says. 'I always had progressive values, but at Birmingham I came into contact with people who were left wing and had interesting things to say, and was confronted with some glaring injustices at the university – vast inequalities between the pay packets of senior managers and other staff on poverty wages.' She joined Birmingham Defend Education, which was the most active local affiliate of the NCAFC and was known for its intensive campaigning culture and its daring occupations of university buildings. When three hundred university staff faced the prospect of redundancy, Birmingham Defend Education launched a solidarity campaign in which Hermanns played an organizing role. Six months later, she found herself in a ten-day-long occupation of the Senate Chambers in the Aston Webb Building. 'That experience massively transformed my relationship to politics', she says. 'And from there it spiralled and basically became my life.' The next few years were full of direct action and encounters with authority, including with local MP Liam Byrne, Labour's Shadow Minister for higher education, whose constituency office the Birmingham students regularly picketed.

In 2014, Hermanns moved to London and became a de facto full-timer for the NCAFC, building national demonstrations in the autumns of 2014 and 2015 and becoming part of the more general extra-parliamentary left scene which included feminist direct action group Sisters Uncut and various housing campaigns. 'My politics never really came from books', she says. 'I didn't join a revolutionary group, but I did feel at home in the movement at large, and I'd have called myself a Marxist. What I did know was that direct action was how we were going to achieve change – and I wasn't interested in all this parliamentary stuff.' Just as it was for most left-wing activists at the time, Hermanns's connection to Jeremy Corbyn and John McDonnell was a personal one, garnered from their presence at picket lines and protests, not one mediated through the Labour Party. When Corbyn won the leadership, she joined the party but did not get fully involved and in internal debates strongly opposed moves to orientate the NCAFC away from broad campus anti-cuts groups (like Birmingham Defend Education) and towards Young Labour and university Labour Clubs.

Hermanns's journey into the heart of the Labour left would begin aboard the number 29 bus on its way through north London in the early autumn of 2015. After a minute or two staring into space, she and a friend noticed that sitting towards the front of the bus was Jeremy Corbyn himself, the newly elected Labour leader. 'We were flat out building the national demonstration for November, and we had this big yellow cardboard frame with us with "grants not debt" on it, which we'd been carrying round the country for people to get their photos taken in to promote the demo', she says. 'We hesitated for a minute, but then we realised what a big opportunity it was – so we chatted to him and ended up getting off at his stop.' On the side of the pavement, within earshot of some teenagers who called out to Corbyn and greeted him, they got their picture with the Labour leader in the yellow frame which promptly went viral on social media. 'It was just such a huge shift', says Hermanns. 'Six months earlier we couldn't even get the Labour Party to demand an end to tuition fees, but here we were with the Leader of the Opposition endorsing our protest. The year before I'd been ambushing Liam Byrne, and now we had the Shadow Chancellor speak at our protest.' From there, Hermanns would go on to volunteer in the Momentum office and would end up as one of the central organizers of The World Transformed festival on the fringes of party conference in 2016 and beyond. During the 2019 general election she would spend ten days volunteering full-time from an Airbnb in the Cornwall constituency of Camborne, Redruth and Hayle, knocking on doors for twelve hours a day in the driving December rain.

Ben Beach didn't even vote in the general election of 2015. He had been present at Millbank when it was occupied, he had been on dozens of picket lines, he had organized rent strikes and housing campaigns in university accommodation and he had been at almost every protest there was going – and had the physical scars to prove it. But after five years of intense struggle against austerity, he could not bring himself to cast a ballot for Ed Miliband's Labour Party. 'I just saw the same thing I saw everywhere in professional politics', he says. 'Everyone could see that the banks had brought the economy down, everyone knew this was true, even the Tories knew it was true, but Labour were so ideologically vacuous they thought it was clever to talk about tightening our belts. No one believes this. It's just fucking pathetic. I mean Jesus Christ – the Ed Stone.' Having joined the SWP in his teens, Beach, like many of his peers, moved towards the anarchist and libertarian left in the years that followed 2010, inspired by the global revolt taking place and the horizontal forms of organization that protest movements were using from Cairo to London to New York.

And yet, at the dawn of Corbynism, even Beach was drawn in. 'When Corbyn appeared, it struck me that we had to be nimble about the situation', he says, 'you can have several different positions at the same time. So I think Labour was crap, but at the same time this is also a bit of an opportunity.' As the summer of 2015 rolled on and the campaign gathered pace, he and thousands of others on the anarchist and libertarian left did the unthinkable and joined the party.

The fact that the movements of the previous five years had seemingly run their course, and the imminent threat of climate change, was also a factor in pushing unlikely new recruits into institutional and electoral politics. 'We have only years left now to act on global warming, not decades', says Beach, 'and action has to happen very quickly on a global scale – so it's going to have to involve the state, even if you don't like the state very much.'

Within a few months of joining, Beach was phonebanked by Momentum, who asked him to attend his local ward Labour Party in Camberwell, where he accidentally got himself elected as youth officer for the branch at his first meeting.

Then, the bureaucratic farce kicked in: the local branch officers, who were on the right of the party, noticed an error in how his membership was registered, and when he showed up to the following meeting he found the entrance blocked. 'The woman who was the chair physically threw me out of the door,' he says, 'and gave me this raving lecture about how I was a fraudster who was registering in different places to hold positions and cast votes in multiple wards.' When he went canvassing locally, he and other left-wing members were denied access to voter data on spurious grounds – another classic in the genre of petty, controlling Labour micro-politics. It was a jarring experience for someone who had spent years organizing rent strikes. 'It just became very apparent,' he says, 'that if you wanted to do anything in this place, it was going to be like pushing a boulder up a very steep hill.' But that was not the end of his Labour Party journey. In spite of his bad experiences at a local level, Beach would spend many days canvassing for the party in Milton Keynes and Harrow and, like Deborah Hermanns, he would end up involved in The World Transformed, eventually coordinating the arts programme for the main festival in 2019.

For Ash Sarkar, the journey was less sudden but no less profound. The daughter of a radical political family in north London, she had grown up with their collective experiences. Her mother had been involved in the Newham Monitoring Project and in efforts to set up Black and Asian caucuses in the trade unions. 'She knew what it was to have to fight racism in the institutions of the left, and she also had to make sense of her situation – what it meant to raise two young women of colour in a world that was deeply racist and misogynistic, while having to face the stigma of being a divorced single mum.' When she was thirteen, Sarkar's mother pressed a copy of Frantz Fanon's *Black Skin, White Masks* to her chest: 'she was like: "this will explain *everything*".' A few years later, when the Iraq War broke out, she had bunked school to go to protests and on arrival at UCL in 2010 had found herself at the heart of the student movement.

Like many of her peers, Sarkar turned to a form of direct action politics that was influenced by anarchism, but by 2015 she had already come up against its limitations. 'For a movement that is based on people coming together and achieving things collectively, it is still intensely vanguardist and gate-keeping,' she reflects. 'It was all about this insular subculture. You had to present yourself in very restrictive ways in terms of how you talk and how you think and what you wear. What you end up doing is that you abdicate the terrain of mass political participation.' When it became clear that Corbyn might win, Sarkar paid £3 to sign up as a supporter but for reasons that would have been alien to many in the party. 'I voted for Corbyn because my honest take at the time was "lol"', she remembers. 'This is either going to break the Labour Party and that's hilarious, or it's going to destroy the British political system and that's also hilarious – so why not.'

It took Sarkar a while to come to terms with the opportunities that Corbynism presented. 'I spent the first couple of years trying to reconcile anarchism with what was going on – so I was a bit sneery about it, I think', she says. 'But Brexit was a splash of cold water to the face. This country is finding meaning in a populism which is based on the idea that people like me aren't really a part of this country, its institutions, its body politics. It was predicated on an image of sovereignty not as a constitutional legal settlement, but as the idea of holding the gate against the barbarian brown other. Suddenly there was this realisation that you can't abdicate the terrain of "where are most people". And so what Corbynism represented to me was a way to find "most people".'

The shift from the anarchist, or anti-statist, fridges to the heart of the new Labour left was as widespread as it was unexpected. 'If you'd said to me ten years earlier that I was going to be in the Labour Party, I would have told you to stop smoking crack', says Seth Wheeler, a veteran of the alter-globalization and anarchist movements, who watched as my generation took the turn into Labour. 'The question is how do we comprehend a social subject who appears to have two completely contradictory political imaginations working at once? On the one hand, they want the destruction of the state and all forms of authoritarian politics, and on the other they have a desire to see a social democratic party in charge in the British state. The easy answer would be to say that they didn't have these two imaginations, they sold out their real convictions for a pragmatic shot at getting a social democrat elected. But to assert that does that whole thing a bit of a disservice, because you then don't really get to see if there are any new forms of politics emerging or mutating in the encounter between these two moments. I think there was something new struggling to take form, but we are only now beginning to understand what that was.'

For myself, I was never fully committed to the anarchist politics that became fashionable after 2010, though I did absorb its predilection for direct action. I joined Labour in 2012, and I had a family history in the party – my father had been a left-wing parliamentary candidate in Leamington Spa in 1983 and had been involved with the Labour Party Committee on Ireland – but until 2015, I had focussed all my efforts on extra-parliamentary causes. Most of my time had been spent in elected positions of one sort or another, from which I had tried to act as a bureaucrat for, rather than against, the movement and had regularly got myself into hot water as a result. For four years, I had been a full-time student activist, first as a sabbatical officer at UCL, then on the national executive of the NUS and then as the president of the University of London Union (as it turned out, the last ever president, as the union was abolished). Throughout that time, I had dedicated myself to building the NCAFC, an independent student coalition which had seen itself as the radical alternative to the NUS.

In the summer of 2015, I went backpacking around eastern Europe and the Balkans before braving the twenty-hour coach ride to Athens. There, in between covering the Greek left's ill-fated confrontation with the Eurogroup for the *New Statesman* and being teargassed in Syntagma Square, I had watched Corbyn's leadership campaign take shape.

When I departed the UK in May in the aftermath of David Cameron's election victory, the left was a grieving mess, and the anti-austerity movement had stagnated. It seemed inevitable that Labour was going to lurch back towards Blairism, and ahead of the leadership contest I had even penned an article arguing that 'there will be no Ed Milibands and no Diane Abbotts in this election, let alone a John McDonnell' and 'we must assess whether remaining in Labour is really a good use of anyone's time'.[5] Shortly after I left the country, Corbyn scraped onto the ballot paper, and I returned in September to find the British left in the middle of a renaissance, full of hope and energy and vastly enlarged. After moving into a flat in north London, I threw myself into the new Labour left, attending my local branch meetings and getting involved in Haringey Momentum.

Having come from student activism, I was particularly concerned with creating a lively youth movement for Corbynism, and there was no shortage of projects to get involved with, many of them organized independently of the new leadership. On 20 September, just eight days after Corbyn's election, about two hundred young activists from all over the country – many of them drawn from the periphery of the NCAFC – formed Labour Young Socialists at a meeting at UCL, debating motions and electing a committee, in what we hoped would be the start of creating a much bigger, unruly youth movement which would orientate itself towards social movements and trade unionism as well as supporting the leadership. Very quickly, these ambitions came up against the intentions of the newly created Momentum national office, which, rather than wanting to create any form of democratic youth organization, was focussed entirely on the official Young Labour elections scheduled for early 2016. Its candidates were to be hand-picked by trusted insiders, with barely any emphasis laid on what a left-wing youth movement ought to do, instead focussing everything on occupying committee positions and the crucial youth seat on Labour's finely balanced National Executive Committee. With Momentum becoming more and more the undisputed centre of the movement, I decided that I would have to climb its structures and seek to build for it a democratic youth organization, and there began in earnest my journey into the new Labour left.

The breakthrough of the Labour left gave the social movements of the early 2010s relevance and gave those who were involved in them hope and renewed political energy. But I found that the experience of trying to have any kind of influence over the direction of the project or its official structures carried the sensation of showing up to a party to which you hadn't been invited. This was because Corbynism had a fundamentally different logic to the social movements and industrial struggles we had just been involved in, and the people who ran the project saw politics in a completely different way.

The strands come together

Had Corbynism merely been a legacy project for the extra-parliamentary movements of the first half of the 2010s, it would never have come into existence. It owed its success and mobilizing ability to the fact that it became a point of confluence for every generation and every tradition of the British left and quickly became so big that it exerted a gravitational pull on everything and everyone around it. The prospect of a left Labour leadership rallied the veterans of the Poll Tax movement, of the anti-globalization movement, of the gigantic marches against the Iraq War and of every other conceivable strand of the left. Formerly independent union leaders like Mark Serwotka and Christine Blower joined, as did many of their members. Older left wingers who had burned out after the collapse of the left during and after Thatcherism came back into activity to attend rallies, phonebank and become activists again. Much of the surge in Labour's membership was not new at all but consisted of rejoiners who had left Labour during Tony Blair's leadership of the party. In 2016, one year into Corbyn's leadership, the average age of a party member was fifty-one, and most of the left's activists were either much younger or at least a decade older than that.[6]

Laura Parker had spent almost two decades abroad by the time of the 2015 leadership election. After two years in the civil service fast stream, she left the country in 1997 to work for the European Commission in Brussels and then spent time living in Bulgaria, Italy and elsewhere. She returned to the UK for eighteen months in 2012 and became a member of Ed Miliband's Labour Party, an experience which she describes as 'stultifyingly dull'. But Parker was no dabbler at left politics, and behind her professional exterior was a committed socialist. She was the daughter of a Marxist academic and had become political from an early age, serving as the youth representative on the Campaign for Nuclear Disarmament's national council in her late teens. At Liverpool University in the late 1980s and early 1990s, she had navigated her way through the student left ('my choice was between a bland Labour Club and Militant, who thought people like me were just middle class and clueless', she says) to become the president of the students' union, running on an independent left ticket. 'I joined the anti-Poll Tax campaign in my first year,' she says, 'and that immediately meant I was working with the broad left.' In the following years, she got involved in the movement against apartheid South Africa and against the abolition of student grants. Her politics never left her: she had been involved in campaigning around children's rights and disability rights throughout her time living abroad and had demonstrated against the Iraq War from Bulgaria in 2003.

In 2014, she found a job as the chief executive of a children's charity and returned to the UK. Living in Vauxhall during the 2015 general election, she had voted not for Labour but for a new left of Labour Party called Left Unity, whose candidate was Simon Hannah. It was, explains Parker, a choice between him and the maverick MP Kate Hoey, known for her pro-fox hunting, pro-Brexit and Northern Irish unionist views, 'and over my dead body was I going to vote for Kate Hoey'. But within a matter of months, Parker would be co-chairing Momentum meetings in Lambeth, and in less than a year she would find herself at the heart of the project, working as Jeremy Corbyn's private secretary in Westminster. Her time in a local Momentum group had made her enthusiastic about the task of building a bridge out from the party to the wider movement 'but at the same time', she says, 'it was clear they needed competent people in parliament'. Her appointment, she says, was down to her fitting a very specific profile: 'Try finding someone who has plenty of civil service experience, who is identifiably left and has supported Corbyn, but who hasn't got masses of factional baggage – it's almost impossible.' She wouldn't last long.

Older generations of Corbynites carried with them a vast array of experiences which younger and newly politicized members inevitably did not have, but that does not mean that their political perspectives were alien to each other. Hilary Wainwright, now in her seventies, is one of the British left's most well-known intellectuals, and her political journey is representative of many older activists who had come through the movements of the 1960s, 1970s and 1980s. The daughter of a Liberal MP, Wainwright quickly turned to the left in her teenage years. She arrived at university in 1967, and the student movement of 1968 was a moment of awakening for her and many of her peers. Unlike the 2010 and 2011 movements, the 1968 generation was centrally concerned with international issues: Ireland, the Vietnam War, the Algerian struggle against the French state and the anti-apartheid movement. And yet the subjective experiences and sensations that Wainwright and other 68-ers describe would be familiar to the students who stormed Millbank. The year 1968 was an international moment of protest which broke through a seemingly invincible old order and established a radical generational identity among many of its participants. 'Being part of that generation was important,' she explains, 'because it gave you a glimpse of what was possible. Before that, convention, repression, capitalism all seemed very stable, and then suddenly systemic change became possible.'

It is not hard to see the direct link, both in terms of theory and in terms of disposition, between the new left of the 1960s and the new left that was created by upheaval of the early 2010s. Their age aside, the veterans of 1968 had much in common with the latest generation of social movements: they shared a deep antipathy towards the Labour Party. 'The first impact of 68,' she says, 'and also the experience of the Wilson government and looking at parliamentary politics, was to lead one to be very sceptical about any engagement in the Labour Party whatsoever.' But some sort of orientation towards Labour seemed inevitable. 'In France, a key feature of 68 was the link between students and the movement for workers' self-management, but in Britain the link between the social movements, the intelligentsia and the working class was mediated almost entirely through the Labour Party. It had a kind of monopoly on political representation.' She opted to stay outside of Labour and got involved with the shop stewards' movement, from 1973 to 1979 working as a researcher in Tyneside. Most formative was her involvement with the Lucas Aerospace workers, who, when faced with redundancies, put forward a plan not just in defence of jobs but also in favour of workers' self-management and the transformation of the arms industry towards socially useful ends.

For Wainwright as for many others of her generation, the youth revolt of the 1960s and liberation movements in the Global South reinforced the conviction that 'there was something beyond the Cold War choice of Cabinet versus Politburo'.[7] Describing herself as a 'socialist of militant and libertarian blend', she was, like many others, greatly influenced by Ralph Miliband, whose 1961 book *Parliamentary Socialism* served up a devastating critique of the Labour Party and the left's strategy of working inside it. Labour was, he argued, 'not about socialism, but about the parliamentary system.'[8] Looking back at the party's history, he saw an organization that was wedded to the existing order and seemed structurally incapable of breaking free of the constraints of the political system of which it was a part. By participating in Labour, the left was exposing itself to the logic of Labourism – its party loyalty, bureaucracy and conservatism. By the early 1970s Miliband was ready to argue for the formation of an alternative to Labour. Despite all of the attempts to transform it, he wrote, 'the Labour Party remains, in practice, what it has always been – a party of modest social reform in a capitalist system within whose confines it is ever more firmly and by now irrevocably rooted'.[9]

Throughout the second half of the twentieth century, the British left's tidal system drew generation after generation into and out of the Labour Party, as different cycles of social movements sought representation and a political voice. In the summer of 2015, it was as if all of them arrived, or returned, all at once, and there was an important difference with previous tides. In the preceding decades, most activists from extra-parliamentary movements would have entered the Labour Party with a developed, or at least historically grounded, critique of the organization they were joining, many of them as part of an organized group or tendency. By the time that Corbyn ran for leader, however, the traditions and organizations of the left were historically weak: the Trotskyist groups had undergone a process of stagnation and then collapse, and many of those who had come into activity in the first half of the decade had no experience of organized politics outside of the immediate parameters of the social movements. For the 'generation without a history' – who had grown up in the wake of the defeats of the 1980s and 1990s and had to a great extent been cut off from the left's collective memory by those defeats – Corbynism was the first and only Labour Party project they had known. Young and old, many were instinctively hostile to the idea of joining the Labour Party but paradoxically doubly vulnerable to being consumed by its electoralist and parliamentarist logic. The change that the left underwent in the latter half of the 2010s was, as a result, all the more total: less a conversion than an inversion.

As the veterans of the extra-parliamentary left surged into Labour, they joined forces with the existing Labour left. Jon Lansman was from the same generation as Hilary Wainwright but had taken a very different path. 'I suppose I was a child of the 60s,' he says, 'and I was imbued with that rejection of deference and respect for authority. It was less the 1968 stuff, because I was still a bit young – but I listened to the music, I read things.' The son of a petit bourgeois Jewish family in north London – his father owned a small schmutter business with shops in

Hackney and Finsbury Park – Lansman's appetite for politics was sparked by reading widely about anti-Semitism and by the burgeoning field of satire. 'I remember as quite a small child creeping down the stairs to watch David Frost's *That Was The Week That Was*, and later reading *Private Eye*', he recalls. His parents voted Tory, but the ideas he was exposed to, along with the experience of revising for his O-Levels by candlelight during the three-day week, led Lansman into the left and into Labour. Although he went to university in Cambridge, he remained active in his home constituency, including in the local branch of the Young Socialists – the only branch in London which was not controlled by the Militant Tendency. There, he became friends with Andy Harris, who would later serve on the Greater London Council under Ken Livingstone in the early 1980s. Harris persuaded him to get active in the Campaign for Labour Party Democracy (CLPD), which Lansman joined in 1977.

CLPD had been established in the early 1970s in response to Harold Wilson's announcement that he would refuse to enact the party's policy on public ownership. Its leading light was Vladimir Derer, who had fled Czechoslovakia in the 1930s and been active on the British left for some decades, first in the early Trotskyist movement and then in Labour. He and others in CLPD concluded that it was not enough for the Labour left to win on matters of party programme if the structures of the party continued to be impervious to implementing them. And so, while much of the then-new Labour left in the 1970s and 1980s emphasized reaching out to a wider layer of campaigns and social movements, CLPD focussed everything on a campaign to democratize Labour. Over the years, it would lead high-profile campaigns in favour of mandatory reselection for Labour MPs, the sovereignty of party conference and a widening in the franchise for leadership elections beyond the parliamentary party. As Leo Panitch later wrote, their decision to concentrate solely on party democracy was a conscious tactical choice. 'By sticking to a "strictly formal democratic platform" the CLPD hoped that "party members and trade unionists holding very different views on policy issues could unite in support of this vital democratic reform".'[10]

The campaign's internal culture was, Lansman recalls, 'amazing – you could just turn up, be an activist and if you were prepared to put in the time, you were welcomed with open arms and you were in all of the discussions'. Lansman was quickly on CLPD's Executive Committee and before long had quit his job as a van driver to work effectively full time on the campaign.

In the aftermath of Labour's defeat in the 1979 general election, CLPD won a string of victories and over the course of three years pushed through mandatory reselection of MPs and a widening of the franchise in the election of the party leadership beyond just MPs, both devastating blows to the Labour right's traditional conception of the party as being essentially led by the parliamentary party as a separate, professional class. The latter reform enabled Tony Benn to launch a challenge for the deputy leadership of the party in 1981, and Lansman became secretary of Benn's campaign, dividing his time between Tony Benn's basement and his girlfriend's house in Greenwich.

'It was a baptism of fire', he says, which quickly landed him in the public eye after Denis Healey, Benn's opponent, was booed loudly at a demonstration against unemployment in Birmingham. Healy went on national television to accuse Lansman of orchestrating the booing, and while the accusation was entirely false, it became the top story within a day. 'That was when they started doing all of the dirty stuff, and you got these stories about "the silver spoon life of Red Jon"', he remembers. Unbeknownst to Healey, Lansman was not in Birmingham at all that day, though he had driven around it on his way to visit his girlfriend's grandmother just outside Aberystwyth. Spookily, within hours of his arrival there, a *Daily Mail* photographer showed up, followed swiftly by a reporter from London, and the next morning a hundred journalists were camped outside the house. 'The only people who knew where I was were Chris Mullin (then a CLPD activist, later an MP) and my girlfriend's lodger, and I can only assume the press found out through nefarious means', Lansman says. 'To be in that situation at the age of 24, it was a terrifying ordeal, and it stayed with me for a long time.'

Benn's narrow defeat in 1981 coincided with a broader turning point. Soon after came the 1983 general election defeat and the miners' strike. Labour's centre of gravity shifted rightwards, as Neil Kinnock took over and the left lost seats on the NEC. In 1988, Tony Benn challenged for the Labour leadership – a campaign which Lansman also ran – but received just 11 per cent of the overall vote in the three-way electoral college between MPs, trade unions and constituency parties. His support among party members dropped from 81.8 per cent in 1981 to 19.6 per cent in 1988. For another two and a half decades, the Labour left would continue to be pushed back into the margins, as its supporters left the party en masse or blew with the wind. And yet Lansman, like Jeremy Corbyn, gritted his teeth and stayed in the party throughout the Blair years, biding his time for the next opportunity. 'I always saw Labour activists in the Blair period as a deferential bunch, hat doffers even', he says. 'But they didn't agree with the privatisation of the NHS – they voted for Blair because they wanted to win, but they never agreed with what he did.' In organizations like CLPD and the Labour Representation Committee (LRC) – which was formed in 2004 and was chaired by John McDonnell – a few hundred left wingers remained active in Labour, keeping the flame alive. Only a handful of young activists got involved in the LRC, among them Owen Jones, and the organization's conferences got greyer and smaller every year. The anti-austerity movement barely related to these organizations at all.

In the years that followed Jeremy Corbyn's election as Labour leader, the existing Labour left would go from the irrelevant fringes to the heart of the most important political project in the left's recent history. Jon Lansman, who until 2015 had been working to coordinate what remained of the Labour left from Michael Meacher's parliamentary office, was one of the key figures in Corbyn's leadership campaign. He was then handed the keys to its successor organization – what would become Momentum. For him, and many like him, Corbynism's existence was not so much a product of the social movements as it was a 'validation of my instinct that it was possible to turn it round, that it wasn't hopeless, and in particular of everything we had done in CLPD – that shifting the balance of power inside the party was the key to the left's success'. Lansman's perspective, from the late 1970s to this day, has retained a laser-like focus on Labour's structures.

To understand what happened to Corbynism, one must understand that for many of its key protagonists, its crucial promise was not about social movements or a new mass politics but about winning elections inside Labour and changing the party's structures. To achieve this, they would need to create and, as it turned out, to control a vehicle that could effectively mobilize Labour's new members in a narrow and targeted way.

If the coalition behind Corbynism had consisted only of the dwindling remains of the Bennite tradition and the veterans of recent social movements, history would have been very different. However, in large part because Labour had drifted so far to the right from the mid-1990s, the project very quickly became a big tent. Much of the soft left – the amorphous political tradition occupying the space to the left of New Labour, which had to a great extent defined itself against the Bennites in the 1980s – fell in behind Corbyn during the summer of 2015. Even more important was the backing of the major unions. Len McCluskey had initially been tempted to back Andy Burnham, but Unite threw its weight behind Corbyn in July, joining the train drivers' union ASLEF, the Bakers' Food and Allied Workers' Union (BFAWU), the Communication Workers' Union, the white-collar transport union TSSA and three unaffiliated unions – the FBU, the Prison Officers' Association and the RMT.

Much more surprising, and therefore symbolic of the momentum behind the campaign, was the endorsement of the public sector giant Unison, whose leadership was widely disliked among the grassroots of the activist left and had been held responsible for selling short the biggest industrial dispute in decades over pensions in 2011. In announcing the decision, Unison's general secretary Dave Prentis was clear about why his executive had voted as it had. 'Jeremy Corbyn's message has resonated with public sector workers who have suffered years of pay freezes, redundancies with too many having to work more for less', he said. Prentis may well have preferred to back Yvette Cooper, but in the cold light of day only Corbyn went anywhere near supporting Unison's actual policy on cuts, wages and public services. In a Labour Party that had moved towards accommodating austerity and neoliberalism, the Bennites found themselves the most effective political representatives of even the more moderate trade unions.

The presence of the major unions within Corbyn's alliance was crucial to securing the leadership but had a profound impact on how the project developed. Whereas other building blocks of the project were drawn to Corbynism by an ambition to transform politics – to build mass movements or open up Labour's democracy – it is impossible to understand the motivations of trade union bureaucracies without reference to more conventional political aims: control and influence. The political culture of Labour's big affiliated unions has always been informed to some degree or another by a drive to build and maintain political fiefdoms: to have more influence than other unions; to keep the power of Labour's members in check; and to maintain rather than undermine the system of patronage and horse-trading that has dominated Labour's policy process and candidate selections for over a century. This way of doing politics is internally coherent as far as it goes: after all, it is the job of a trade union to fight for policy and influence on behalf of its members, and if (setting aside the fact that barely any officials in the big unions are even elected) the bureaucracy views itself as the embodiment of members, then it logically follows that the real task is to gain influence for a narrow set of people at the top of the union.

The role of the Unite leadership would be particularly decisive in the years that followed. Throughout the Corbyn period, Len McCluskey would pump money and resources into the project to keep it running. With the party machine run by hostile staff and the parliamentary Labour Party determined to undermine Corbyn, Unite supplied the money and bureaucratic clout that the Leader's Office needed to see off a barrage of plots and attempted coups. McCluskey's backing was rewarded with probably the closest relationship between a Labour leadership and a single trade union in the party's history. It was not just that the

Leader's Office and Unite worked in lockstep throughout Corbyn's leadership: Unite to a great extent *was* the Leader's Office. In just a few years, close allies of Len McCluskey came to occupy the positions of Corbyn's chief of staff and the Labour Party general secretary and controlled much of the Labour machine as well as holding a decisive influence over the party's NEC. Some of Unite's appointments were in their own right well-known left-wing activists, but others were not. Karie Murphy, who would serve as chief of staff, was best known for her attempts to get selected as Labour's parliamentary candidate in Falkirk. Her experience of working in politics came not from the offices of John McDonnell and Jeremy Corbyn but as an aide to Tom Watson, who was by now Labour's deputy leader and an opponent of the Corbynite left.

Andrew Murray, chief of staff at Unite, can be best understood as a kind of hybrid figure, sitting between the activist left and the trade union bureaucracy. A long-time member of the Communist Party, Murray had been a senior figure in the Stop the War Coalition alongside Corbyn and Benn and had been appointed to his job in Unite following McCluskey's election as general secretary in 2010. Prior to that, he had gained a reputation as a highly effective trade union organizer and had been a journalist at the *Morning Star*. Murray was from the orthodox wing of the communist movement. He joined the Communist Party of Great Britain (CPGB) in 1976 (around the same time that Jon Lansman joined CLPD) and when the party underwent a series of splits and internal faction fights between its Eurocommunist leadership and a pro-Moscow minority in the 1980s, he had found himself firmly on the pro-Moscow side. He and Seamas Milne (who, unlike Murray, was a member of Labour) had links to the same faction anti-revisionist grouping, which published a magazine entitled *Straight Left*. In 1988, following years of internal strife, the Communist Party of Britain (CPB) was set up as an orthodox split from the official party, and when the official party dissolved itself in 1991, only the CPB remained. Murray remained first in the CPGB and then the CPB right to the end and never joined Labour. But in 2016, a year after Corbyn's election, even Murray was swept along, and not because he had changed his mind about communism. 'I left the CP to join the Labour Party because the union had been asking me to for quite a long time', he tells me:

> Because I'm a senior official in the union, the logic was that you ought to be batting for the union in Labour. I'd always said to Len and others: 'if the Labour Party can go five years without invading another country or supporting an invasion, I'll think about'. Well Jeremy's election called my bluff. I'd known

Jeremy for years and years, and campaigned with him. It seemed like here was an opportunity, and everyone had to put their shoulder to the wheel.

As Corbyn's team took shape in the year or two after his election, it became widely reported in the press that his inner circle was increasingly dominated by the 'four Ms'. John McDonnell was not among them. Instead, the epithet referred to Len McCluskey, Karie Murphy, Andrew Murray and communications director Seamas Milne. Their influence over policy and strategy derived not from a sense that they spoke for the movements that lay underneath the project but from their pre-existing relationships with Corbyn and the organizational clout of Unite.

In every previous generation, the Labour left had seen its role as intervening in the trade unions at a rank-and-file level. In the days of Aneurin Bevan, an overwhelmingly left-wing party membership had been outvoted again and again by the block votes of the major unions, and although Bevan was reluctant to intervene directly in the affairs of unions, he understood the dynamics and conservatism of the bureaucracy. In the 1970s and 1980s, the left had much more directly prioritized developing and working with shop stewards networks, building industrial and political power at the base of the labour movement. Tony Benn had run for deputy leader in 1981 against the urging of many of the nominally left-wing union leaders and had played a prominent role in supporting shop stewards in the face of considerable hostility from the national offices of unions. CLPD understood that the positions of trade unions were pivotal to changing Labour's structures and had run operations inside unions to shift them. As Reg Race, the left-wing MP for Wood Green, put it, '[t]he Campaign for Labour Party Democracy believes that the two principal obstacles to real socialist change in Britain are the Parliamentary Labour Party and the TUC General Council.'[11]

In the decade prior to Corbyn's election, John McDonnell had publicly criticized the leaderships of Unison and other unions when they sold strikes short, repeatedly backed left candidates in union general secretary elections and toured the country speaking at rank-and-file mobilizing conferences and left faction meetings. But in the period after 2015, all of that would disappear. Trade unions – some of them on the left, some of them not – would become stakeholders, whose patronage and support the new leadership needed. With that support would come a style of party management which would run directly against the aspirations of the movements that had created Corbynism.

The coming together of these worlds – of the social movement and labour movement activists, the Bennite left and Corbyn's institutional and bureaucratic backers – was sudden and overwhelming. For everyone, the project represented an unimaginable advance on what had previously seemed possible, a seemingly once-in-a-lifetime opportunity to rebuild the British left.

Into Momentum

In one organization in particular, this swirling mix of traditions and activists would collide again and again. Momentum began life as the successor organization to Jeremy Corbyn's first leadership campaign, and it drew its strength from a mixture of, on the one hand, organically grown activist networks and, on the other, centrally accumulated assets and prestige.

The summer of 2015 had witnessed a blossoming of local activism. In pretty much every area of the country, local groups had sprung up. Many of them had been initiated by the existing left – the remains of anti-cuts groups left over from the anti-austerity movement, local trade union networks and left-wing constituency parties – but over the course of the summer they had swelled to a size well beyond anything the left had seen in recent years, organizing rallies and phonebanks and stalls and discussing how they might take over their local parties. Just as they had during the anti-austerity movement, the local groups had mobilized under a blizzard of different names and acronyms and with no consistency in terms of structure or national affiliation.

There was a clamour from these local groups, and from many floating activists, about the need to build new organizations to take forward the task of organizing the Corbynite left, and it was not always obvious from their perspective that Momentum would become the undisputed centre of the new movement. The weeks following Corbyn's election witnessed the birth of a series of new organizations and fronts. Labour Young Socialists was an attempt to build a new youth organization. Communities for Corbyn was an attempt to launch a horizontal network of local pro-Corbyn 'circles', named after the local branches of Spanish left party Podemos, which would upload their activities to an interactive map. Its launch took the form of a statement, published in September in *Red Pepper* (the magazine founded by Hilary Wainwright) and was signed by myself, Novara editor Aaron Bastani, Heathrow-activist-turned-John McDonnell aide Joe Ryle, Occupy cofounder David Graeber, NCAFC organizer Deborah Hermanns, Lambeth activist Ruth Cashman and IWGB general secretary Jason Moyer-Lee, among others. 'Jeremy's victory was made possible by people inside and outside the Labour Party who share a common hope in the future', the statement read.

'It demands that all of us take our share of responsibility [. . .] We call on like-minded people to join us, creating a democratic and diverse network through action across the country.'

Running in parallel, Corbyn's leadership campaign had a vast bank of centrally acquired data – something like a quarter of a million email addresses – and the official blessing of Jeremy Corbyn and John McDonnell. The man charged with bringing together the legacy project of the campaign was Jon Lansman. 'For lot of the period prior to 2015, I had played a role similar to the one I'd played in the 1980s, of liaising between different organisations on the Labour left,' he says, 'and, ironically given what happened later, I was seen as something of a diplomat – which is why John McDonnell asked me to lead on the establishment of Momentum.' The institutional weight, in the form of data and profile, which Lansman had at his disposal made it inevitable that within a matter of months, Momentum would have the gravitational pull it needed to suck in all of the various fledgling independent projects. But this did not mean that the new organization would automatically reflect the orientation these projects had towards building social movements or creating a democratic network of activists. Lansman's instincts were quite the opposite: having stayed in the Labour Party for decades, and having just had his strategy vindicated, he wanted to take the energy and dynamism of the campaign and turn it towards building a Labour Party faction that could dominate internal elections and party conferences. 'My initial primary objective,' he says, 'was to create a vastly bigger, digitally capable CLPD.'

Long before Momentum developed a grassroots base or a formal structure, it was wracked by disagreements about its purpose and about who was in charge of it. Jon Lansman had set up a limited company which owned the email addresses and other data from the leadership campaign – effectively the legal core of the organization. At the same time, a Reference Group had been set up, consisting of four new left-wing MPs – Clive Lewis, Richard Burgon, Rebecca Long Bailey and Kate Osamor – who were supposed to act as trustees. Sam Tarry, the political officer of the white-collar transport union TSSA, was also a de facto member of the group, alongside Lansman. Then there was a sprawling mass of leadership campaign volunteers, many of whom were younger and newer to politics, who felt like they had a stake in what happened next. In the weeks and months around Corbyn's election as Labour leader, these various constituencies met dozens of times in a baffling array of different formats and configurations, each of which took separate, often conflicting, decisions about the future of the organization.

Into this chaotic situation were thrown Emma Rees and Adam Klug. The pair had met at Sussex University in the mid-2000s and were not, in a conventional sense, obvious choices to run Momentum. 'I suppose you could say we were the kind of people who attended protests, but never really organised them', says Rees. They had graduated a couple of years too early to have taken part in the student movement of 2010 and had been brought into politics via other means: like many people of his generation, Klug had walked out of school against the Iraq War and became much more politically engaged after a period of travelling, visiting Bolivia a few weeks after Evo Morales had been elected, spending time in Venezuela and Cuba and witnessing the real-life effects of global capitalism on populations in the Global South. The pair had lived with a leading organizer from UK Uncut during its heyday, and from 2013 until 2015 they had been primary school teachers, an experience which had cemented their radical politics. 'You're just constantly confronted with kids who are having their creativity and humanity squeezed out of them by an education system that is brutal and rigid', reflects Klug, while Rees remembers her experience of austerity in the education system: 'Like a lot of teachers, I found myself buying food and nit cream and other odds and ends because parents just couldn't afford it', she says. 'The majority of my kids were poor and many had suffered childhood trauma, and the system was just unable to cope with it – I was spending my lunch breaks filling out forms to get kids a few sessions of counselling with children's charities, as public services had suffered so many cuts.'

Rees and Klug had been about to move to Barcelona when Corbyn's leadership election kicked off (they had even booked their transport) but stuck around to be a part of the action. Klug had gone to sixth form with one of Jeremy Corbyn's sons and so had a personal link into the campaign. In its final days, they were asked to organize Corbyn's arts policy launch. 'The fact that we managed to get a comedian and a DJ and lots of young people in the audience was regarded as an impressive outcome for a Labour Party event at the time', says Rees. 'The event took place at the turning point in the campaign, where people started to believe that Jeremy was actually going to win. There was a palpable energy and enthusiasm at that time and (however it sounds now) the "new kind of politics" slogan was really resonating with people.'

As time went on, however, tensions over the purpose of Momentum began to surface more. 'There were basically three different visions', Rees reflects: 'was it about being a social movement, was it about bridging social movements and the party and bringing activists between the two, or was it basically supposed to be a fancy version of CLPD or a left faction in the party? I always got the impression that we were asked to stick around because the Labour leadership wanted Jon Lansman's internally-focussed version of the organisation, but they wanted it to look and feel like the arts policy launch we'd put on.'

Owen Jones, who was by now the left's most famous spokesperson outside of parliament, put an enthusiastic case for the new Labour left to organize in wider society. Labour's army of activists, he wrote in his *Guardian* column about a month before Momentum was launched, 'are brimming with enthusiasm, rather than simply grumpily opposed to the Tories – and it needs to use them to build a genuine social movement. Britain has up to 11 million private renters, often being charged rip-off rents and deprived of basic housing security. Why shouldn't Labour set up private tenants' associations, again to help organise people? The party is talking about the rights of self-employed workers who value their independence, but not the insecurity of those with no pension and limited social security. Why not try to organise them, too?'[12]

Many of the tensions within Momentum were inbuilt. The governance of a campaign for a party leadership is by its nature centralized, however much it may claim to be for or by the grassroots. Whereas almost any other project of the left starts from the bottom – from local groups and networks of activists – and builds upwards, Momentum began its life as the voice of the Labour left upside-down, as the property of the candidate and their appointees. To bring it into existence, those charged with running Momentum had to actively give away their power to decide policy and direct the masses; and, although they knew that this was the right thing to do, some (though by no means all) never really reconciled themselves to this outcome. The temptation to recentralize power would grow stronger and stronger as the inevitably messy process of internal democracy played out.

Momentum was eventually launched in the press with much fanfare on 8 October 2015, promising 'a mass movement for change, for real progressive change in every town and city'. But beyond a name and a bit of hype in the press, its existence was unclear – and the debate on both its role and its internal structures had yet to be resolved. Eventually, as the year wore on, Jon Lansman proposed that a National Committee be convened for the organization in early January 2016, consisting of representatives of the existing organizations of the Labour left and a number of activists representing regions who would be appointed to the committee by the existing Reference Group. Momentum's new staff team were aghast at the prospect of an appointed leadership. 'The whole mantra from Corbyn's leadership campaign had been about a new kind of politics and getting new people involved,' says Emma Rees, 'and we had all these new groups setting up and registering with us. But it was clear to us that if we had a committee that was appointed, it would just consist of people who were already known to the Reference Group – the old Labour left.' The staff team dug their heels in and pushed the proposal back by effectively downing tools.

Eventually, John McDonnell stepped in and broke the deadlock, and a compromise proposal was agreed by the Reference Group: the National Committee would meet in early February, and representatives of members would be elected rather than appointed. The new structure would involve the local groups that had been established all over the country. But rather than allow all local activist groups to be represented at a national level, Momentum was given a layer-cake structure, in which local activists would elect delegates to regional committees, which would in turn elect delegates to the National Committee. The National Committee would take charge of the future of Momentum and would elect from its number a Steering Committee to be responsible for the organization on a day-to-day basis.

Momentum's obsession with its own structures and governance stemmed from the sharply contrasting priorities that existed at the base of Corbynism. The first great debate on its new National Committee would not be about campaigns or activity but the requirements for membership of the organization. On one side sat Lansman and his allies, who wanted to limit Momentum to Labour members. He was agnostic on the issue himself, but the new Labour leadership was concerned about opening Momentum's membership to those outside the party, viewing it as a liability because of Labour's tribal culture and the possibility of infiltration by groups like the Socialist Party. 'An awful lot of what I am blamed for actually came from above,' Lansman laments, 'and throughout that whole period I felt absolutely caught between that and the membership.' On the other side sat a sprawling alliance of activists and staff who wanted Momentum to be open to people outside Labour, providing they were not supporters of a rival political party. On paper the debate seems rather dry – but, as is often the case in Labour Party politics, this seemingly procedural point was just the starting point for a series of debates which would define the fate of Momentum and to an extent the wider project of Corbynism.

Divisions on the structure and orientation of Momentum were playing out at every level of the organization and were already tearing apart the activist networks that had propelled Corbyn to the leadership. In my local Momentum group, Haringey, the Momentum franchise had been given by Lansman to two local stalwarts of the pre-existing Labour left. Over the course of three consecutive meetings in the autumn of 2015 – with between a hundred and two hundred local activists packed into a sweaty room in a community centre on Green Lanes – they had refused to allow Haringey Momentum to plan activities or elect a local committee. This was because, they said, Momentum had not yet decided on its criteria for membership and there were a handful non-Labour members in the room. Attendance was beginning to drop, as requests for votes were repeatedly ruled out of order and the events descended into a shouting match, with the chairs overruling an increasingly frustrated audience and insisting that the meeting limit itself to a debrief from the leadership election and discussion of how those present might support the new leadership. For the large number of young people who had come to the meetings, many of whom had cut their teeth organizing university occupations or in the Occupy movement, it seemed absurd that a group with so many activists and such energy – and with so much to be done in the local area around cuts and housing estate demolitions – would demobilize itself for several months in the name of maintaining a Labour-only membership structure. Clearly, under the surface, something else was going on – a struggle for power between the left's new activists and its old guard. We knew that many right-wing MPs and apparatchiks were deeply suspicious, if not outright hostile, to the influx of new party members. But it rapidly became clear that some on the left were, too.

Momentum's move to establish structures broke the impasse in Haringey and many other local groups by forcing elections to take place. Clocking off early from my shift at a local branch of Wetherspoons on a cold evening in early January, I rushed over to the crunch meeting, where I and another young activist beat the old guard candidates and represented the group at the all-London meeting, where I was elected as one of four London delegates to the National Committee. The National Committee took place at a room in the labyrinthine basement of Birkbeck College in Bloomsbury on Saturday, 6 February (by coincidence the sixth anniversary of the founding conference of the NCAFC), and was host to a theatrical enactment of the split between Labourism and social movement politics. Entitled to attend were twenty-six elected delegates from regions and twenty-seven representatives of trade unions and other organizations, many of whom were appointed rather than elected. The existing organizations of the Labour left – CLPD, Red Labour and the LRC – were given seats but so too were soft left groups Open Labour and Compass. On arrival I was taken to one side by a tall man about my age, with whom I conferred in a conspiratorial tone to confirm that the London delegation was indeed voting for an open membership system.

I had never met James Schneider before, but in the coming years we would work together frequently – mostly on the same side. He had joined the Momentum staff team by accident after volunteering on the leadership campaign and had almost no history of activism in politics at all. Originally politicized by the Iraq War, Schneider had initially been a Lib Dem, but his politics shifted to the left following the financial crash. He had already left university by the time of the 2010 student movement and, regarding the UK as a bleak place politically, had become an Africa-focussed journalist. 'I thought UK Uncut was amazing,' he says, 'but I wasn't involved, admiring it from afar. And it did reach a long way. I remember interviewing a Zambian tax justice activist who told me how much of a boost seeing UK Uncut take on tax dodgers had been for the African tax justice movement.' After the general election result in May 2015 ('I surprised at just how incredibly upset I was by it') he had joined Labour, without much hope it would ever really reflect his politics, and had jumped at the opportunity to support Jeremy Corbyn, whom he had met in passing at events about the Central African Republic's civil war. Arriving back to the UK after a long stint covering Boko Haram, he had some leave built up and spent it on Corbyn's leadership campaign, inside which he was rapidly promoted. By February 2016, Schneider was operating as an unpaid nationwide organizer for Momentum and was managing its press operation. In less than a year, he would be Labour's head of strategic communications – effectively acting as deputy to Labour's director of communications Seumus Milne.

At the first national committee meeting of Momentum, Schneider was organizing the floor for the open membership side, his concentration on the task at hand intermittently compromised by the fact that he was having to run out of the room to engage in a press management war with Andrew Gilligan, who was writing an exposé of 'the radical hard-Left Momentum activists mounting a ruthless purge of Labour' (of which I was one) for the *Telegraph*.[13] The tense debate that followed went much wider than the merits of any membership system: those of us in support of an open membership structure by and large argued that Corbynism had been created by movements outside Labour, that we now needed to turn outwards and that, because of Labour's dreadful record in both office and opposition, the onus was on us, the new Labour left, to convince others to join the party – not to turn them away at the door of Momentum. On the other side was the opposite case: that Corbynism was the product of years of painstaking work inside the party, that Momentum's job was to almost unconditionally support the new leadership and help it win elections and that Labour was the undisputed centre of left politics in Britain. In a tub-thumping crescendo, one delegate from the North West argued: 'there is only one party in this country's history, only one, that has done a damn thing for working class people – and that party is the Labour Party.'

His speech fell on deaf ears, and the meeting voted by a clear margin to endorse an open membership system. By a similar split, it also endorsed my paper supporting the creation of a democratic youth organization. The result of the vote prompted a gloomy response from some. Jon Lansman was already Momentum's figurehead and had spent months fighting behind closed doors for a Labour-only membership system. In the aftermath of the vote, the rationale behind his position became clearer: that without a Labour-only membership structure, Unite would not affiliate to Momentum. For Lansman, ever the broker of alliances on the Labour left, this was a major setback; for those of us who were more interested in Momentum's independence and role in bridging the party to wider movements, it was either a minor inconvenience or a positive boon.

Looking back, what is remarkable is the fact that – despite Momentum's claim to want to bring together the party and social movements and the clear support given for this course of action by its democratic structures – its leadership and office did not contain many people who had come from the movements of the early 2010s. Of those elected to the Steering Committee, I was, at twenty-seven, the youngest. The next youngest was Sam Wheeler, a Manchester Labour activist and Unite member, whose outlook on Momentum's priorities and on questions like internal democracy was in many ways the opposite of mine. Jackie Walker and Marsha-Jane Thompson had both held positions in the LRC. Cecile Wright was a well-known academic in the Midlands. Christine Shawcroft was a representative of the Bennite bulletin Labour Briefing. Jon Lansman was the beating heart of the pre-existing Labour left. Jill Mountford, a member of the socialist group Workers' Liberty, was the veteran of many extra-parliamentary campaigns, most recently a high-profile fight to save Lewisham A & E, but was from an older generation. And then there were the trade union representatives: Matt Wrack from the Fire Brigades' Union and TSSA political officer Sam Tarry, whose stint as chair of Young Labour was by now six years ago. Momentum's office was dominated by people my age or younger, but its core staff team had not been involved in the 2010 student movement or anything after it: Schneider had focussed himself on Africa-focussed journalism, and Klugg and Rees had been on the fringes of political activity.

Many of the much younger office volunteers regarded the storming of Millbank, the pensions' dispute and Occupy as ancient history, but this lack of conventional political training among Momentum's staff was not all bad. 'If I knew then what I know now,' says Emma Rees, 'I would not have been so ambitious and gung ho. We weren't jaded, we didn't have baggage and political scars.'

Just as in the student movement of 2010, the separation of a generation of left-wing youth from the history and traditions of the organized left had the effect of creating a free-flowing, unconstrained atmosphere. But it would also make the Corbyn project – with its promise of a new kind of politics and its attempts to create an all-embracing mass movement – vulnerable to being defeated and co-opted by the much better organized, more institutional left.

By accident, I would end up getting much more closely acquainted with Momentum's office than I had initially expected. When the Steering Committee first met, it appointed its 'officer group', three people tasked with taking more day-to-day responsibility. It was obvious that Lansman would be the chair, and as the result of some horse-trading it was agreed that Jackie Walker would be vice chair. Unbeknownst to me, Lansman's preferred candidates for the more arduous role of treasurer, Marsha-Jane Thompson and Christine Shawcroft, had both refused, and so when I volunteered I was simply nodded into the role. It was an unglamorous job in itself, but it meant that for the whole time I was on the Steering Committee I came into the Momentum office in the TSSA's headquarters in Euston on an almost daily basis. Throughout 2016, I spent hundreds of hours huddled in the corner with a laptop, following the development of the organization and squabbling with Lansman about assorted procedural matters, before either going down the pub with the staff and volunteers, rushing off to speak at the meeting of a local group or organizing events for the new anti-Brexit campaign Another Europe is Possible.

What I discovered was that the divisions that were raised at the foundation of Momentum – the party focus versus the wider movement, autonomy versus central control, open procedures versus backroom deals – would dominate its office politics and the activities of the wider organization throughout its first year in existence, and that the attitudes of most of the Steering Committee were profoundly at odds with the sentiment at the grassroots of the organization. The very existence of Momentum was, initially, an attempt to use these divisions as a source of creative tension – and the fate of Momentum in many ways sums up what happened to the Corbyn project more widely. In the end, the two sides could not be straddled forever. One vision would have to defeat the other.

Debate of the decades

On the evening of Monday, 17 March 1980, Westminster Central Hall was packed to the rafters. The event that had filled the 2,600-seater hall was not a rock concert but a debate organized by the official organization of the Labour left, the Labour Coordinating Committee. It took place just under a year after Margaret Thatcher's victory in the 1979 general election, and the left was at a crossroads. The 1970s had been a period of industrial militancy unprecedented in the post-war era, as successive Labour governments disappointed left-wing members with cuts and wage restraint. Now, however, a new tide was beginning to draw activists back into Labour and a new Labour left, at its head a newly radicalized Tony Benn, began to take shape. The debate was entitled 'The Crisis and Future of the Left' and would quickly become known as 'The Debate of the Decade'.[14] It witnessed one of the clearest distillations of the differences between the Labour left and the extra-parliamentary left and was chaired by leading anti-apartheid and anti-fascist activist Peter Hain, who would himself become a Labour MP eleven years later. The speakers were, on the Labour side, three current or former MPs: Audrey Wise, Tony Benn and Stuart Holland – and, on the extra-parliamentary side, 1968 icon Tariq Ali, revolutionary intellectual Paul Foot and socialist feminist Hilary Wainwright. 'I remember feeling a bit of a minority voice,' Wainwright remembers, 'and feeling kind of small between these two guys who were big, both physically and in terms of their rhetoric.'

In many ways, the debate at the beginning of the 1980s was quite different to the one that took place at the birth of Corbynism in organizations like Momentum. By the end of the 1970s, the organized revolutionary left was reaching its high water mark, and two of the speakers for the extra-parliamentary left were representatives of Trotskyist groups (Tariq Ali for the International Marxist Group and Paul Foot for the SWP). These organizations had many thousands of active members, were serious forces in the labour movement and occupied a much greater role in public life than they would in 2015. This was an era in which Tony Benn felt the need to impress upon the audience that 'reform is an honorable and radical course', as opposed to 'some coup d'état by vanguard forces'. 'The British working class movement created the British Labour Party and we have the means to win consent for socialism by democracy', he concluded, amid a raucous atmosphere of cheering, booing and disruption from hecklers. 'Any other sort of socialism is unachievable and would not be worth having even if it was achieved.' Tariq Ali responded that revolutionary politics was not about coup d'états but about 'a right to vote which is infinitely more democratic than the right which exists once every five years'. 'There have been social democratic governments in Sweden, Australia, Norway, Belgium, Britain now for many decades. Not in one single case have any of these social democratic governments brought about a fundamental shift in the relationship of class forces in favour of the working class', he said, arguing that 'a new type of party is needed, a mass revolutionary party which organises people at the point of production, in the neighbourhood, which can take up all the central question which face the working class movement in Britain and internationally'.

But underneath the standard debate between reform and revolution ran a series of arguments and ideas that would resurface again with the emergence of Corbynism. The emergence of Bennism and the (now old) new Labour left of the 1980s was, like Corbynism, an attempt to bring together the Labour Party and the parliamentary left with social movements and industrial struggles. This generation of the Labour left had, like the left outside the party, been influenced by the disappointing experience of the Wilson and Callaghan governments and by Ralph Miliband's critique of Labourism, even if they did not share his conclusions. Tony Benn was interested in defending a parliamentary road to socialism, but the emerging Labour left of which he was a part pursued this strategy with a critical eye on the nature of the state and with the acknowledgement that holding power in parliament would be impotent without a more generalized mobilization at the base of society. Consequently, the Bennite left was greatly concerned with joining itself to, as Tony Benn put it in the debate, 'the radicalisation of the main body of the labour movement' and 'the women's movements, the blacks, the environmentalists, the peace movements and those who are trying to bring about a peaceful united Ireland'. It was this emphasis, in addition to its emphasis on a thoroughgoing internal democratization of the party, which set the Bennite left apart from the Labour left that had gone before it, embodied by the likes of Aneurin Bevan and Michael Foot.

The attempts to meld social movements with a parliamentary strategy not only brought the extra-parliamentary left and the Labour left closer than they had ever been but also threw up a series of contradictions. It was Hilary Wainwright's contributions to the debate that most articulately explained the tension:

> Is the extra-parliamentary activity, the mass movements to which the Labour left give support, merely like 'extra-curricular' activity, just a worthy back up to the real thing, the work that goes on in parliament, the work aimed at bringing to power a radical Labour government? Or are extra-parliamentary movements like the women's movement, some shop stewards' combine committees, tenants' groups and others *themselves* the basis for a new form of political power? Are *they* the real thing for which parliamentary activity is just one source of support?[15]

Wainwright drew on the recent example of a recent campaign against the closure of Vickers Scotswood factory on Tyneside where, rather than focussing on building a campaign of direct action and worker takeover of the profitable plants, the shop stewards had put their faith in the then-Labour government (and the left-wing minister, Les Huckfield, who was in charge of the case) to nationalize the factories. Labour did not come through, and the workers joined the dole queues. Extra-parliamentary movements like the shop stewards' committees, argued Wainwright, 'are themselves the beginnings of a form of political power far more democratic, far more directly accountable, and a hundred times more powerful against private capital than parliament can ever be', and yet because the logic of the labour movement was imbued with parliamentarism, the transformative potential of the mass movement was hamstrung.

Thirty-five years later, as the tide dragged the veterans of the anti-austerity movement into Labour, a new iteration of this tension took place. Just as in 1980, social movements and industrial militancy were seen as 'extra-curricular activities' as far as the logic of Corbynism was concerned. The student protests of 2010; the strikes, tent cities and mass movements of 2011; and the housing campaigns and other initiatives that had come after it were all useful but were essentially warm-up acts. The real job was cheering on the Labour leader, and this mode of politics was backed up by the endless news cycle that surrounded him.

In the 1980s, the Labour's inward tide was also strong and proved stronger than the critiques offered by many on the extra-parliamentary left. Just over a year after giving his passionate speech in Westminster Central Hall, Tariq Ali resigned from the International Marxist Group and joined Labour, citing the fact that the new Labour left was 'drawing wide new layers into the struggle for socialism and galvanising the base of the Labour Party'.[16]

What Wainwright and Ali both went in search of was, more or less, a space somewhere in between the emerging Bennite Labour left and the often sectarian revolutionary left outside it. They were not alone. The widely popularized history of the 1980s focuses predominantly on the personal fortunes of Tony Benn and on a few high-profile flashpoints such as the 1981 deputy leadership election and the general election of 1983. But away from the set-piece battles at party conference and at the ballot box, another tradition was emerging from within the Labour left which would reach outwards and which would go much further than Benn in terms of its break with parliamentarism and its focus on working with social movements.

At the heart of this other Labour left were a series of radical experiments in local government, most prominently the Greater London Council under Ken Livingstone. In 1981 Hilary Wainwright got a job there, though she remained an 'obstinate refusenik' when it came to joining the Labour Party itself. 'It felt as if I had joined an open, campaigning socialist party without having to join the tight, conservative party that has its HQ in the Palace of Westminster', she later wrote.[17]

John McDonnell was the deputy leader of the GLC in the 1980s. 'I got elected by accident', he says. 'I was going to be the election agent for my friend Chris Rogers, but he ended up getting elected to a trade union position so we were short of a candidate.' As well as being the capital's de facto finance minister, he was also put in charge of campaigning. 'The GLC tradition was linked to the rest of the Labour left but distinct in the sense that it was much closer to social movements, and we did things that were within the Labour tradition not just frowned upon but frequently condemned' – things like championing gay rights, a stance that was widely attacked as divisive by establishment figures in the Labour Party. 'We were in and against the state',[18] McDonnell says. 'We were going into the state to transform it and we were doing that by building and supporting social movements across London. We employed two community organisers in every borough, and we opened up County Hall every night to campaigns and groups of people who wanted to organise, develop policies and develop campaigns.' Breaking with all convention, the GLC opened up its committees to members of the public, some of them elected at mass annual assemblies, and gave community groups and campaigns real decision-making power in planning decisions and housing matters.

As Hilary Wainwright later wrote, the radicalism and openness of the GLC was driven by a generation of left politicians who 'felt closer to and more allied to socialists and feminists outside the Labour Party than functionaries within it'.[19] As the Corbyn era wore on, many onlookers observed a gap opening up between the approaches of McDonnell and that of Corbyn and his inner circle. This manifested itself on an array of issues from Brexit policy to Momentum's internal democracy, and one of the main reasons for it was that McDonnell – as a self-conscious member of the 'in and against' tradition – had a much sharper critique of Labourism than the main flow of the new Labour left of the 2010s. The brand of politics that the likes of Wainwright and McDonnell practised in the GLC – the attempt to connect electoral projects to social movements and the need to constantly learn from grassroots campaigns – has defined McDonnell's approach throughout his political career. Boosted by the legacy of the social movements of the first half of the decade, it was one of the crucial building blocks of a new left, and in 2015 it would, for the first time, be given a hearing and a champion at the very top of the Labour Party.

Decades after the 'debate of the decade', when Jeremy Corbyn put himself forward for the Labour leadership, both Hilary Wainwright and Tariq Ali (and with them figures from the orthodox communist tradition like Andrew Murray) threw themselves behind him. For many of the veterans of the movement against the Iraq War and other episodes of public protest, Corbynism was an even easier sell than Bennism. Benn was, after all, a third-generation parliamentarian. Although he was highly critical of the British state and the supposedly impartial civil service, he often displayed a kind of deference for the House of Commons. He had moved decisively to the left by the time that 'Bennism' became an organized movement within Labour, but he had spent most of his career as a pretty conventional Labour Party politician, serving in Harold Wilson's Cabinets. Corbyn, on the other hand, was an outsider, whose politics and profile had been forged on picket lines and at protests. His pitch to both Labour members and the wider public made a virtue of the fact that he shared none of Benn's oratorical skills or experience holding public office, his appeal resting on his consistency and authenticity during the left's long years in the wilderness. Crucially, whereas the social movement tradition that had found a home in the GLC was a relative sideshow in the wider project of Bennism, Corbynism was built in the shadow of recent mass movements – and John McDonnell would be the new shadow chancellor.

Bevanism, Bennism, Corbynism: every few decades, a new Labour left sprung up, bringing a new wave of recruits into Labour and transforming politics around it. Each successive generation had placed greater emphasis on opening up the Labour Party, utilizing and supporting mass movements from outside. Corbynism's promise to break free from the straitjacket of conventional Labourism – of bureaucracy, top-down decision-making and the demobilization of social movements and organized workers – was, on the surface, stronger than any iteration of the Labour left before it. As we shall see, what actually happened was quite different.

5

The movement versus the machine

Corbynism was, more than any generation of the Labour left before it, the result of mass movements outside the party. Its promise to transform Labour, and its potential to put it at the centre of a movement of protest and industrial struggle, was correspondingly strong. But this is not how things turned out. If the last chapter was the story of how a new force emerged out of the social movements of the first half of the decade and entered Labour, this chapter is the story of how that energy and bottom-up politics was ground down and absorbed into what would become an orthodox and conventional electoralist project. This would not just be an innocent meeting of different worlds – it would be the defeat of one world by another, enacted at times quite consciously. To understand how and why this happened, we first have to look at the context in which the new leadership found itself, for Corbynism was a project constructed under siege.

The election of a left-wing socialist as leader of a mainstream centre-left party sets Corbynism aside from every comparable political project. Bernie Sanders never had to run the Democratic Party. Pablo Iglesias, Jean-Luc Melanchon, Alexis Tsipras and other popular figures of the European left all led new parties and so did not have to share a bed with the same technocratic politicians whose neoliberal consensus they aimed to break. Tony Benn and Aneurin Bevan failed in their attempts to take over the Labour Party and spent much of their time as bitter opponents of its leaders. Corbyn's elevation to the leadership therefore presented both the left and the left's internal opponents with a situation they had never faced before: an unprecedented moment of hope bringing us suddenly close to power and an unprecedented menace which must be extinguished by any means necessary.

Moments of unforeseen and sudden change are prone to producing a great number of ironies. Perhaps one of the greatest is the fact that Jeremy Corbyn – who is by all reliable accounts a genuinely nice man with very normal human flaws – was portrayed throughout his time as leader in a deeply inhumane way. For the most part, his public image was split in two, and the two images conveyed to two different audiences by different commentators and media outlets. To much of the new activist base of the Labour Party, Corbyn became a figure beyond reproach, whose name was to be sung out in unison and whose pronouncements – no matter how much they conflicted either one's own views or his previous pronouncements – were to be defended and evangelized.

But to his opponents in the parliamentary Labour Party, to the right-wing press and to much of the public, Corbyn was the subject of a portrayal that bordered on the demonic. Former MPs like Ian Austin lined up to accuse him of working with terrorists. His historic position on Irish unity and Palestinian liberation was regularly reported alongside an innuendo that he was 'a threat to national security', a claim that was backed by intelligence bosses who were wheeled out of retirement specially for the task.[1] Much of the criticism levied at Corbyn was not just point-scoring or headline-seeking, but betrayed a deeply personal and visceral hatred of him on the part of his detractors. Former Labour MP Tom Harris referred to Corbyn not just as an extremist but as 'a nasty bully'[2].

The propaganda campaign directed at Corbyn was not, of course, really about the man himself. The sudden shattering of the consensus behind neoliberalism and austerity was driven by the politicization of hundreds of thousands of new Labour members and was a mortal threat to the existing Labour Party establishment which resided at Westminster and at the party's headquarters at Southside. On the one hand, the bulk of Labour MPs honestly believed that a left-wing manifesto would mean a disaster that could cost them their seats and any prospect of wielding governmental power. On the other, MPs also knew that any prospect of electoral success under Corbyn would mean an entrenchment of the left's power and a growing demand for a new generation of parliamentarians who shared the membership's appetite for a radical programme – that is, not them. Meanwhile, the party machine, which had been moulded by New Labour, was populated by people who knew that unless the left could be removed from the leadership, and quickly, they were living on borrowed time. The approach of the pre-existing Labour establishment to the Corbyn leadership therefore went well beyond anything that could be labelled as criticism or scepticism. It was sabotage.

Clive Lewis was already well-acquainted with the methods of the more bureaucratic wing of the Labour Right by the time he was elected as the left-wing MP of Norwich South in 2015. He had grown up around the time of the miners' strike and has strong memories of his dad – who was an official for the BFAWU – doing food collections for the miners. He arrived at university in Bradford in the mid-1990s, just at the moment when the NUS began to be dominated by young Blairites, who set about preparing the ground for the introduction of tuition fees. 'As someone who had come from a council house, had a comprehensive education and a grant, it just felt like everything I had was coming under attack', he said. 'And here was a group inside NUS – in fact the leadership of NUS – who seemed, at best, ambivalent about it.' Lewis joined the Campaign for Free Education, a left-wing faction,[3] and was eventually elected as an NUS vice president. The president of the NUS at the time was Jim Murphy, later an arch-Blairite MP and leader of Scottish Labour.

Lewis regularly found himself at odds with the rest of the NUS leadership and eventually found himself summarily suspended. He remained committed to socialist ideas, though he left active politics for a life in the BBC and the army reserve and was only able to get selected as a parliamentary candidate because of the opening up within the party that occurred under Ed Miliband. He fondly remembers the look of thunder on the face of the senior party staffer who had been sent to oversee his selection count. 'You could just tell he was thinking "in my time you'd never have been allowed anywhere near this" – it was great', he says.

'I suppose after all that', says Lewis, 'you might think that nothing could surprise me.' But 'maybe with the exception of the two Johns [McDonnell and Lansman] we didn't realise the scale and depth of the determination of the right to take back control of the party. The left couldn't match that vehemence, that dedication, that one track mentality and ruthlessness. It was like nothing any of us had ever experienced before.'

The response of many MPs and senior staff towards the events of summer 2015 is well documented. From the moment Corbyn entered the leadership, he faced a barrage of negative briefings and attempts to undermine him from within the PLP, which intensified throughout his time in office. 'I think people have underestimated just how much energy had to be put into day to day survival, and in every respect – not just in terms of losing votes at the NEC', says John McDonnell. 'We could barely hire staff. I wanted to hire a hundred to two hundred community organisers, but it took us nearly three and a half years to get barely thirty or forty, because they blocked it at every stage.' McDonnell remembers how his Shadow Treasury team worked hard to hold George Osborne to account, but that 'when we went into the chamber for Treasury questions or debates, the PLP boycotted the debates. We'd have the whole rash of Tories in front of us shouting and bawling and empty chairs behind us.'

The old regime's continuing hold on the Labour machine set up constant barriers to the task of running an effective opposition, but by conditioning the Corbyn project in a constant state of siege, it also created another danger. 'It distracts you from getting out there and mobilising as we perhaps needed to,' says McDonnell, 'and it pushes you into a bunker mentality at times and that means you're prone to bureaucratising your own project'.

Momentum's existence was greeted with hysteria by many MPs and party staff, who rightly saw an enlarged organized left as a threat to their role in the party and dedicated much of the period up until the 2017 general election – when Momentum's role in mobilizing members on the doorstep turned its mainstream reputation from outcast to saviour – to an attempt to have the organization proscribed. In 2020, a leaked internal report seemed to reveal what many had already suspected: a deliberate attempt by party staff to undermine Labour's electoral performance. It also unveiled an unpleasant culture of outright nastiness towards the left and the leadership, with informal staff WhatsApp threads containing a litany of derogatory comments aimed disproportionately at the Black and women members of his team.

At least to begin with, the hostility that existed between the party establishment and the mass of members who supported the new leadership was largely a one-way street. Jeremy Corbyn was elected on a promise of a 'kinder, gentler politics'. Many of his supporters, critical though they may have been of New Labour's policies, were brought into the party quite naive to the idea that there would be such a campaign of sabotage against the new leadership. The turning point for the internal culture of Corbynism, and the moment when most left-wing members' factional consciousness came alive, took place in the summer of 2016 in the immediate aftermath of Britain's vote to leave the EU. The day after the referendum, MPs Ann Coffey and Margaret Hodge announced that they would submit a non-binding motion of no confidence to the parliamentary Labour Party, which was passed on 28 June by a margin of 172 to 40. Corbyn refused to resign, and so in early July a formal leadership challenge was launched, with two candidates putting themselves forward against Corbyn: Angela Eagle, a well-respected MP in the centre of the party who had served as a minister under Gordon Brown and had voted for the Iraq War; and Owen Smith, a charismatic former pharmaceutical lobbyist who presented himself as the soft left candidate.

The moment was a watershed. The actions of the parliamentary party were out of touch with the mood of the party membership, who less than a year previously had given Corbyn an unprecedented mandate as leader. They also left Labour in a perilous situation: with David Cameron having resigned, the accepted wisdom was that a snap election was round the corner and could come in the middle of the leadership challenge or soon after it. The Labour Right had spent decades touting itself as the wing of Labour that cared about winning elections, and yet here it was brazenly pursuing power in the party at the expense of power in the country. The methods by which the left's opponents sought to take back control of the party betrayed a truly patrician attitude towards politics. Having first used their majority among MPs to denounce Corbyn, they then sought to prevent him even being on the ballot paper by asking the party's National Executive Committee to rule that sitting leaders were not automatically candidates. In this task they had the full support of the party's general secretary, Iain McNicol, and had they been successful, the ruling would have precipitated the most serious civil war in Labour's history, if not an outright split.

As it was, Labour effectively underwent a kind of internal split. On one side sat the party machine, most MPs and the overwhelming bulk of Labour's local councillors; and on the other, a mass membership more mobilized than it had ever been. As Corbyn emerged from being berated at a meeting of the parliamentary Labour Party on Monday, 27 June, he was greeted in Parliament Square by a rally of more than ten thousand, which had been organized at less than twenty-four hours' notice. 'Jeremy was really at his lowest ebb – and there was a danger of him resigning', says Joe Ryle, one of John McDonnell's press aides. 'To this day I've never been to another demo that was so electric.' In a time of crisis, all of the left's networks had pulled together: Joe Ryle had been at Glastonbury when the leadership challenge started but had spent much of his time there on the phone; the People's Assembly Against Austerity pushed Momentum to organize the protest and helped arrange the sound equipment; the FBU brought a fire engine which acted as a stage; and James Schneider and ten others, working out of a rundown office in Bethnal Green, had helped mobilize numbers. 'Over the course of that week, there were rallies in forty towns across the country', Schneider says. 'You had hundreds of people getting together in towns that barely had an active Labour Party in them. It was almost spontaneous – and I liked it because it showed that Momentum existed and had capacities well outside the centre of the organisation.'

The summer of 2016 oscillated between being a moment of formative crisis and wild farce, and as a press officer on the Corbyn campaign (I spent most of my time ghost writing opinion articles and preparing speeches) I had a front-row seat to watch the farces unfold. It began with Angela Eagle's launch press conference, during which most media left to cover the fact that Andrea Leadsom had withdrawn from the Conservative Party leadership race and Eagle was left on stage forlornly calling out the names of journalists and TV networks only to be greeted with an awkward silence. Her withdrawal left Owen Smith as the only candidate against Corbyn, and to say that Smith was prone to gaffes would be a generous understatement. He made a joke at a press conference about having a 29-inch penis and boasted about how his ability to 'pull' his wife while at school demonstrated leadership qualities. Shortly after Smith was nominated, video footage surfaced from a 2015 Welsh general election debate in which he discussed with Plaid Cymru leader Leanne Wood why they had been invited and told her 'your gender helps'; 'yeah', Wood replied, sarcastically.[4] Suffice it to say that by the end of the campaign, *Vice* magazine was publishing articles with headlines like 'A Quick Guide to All the Times Owen Smith Mentioned His Penis'.[5]

Between June and September, Corbynism transformed from a fresh, perhaps naive, mass of people from different backgrounds and movements looking for parliamentary representation into something much tighter and more cohesive. Many new members were drawn into factional politics at a local level for the first time, and the behaviour of MPs and the party machine underlined the perspective of many activists that their main task was to defend the leadership against its internal opponents at all costs. The crowds that flocked to Corbyn's rallies in 2016 were bigger than in 2015, the phonebanks better attended and the mobilization much broader in terms of geographical reach. More people continued to flood into Labour, many of them getting active in politics for the first time. After the first leadership contest election, Labour had 388,000 members, but after the second it had more than half a million.[6] Whatever one thought about Corbynism's policies, or the personalities at the top, it was indisputably built on popular demand and on a political awakening among hundreds of thousands of people.

Living on air

The paradox of the Corbyn moment, then, is that the rebirth of the Labour left – despite its roots in the strikes and protests of the first half of the decade – did not translate into a flourishing of social or industrial struggle. This is not because the new Labour leadership was hostile to strike action: on the contrary, Jeremy Corbyn and the rest of the Shadow Cabinet were frequent visitors at picket lines and often seized opportunities to make a symbolic gesture of solidarity. John McDonnell was a regular supporter of strikers in precarious and low-paid workplaces, for instance, workers at Picturehouse cinemas and McDonalds, who were engaged in high-profile if numerically small disputes. The IWGB and United Voices of the World (UVW) became much more prominent during the Corbyn years, and McDonnell was, diary-permitting, always around to be at their pickets and protests, ignoring the official position of some TUC affiliates who were hostile to these new and more militant unions. When junior doctors struck in 2016 against the imposition of new contracts, the new leadership saw an opportunity not only to stand with the strikers but also to make a point about the Tories' agenda for the NHS. Corbyn and McDonnell both attended rallies and pickets for the doctors, defying the position of their Shadow Health Secretary, Heidi Alexander, who did not publicly support the strikes.

And yet the overall trend in industrial militancy during the Corbyn years is unmistakable. The number of workers involved in taking strike action in 2015 was already at an all-time low of 81,000 (down from the almost two million who took action over pensions in 2011). That number went up slightly in 2016 but then plummeted again to 33,000 in 2017 and 39,000 in 2018.[7] This was an era in which hundreds of thousands of people were getting active in the labour movement for the first time, many of them in order to support a leadership that attended picket lines on a regular basis. The social conditions which had driven the mass movements of previous years had not gone away: austerity was still in full swing when Corbyn was elected Labour leader, and it continued under Theresa May. By the end of the decade, wage constraint had begun to be eased but only in selected parts of the public sector; welfare claimants were still being squeezed, local government was still facing cuts and public services were still under attack across the board. It should be noted that trade union membership did rise very slightly over the final three years of the decade, but given the context one might have expected the development of a new workers' movement. The reality was the inverse.

Social movements, too, did not blossom in the new Labour left after 2015. Corbyn's first speech as a candidate for the leadership had been made from the stage of a People's Assembly Against Austerity rally in Parliament Square, and the following five years would witness a number of marches for the NHS and public services, many of them organized by the People's Assembly, but these protests got gradually smaller. In reality, they amounted to an annual re-enactment of a movement which some years previously had ceased to exist and lacked the disruptive and transgressive potential of the protests that had come before them.

The Labour leadership was on some level interested in building power in communities and workplaces outside of the electoral cycle. The creation of a Community Organising Unit in 2018 might have been a landmark event in Labour's rebirth, but it happened late and with a fraction of the resources it needed. In hiring a few dozen professional organizers to 'empower people to campaign and win in their communities and workplaces on issues that matter to them,'[8] it was to a great extent an attempt to engineer 'from above' what ought, in order for the effort to have been successful, been the task of every activist. As it happened, there was no widespread rebirth of local anti-cuts networks, and the Momentum groups and constituency Labour Parties which became the focal points for the new Labour left were very often either uninterested or too busy.

But why? Why, given the context of a burgeoning left-wing political movement, did social movements and industrial militancy not only fail to grow but also go into reverse?

One thing worth noting is the 2016 Trade Union Act, which introduced new thresholds on strike ballots – but this legislation did not change the picture fundamentally. At the root of the problem was the basic logic of the Corbyn project and its sense of priorities. As time went on, both Momentum and the left's wider activist base became increasingly obsessed with winning seats on committees and occupying them, often without much sense of purpose beyond providing a supportive voice for the leadership. Over the course of its dominance over Labour's internal structures, the left came to control many layers of the party, primarily at ward and constituency level, which were in their own right mass organizations. As membership figures rose above half a million, there were on average almost a thousand party members in every constituency, and in some seats there were many times that. Where the left controlled the local party, they had the ability to contact local members at will. Labour's mass membership could have been the core of a renaissance of trade union militancy, or a renewed movement against austerity, or a range of more proactive demands on housing, the NHS or climate change.

Instead, we turned inwards. In 2016, I was part of a slate of left-wing candidates who took over Young Labour, the official youth wing of the party which, on paper, spoke for all Labour members under the age of twenty-seven – but once in office, the new committee remained entirely focussed on internal party matters and issuing statements pertaining to this or that controversy. In most local parties, the left threw its energies into turning out members to constituency Annual General Meetings, getting them to vote in the NEC elections and, at election time, knocking on doors – a set of activities essentially identical to those of the pre-Corbyn Labour Party.

In Lambeth, which had been the scene of a very lively anti-cuts movement, the transformation of the local left was clear to many local activists. 'At the start of Corbynism, people did talk about organising protests,' says Dan Jeffery, a leading activist in Lambeth Save Our Services who joined Labour in 2015, 'but there was nothing on the scale of what we'd done before. A lot of energy got sucked up into machinations and committees of Labour, and eventually even the radical talk dissipated.' Ruth Cashman was the branch secretary of Lambeth Unison and had been part of setting up Lambeth for Corbyn in 2015, but she also found the dynamics of Corbynism troubling. 'What struck me,' she says, 'is how few trade unionists there were in Lambeth Momentum. It was much less action focussed, partly because it was bigger and full of newer people, but also because of its makeup.'

When local issues did arise, the local Labour left largely remained impassive. From 2016, the Ritzy Cinema in Brixton was home to a high-profile strike for living wage, organized in large part by Kelly Rogers, who had cut her teeth organizing students at Birmingham University in 2010 and the years that followed. The strike garnered widespread support, spreading to six new Picturehouse cinemas in six months, and was heavily dependent on community-led support and protests. 'It was social movement unionism, a method I learned in the student movement,' Rogers reflects, 'that if you're up against a big company and you don't have much industrial leverage, you need to get leverage in other ways – with direct action by supporters, big protests and appealing directly to customers to boycott.' While the Labour left was willing to pass motions and individuals would often donate to the strike fund, it never made it a priority in terms of mobilization.

'It was a really political moment, with the EU referendum and the rise of Corbyn,' says Rogers. 'We felt very connected to Corbynism, and pretty much all of the workers in the Ritzy and other Picturehouse cinemas were Corbyn supporters. I'd hoped that this might be something Labour would knock on doors about locally.' The strike was supported by John McDonnell and a number of Labour activists did get involved individually, but 'those hundreds of people going to Labour meetings never really showed up in the way that we needed them to'. When the Ritzy sacked its trade union reps in the summer of 2017, supporters staged a daily protest outside for eight weeks. 'It was a really moving show of solidarity,' says Rogers, who was one of those sacked, 'but it was organised by a layer of people who were either in or came from organised socialist groups, not from Labour.'

Local trade unionists witnessed a similar pattern when it came to campaigns around social housing and other issues. As activists' focus shifted from mobilizing for strikes and protests to mobilizing for Labour NEC elections, says Ruth Cashman, 'the lack of action created its own kind of momentum. Unlike in the anti-cuts movement, being radical and action-focussed and bringing people together didn't mean that you rose to the top – and instead what you got was the people who were hyper-loyal, and most obsessed with committee meetings becoming the local leadership.'

Those upticks in extra-parliamentary mobilization which did take place were either not sustained or were largely disconnected from the Labour left. Many hundreds of thousands of people demonstrated on multiple occasions against Donald Trump – either in response to his ban on arrivals from Muslim countries in early 2017 or in opposition to his state visits in the summers of 2018 and 2019 – but these protests were one-off events which did not generalize into movements. The anti-Brexit movement mobilized the biggest marches in Britain since the Iraq War and were part of a more generalized social movement which sought to pressure the government for a second EU referendum – but the relationship between this movement and the Corbyn leadership was at best distant, and it was left to organizations like Another Europe is Possible to engage in it on behalf of the left. Black Lives Matter began to break through in the UK when a group of activists blockaded London City Airport in August 2016 but had very little to do with the Labour Party or Momentum. Neither did the growth in renters' unions and community unions like ACORN. The final two years of the decade witnessed an explosion of climate activism driven by school student strikes and Extinction Rebellion's direct action crusade – but while the Corbyn leadership was keen to support these endeavours symbolically, the new Labour left did precious little for them in practical terms.

Some observers will be puzzled by the diagnosis that Corbynism did not engage in social movements. Many journalists saw massive crowds at rallies and read statistics about the sheer number of people flooding into Labour and concluded that Momentum *was itself* a social movement. Any confusion arising from this perspective is the result of the fact that we are simply talking at cross purposes. The social movements that nourished the development of the left in the early part of the 2010s, and which in every generation have produced the dissent and mobilization that has built the left's support base, were fundamentally concerned with building power in society and workplaces – and using the power of public pressure and the threat of disruption to change the debate on a given issue and extract concessions from the political system. The movement that developed inside Labour after 2015 might have shown its solidarity with social movements and strikes but was fundamentally concerned with defending Jeremy Corbyn and getting him elected.

The decline of social movements, and their replacement by an emphasis on parliamentary politics, was clear to anyone who had come through the previous few years. 'I think it was a failure that everyone put all their eggs in one basket', says Joe Ryle, who had spent years in climate camp and student activism before working for John McDonnell. 'In terms of pushing movements pushing their own agendas, that largely dropped off and it was just all about Jeremy – expecting him to deliver everything that everyone wanted.' Knowing that the intense parliamentary cycle was in danger of eroding the Labour leadership's connections to the wider movement, Ryle organized a series of monthly meetings at which Corbyn and McDonnell would meet NGOs and campaigns, but even here, the logic of the project weighed down what seemed possible. 'The meetings never came up with anything practical really', Ryle says. 'It was mostly just a lot of questions to John and Jeremy about what *they* were planning to do.'

As a Communist Party activist and Unite official who had seen many movements come and go over the decades, Andrew Murray came from a quite different perspective to someone like me or Joe Ryle, but he reached a similar conclusion. 'The last really big anti-austerity demonstration was the one in 2015 on the same day that Jeremy reached the ballot paper. And so we had a political phenomenon that was the product of mass movements', he says, 'but in the moment of its victory, the source of its strength was switched off. Right the way to the end, there was no significant degree of mass struggle. And without that a radical political project is living on air.' This lack of a struggle was not just a problem for the movements themselves but for the whole concept of a socialist electoral project. 'We were trying to sell a politics of hope', says Murray, 'but you cannot just suck that out of your thumb in an election campaign. It needs to be rooted in people doing things for themselves – in their workplaces, in communities, on the streets.'

In a social movement, agency is built and, ideally, retained at a grassroots level; and to exist in any real sense, a social movement must have independence from any political project to which it is adjacent. But over the course of the Corbyn leadership, despite a lot of mobilization at the grassroots level, faith and hope were placed in leaders to deliver transformation from above. Policy positions largely came from the top down, announced to members at the same time they were announced to the public and were never really a matter for debate within the movement. Momentum almost never took a policy position which conflicted with the leadership's and never engaged its own members in a democratic process to develop a policy programme.

By party conference 2019, a number of projects did exist which were independent of the leadership and aimed to push policy from below. Labour for a Green New Deal, Labour for a 4 Day Week, the Labour Campaign Against Private Schools and so on all had a real impact on Labour's policies in education, work and the environment and were often encouraged by the Leader's Office. But in a way, their existence only serves to illustrate the problems that existed in the Corbynite left: the most prominent and successful campaigns were tight-knit pop-up organizations with no internal life, which had the tacit approval of the leadership and whose sole aim was to change Labour's formal policy position. Only on rare occasions – on the issues of Brexit, migrants' rights and party reform – did activists force an open debate within the left, and, as we shall see, the bureaucratic hurdles placed in their way would prove overwhelming.

Losing Momentum

To an extent, the process that the British left underwent during the Corbyn years is the natural logic of parliamentarism: agency is sucked upwards as the left moves closer to government. But in another sense, it is the story of what happened inside a specific organization: Momentum. From the moment Jeremy Corbyn was elected as leader in 2015 until January 2017, a battle had raged about the organization's purpose: would it play a part in linking Labour to the world outside and building social movements, or would it become a vehicle to win internal elections and parliamentary selections inside Labour?

By the time that Laura Parker became Momentum's national coordinator, moving over from her role as Corbyn's private secretary in late 2017, that decision had already been taken. 'When I arrived, all of the energy on the staff team was going into things like the NEC', she says. 'The leadership of the organisation had not committed to investing resources in maintaining or building local groups, and we had all these regional organisers who were doing factional stuff, but then no campaign team.' By now, Momentum had already won clean sweeps in NEC elections and was organising delegates for party conference in September. 'There were a few of us on the staff team who tried to talk a social movement strategy into being, but a lot of our efforts were strangled at birth really, because it just wasn't what the leadership of the organisation wanted to put resources into.'

This is not to say that Momentum did nothing to organize in the trade union movement or wider society: in 2018 it organized some events and solidarity actions with the BFAWU, who were organizing workers at McDonald's, and the following year organized a few flash occupations of Barclays branches in protest at their relationship with the fossil fuel industry. 'It was groundbreaking in the sense that we were organising protests with a campaign rather than just doing something with an affiliated union,' says Parker, 'but it was too small, in large part because we remained overwhelmingly focused on party-facing stuff'.

By the time of the 2017 general election, Momentum had abandoned whatever was left of its social movement mission and had become, in effect, Corbyn's praetorian guard. This shift was not just a matter of chance, or the result of an abstract logic, but the consequence of a deliberate drive by the organization's leadership and the Leader's Office.

To understand what happened to Momentum, we must return briefly to the events of the summer of 2016. The new leadership had already faced a constant low-level siege, with regular negative press briefings and leaks and a campaign of non-cooperation from the party machine. But when the parliamentary party launched a formal challenge to Corbyn's leadership, the situation became much more overwhelming and urgent. 'For the first year, so much of the operation was a mess', explains Clive Lewis. 'And then when the coup happened we realised it was going to be a pitched battle between this new project based on people power and hope, and the establishment of the party and the party bureaucracy all coming at us all at once.' The sudden need to tighten up the left's operation led the project to seek new internal management and allies that could offer it institutional clout and know-how and resources to run a campaign. Unite was where the leadership turned, and its staff, cash and political culture flowed into Corbyn's office. 'The Corbyn project outsourced the fight, essentially,' Lewis says, 'Momentum just didn't have the experience and the people and the tools to see off this threat, so we had to turn to one wing of the bureaucracy to defeat the other.'

The professionalization of the Leader's Office and the influence of Unite changed Corbynism. The presence of figures like Karie Murphy and the increased influence of Len McCluskey did not make all of the problems of competence disappear; many court histories of Corbynism are full of stories of internal dysfunction, policy made on the hoof and allegations of bullying. But the backing of Unite did bring a level of stability, institutional experience and ruthlessness to the project, enabling it to win the 2016 leadership election decisively and with a lot of resources and accelerating the turnover of party staff which culminated in Jennie Formby's appointment as general secretary in 2018. It also brought a new level of bureaucratization and conservatism into the heart of the project: not just in terms of the many allegations of control freakery and overzealous secrecy but also in terms of the leadership's increasing unwillingness to see through reforms to party democracy, including the open selection of MPs, and to let members decide party policy at conference. 'It was a trade-off', says Clive Lewis. 'They came in and in effect said "yeah, sure, we'll bail you out – but we're gonna do this our way."'

The summer of 2016 also had a profound impact on the internal life of Momentum. By the time of the leadership challenge, the organization had more than a hundred local groups across the country and regional networks which enabled local activists to coordinate horizontally without constantly having to be overseen by the central office. A formal membership system had been introduced, and at the centre of the organization there was a national committee which could democratically discuss policy and priorities. Momentum was by now perhaps halfway through the process by which it planned to resolve the various debates about its purpose: in May that year, the national committee had voted to call a founding conference, which would establish a proper constitution and a new democratic structure to replace the existing one, which everyone agreed was too layered and complex.

Having a sprawling grassroots that was so diverse and so active inevitably made Momentum a messy, difficult and at times unpleasant place. The organization was haunted at every level by clashes of personality, culture and political priorities, as generations of left-wing activists from all kinds of backgrounds were pushed into the same organizing spaces. As an officer of Momentum, I would often end up adjudicating on these issues from the office: in this group someone had stolen the social media passwords, in that group it was an accusation of racism, in that group the chair wouldn't let the group meet, in that group someone was complaining about data protection. Democracy might have been integral to creating any socialist movement worthy of the name, but it was a PR nightmare and provided the right-wing press with an endless number of stories about the antics of Momentum activists which alarmed both the Leader's Office and the office of Momentum.

When the leadership election of 2016 was called, Momentum transformed itself in a matter of days into the second leadership campaign, flush with Unite money and full of purpose. After almost a year of managing a messy grassroots organisation, the staff and top brass were given a glimpse of a more efficient and streamlined future. Momentum's local groups stopped squabbling, and even the scandals were slicker. Over the course of the summer, two journalists managed to infiltrate the campaign: one was a *Daily Mail* journalist who posed as a volunteer with learning difficulties; and the other was an undercover reporter for Dispatches who got a job on the campaign (as the person responsible for running background checks on staff, no less) and went around the office with a camera hidden in a reusable coffee cup. Momentum's press officer James Schneider, commanding a war room of press officers, led a response which successfully flipped the Dispatches episode into being a good news story about media bias and was soon offered a job in the Leader's Office.

For Jon Lansman, Momentum's chair who became the leadership campaign's director, the conclusions drawn from that summer were blunt and chimed with his experiences over decades of organizing on the Labour left. 'I do like democracy in organisations,' he says, 'but what matters just as much as democracy, if not more, is effectiveness.' The campaign was, in many ways, a major step forward for Momentum: its membership soared and its staff excelled in the heat of the moment. But the organization's internal democracy never recovered. Its elected Steering Committee was not consulted about the decision to second its staff team or hand over its cash and was shut out of any leadership role in the campaign. As Momentum's treasurer, I was moved away from the finances and given a junior job on the press team. Other democratic functions were also shut down: a National Committee meeting scheduled for in July was called off entirely, and no date was named for a next meeting. In its place, a command structure took form: orders were signed off by the Leader's Office, Unite and the campaign leadership; communicated through the campaign to staff; and implemented unquestioningly by a mass of activists.

At the ACC arena in Liverpool in September that year, as the staff of the leadership campaign gathered nervously in the conference hall, it was clear that Corbyn's re-election was not in doubt. Frantic whispers broke out in the crowd about John McDonnell (who, as Corbyn's agent, was the only person on our side who already knew the result) and if and how he was wearing his lanyard: 'it's on, it's on – that means it's better than last time-' 'No that just means we've won-' 'No, it means it's less good'. Then, as the result was read out, the realization: it *was* bigger than last time. We had won with around sixty thousand more votes than in 2015. Both exhausted and unsurprised, the cheer was more staid and less emotional than the previous summer, but the achievement was nonetheless impossible to take away from the victors – either from Corbyn himself, for whom it represented an unquestionable stamp of legitimacy, or from Momentum, for whom it acted as a proof of concept.

But the atmosphere inside Momentum had changed forever, and the divisions within the organization would become sharper and sharper. From the autumn of 2016 until the end of the internal conflict in early 2017, Momentum split in two. On one side was the majority of the elected National Committee, a minority of the Steering Committee (myself, Matt Wrack, Jackie Walker and Jill Mountford[9]) and an overwhelming number of the local groups, whose aim was to get Momentum's rudimentary democratic structures back up and running and to continue down the road of building an organization that was substantially independent of the Labour leadership. On the other side were Jon Lansman, the Leader's Office, a majority of the Steering Committee and, in the final analysis, many of the staff of the organization, who were determined never to go back to the messy, insubordinate situation they had faced before the leadership campaign. In the end, that would mean abolishing Momentum as it then existed: shutting down the democratic processes and setting up a new organization in its place.

The outcome of this split defined the fortunes of the Corbyn project. Had things happened differently, the new Labour left would have been a more untamed and uncontrollable place: at its heart would have been a Momentum led by a network of local activist groups, which would have been not only a source of dissent and negative press for the Labour leadership but also a source of bottom-up energy and the basis for a turn outwards to community and trade union organizing. As it happened, the leadership of the project decided – some of them with a heavy heart, some enthusiastically – to prioritize professionalization and control over internal democracy and the development of an independent grassroots. This was the central mechanism by which Corbynism gained control of the Labour Party but lost its soul in the process.

The new Labour left, or the New Labour left?

If you had to choose one character through which to understand the Labour left, it would have to be Jon Lansman. Momentum's founder and chair throughout the first five years of Corbynism embodies in so many ways the contradictions at the heart of the project. Like Corbyn himself, he reached prominence in the era of Bennism in the 1980s – and was perceived by many centrist opponents as a relic of that era – but he led an organization which found itself on the front line of Britain's first major socialist movement of the twenty-first century. He was the bearded and grey-haired figurehead of an office that had an average age barely in its twenties. He was not familiar at first with the world of digital campaigns and big organizing models but was nonetheless a great believer in them. In private, he was a withering critic of the failings of the Leader's Office – its command and control culture, its lack of action on anti-Semitism, its domination by Unite – but he was, in public, loyal to the leadership and expended every ounce of political capital he had to support it and ensure that Momentum did the same.

Navigating these contradictions takes a special kind of political personality. Lansman is a stubborn, unshakable opponent of ideas that he disagrees with, right up until the point at which he is convinced of them. He is a genuine listener who values pluralism and being challenged, but he was also, as far as I could tell, incapable of chairing a meeting without interspersing proceedings with opinionated monologues from the chair. Most of these monologues would be delivered grumpily, in blunt terms and wearing his trademark collection of colourful floral and Hawaiian shirts. They would, unless the meeting had been simply too rancorous, be followed by conciliatory pints in the Exmouth Arms by Euston station.

In one way, though, Lansman was a more conventional Labour figure: he might have supported protests, but he had never been seriously active in movements beyond the party. He was the most famous veteran of the CLPD, but his attitude to the internal democracy of Momentum had always been ambivalent, and it was the staff, not he, who had by and large insisted on it. These two features of Lansman's makeup – his ambivalence towards internal democracy and his party-focussed background – were the perfect ingredients to ensure that he and I (a social movement activist who regarded internal democracy as non-negotiable) found ourselves on opposite sides within Momentum, and I spent much of autumn of 2016 in the basement rooms of Momentum's Euston headquarters (the strip lights flickering, the procedural wrangling seemingly eternal) on the receiving end of his monologues from the chair.

In the aftermath of the 2016 leadership election, it became clear that making Momentum's democratic structures meet again was going to be an uphill battle. Having been prevented from meeting during the campaign, the National Committee had been postponed to November, when it was supposed to discuss the arrangements for Momentum's founding conference. The only body which met with any regularity was the Steering Committee, on which Lansman had a solid majority – and it was often called at less than a day's notice. As one of the three officers who had responsibility for the day-to-day running of the organization, I would trudge downstairs to these meetings after long days in the office poring over budgets and campaign plans or running investigations into disputes between members. But the crucial decisions about the future of the organization were clearly taking place elsewhere.

Having grown beyond the messy world of local groups and regional networks, which they viewed as unrepresentative of the wider Momentum membership, Momentum's leadership had set their sights on a different future: One Member One Vote (OMOV). The idea was to scrap all of the delegate structures and instead hold online elections for a leadership committee alongside, maybe, some all-member votes on certain issues – replacing a deliberative form of democracy with a plebiscitary one. In this way, the Momentum office and party leadership could retain much more central control: the slate with the tacit endorsement of Corbyn's office would obviously win the online elections, and they could then manage the organization efficiently. Rather than having its own democratically decided policy, Momentum could focus on simply supporting the Labour leadership, mobilizing members for elections within the party and more widely. By renouncing the organization's policy independence, it would also serve as a defence against the accusation that Momentum was a 'party within a party'. 'The point was,' Jon Lansman argues, 'that we should focus on the things we agreed on. The Labour Party already had a democratic process in which we could fight it out when we disagreed.'

It is fair to say that there was substantial support for this model: supporting Corbyn was, after all, the mood of the moment, and OMOV was a democratic system that, at a superficial level, enfranchised every member. Had Lansman and his allies simply proposed the new system to the upcoming founding conference, Momentum might not have descended into a period of farcical infighting. Instead, they used their majority on the Steering Committee to cancel the National Committee and conference entirely, a move which provoked opprobrium across the organization. As the rest of the country was digesting the result of the EU referendum and the realities of Theresa May's new premiership, Momentum talked only about itself. The day after the 2016 US presidential election, the Steering Committee met, but no one mentioned Donald Trump. In community halls, churches and pub back rooms across the country, local activists met to engage in bitter arguments and to issue still bitterer statements. Social media filled with bile, as critics of the Momentum leadership went out to condemn the manoeuvring, and its supporters sought to brand its critics as wreckers and Trotskyist infiltrators. Old wounds came unstuck, and all of the tensions between the different traditions and generations within the new Labour left suddenly took form.

When the controversy reached the mainstream press, John McDonnell intervened, summoning Jon Lansman and FBU general secretary Matt Wrack, as leaders of the two sides, for peace talks in his office. There, and in the Steering Committee meeting that followed, Lansman effectively backed down and gave the green light for the National Committee to finally meet again – but the moment of internal peace was fleeting. When the around seventy delegates gathered in Birmingham's Quaker Meeting House on 3 December, they found themselves in a meeting that resembled a cross between a badly directed pantomime and incompetently handled legal proceedings. With the membership polarized against the leadership, no genuine debate took place between proposals: practically all of the representatives of local groups and regions arrived mandated to vote for a delegate conference, while almost all of the representatives of affiliated organizations were lined up to vote for a purely digital set-up. A compromise proposal motivated by me, which would have split the decision-making evenly between the two systems, received no votes at all. By the end of the meeting, the pro-conference side had narrowly but comprehensively won.

For Lansman, defeat at the National Committee clarified the need for more drastic action. Obeying the democratic process now would mean allowing a founding conference to go ahead, and that could have meant losing control of Momentum just as he had lost control of the National Committee. This could not be permitted to happen. 'I went to the leadership with a solution', explains Lansman. 'And Jeremy was persuaded – he isn't always decisive, but he was persuaded.' At 7.39 pm on Tuesday, 10 January 2017, with the blessing of the Labour leadership, Lansman emailed the Momentum Steering Committee out of the blue with a new constitution for the organization, and at 8.54 pm – after a series of angry and incredulous responses from those of us who did not know it was coming – a majority was declared in favour of it. And so Momentum's democratic structures were abolished in the space of seventy-five minutes by an email vote among a committee of ten people.

The imposition of a new constitution onto Momentum was one of the first moments which divided Jeremy Corbyn and John McDonnell. The move was informed in part by fear of infiltration by far-left groups and the need to erect a defensive barrier against them. This fear was almost certainly misplaced: there were at most two hundred organized far-left activists in Momentum, compared to the many thousands who were members of groups like Militant on the Labour left of the 1980s. McDonnell pushed back: 'I was saying "you shouldn't do this: putting these defensive mechanisms in place will undermine the real purpose of having a broad social movement" [. . .] I lost out on that one,' he says, wryly, 'there were those in the Leader's Office who were keen on a more traditional approach.'

Much of Momentum's staff team and many of its media outriders were supportive of the need to build movements outside of the party but went with Lansman's plan as a means to end the organization's infighting. For Owen Jones, desperation was the crucial factor. 'It just felt like it had been months of internal acrimony and division', he says. 'It's been in existence for a year, and it's not working.'

Adam Klug felt a similar sensation. 'What we were experiencing as staff was a toxicity and a dysfunction that was really troubling', he says, 'and it felt like Momentum was moving away from its founding purpose and like it was all going to fall apart. But you've got to remember that a big factor was also where other people were: Jon [Lansman], the Leader's Office, the Shadow Cabinet and so on were all getting involved, and it felt like it had become untenable.' The impression that you get from everyone within Momentum who was responsible for executing the plan, including Jon Lansman himself, is not one of glory but of what felt to them an uncomfortable necessity. 'A big drive for us was making Momentum an appealing, inclusive and empowering place for people who were new to politics', says Emma Rees. 'The situation at that time was doing the exact opposite.'

Nonetheless, McDonnell's warning proved to be correct. In the years that followed, Momentum would become a slick top-down campaigning vehicle, whose efforts in winning control of Labour's NEC and at the 2017 general election were the crucial factor in making Corbyn's leadership viable – but at a cost. We will, of course, never know if Momentum would have been able to pull off its 2017 campaign without the centralization it underwent, but what is clearer is the longer-term shift. In late 2016, Momentum had more than a hundred local activist groups, which had overwhelmingly opposed the restructure.[10] By the end of the decade, almost all of them had evaporated, cut off from any democratic representation. To the extent that Momentum had grassroots organization at all, it was directed into attempts to take over constituency parties. Its internal democracy was, for the remainder of the Corbyn era, token: annual elections took place, but their result was never in doubt and the promised digital democracy never materialized. Getting rid of Momentum's democratic structures would have long-term ramifications: when the left lost control of the party in the wake of the 2019 general election defeat, it was in large part because it lacked the kind of cohesion and resilience that could only be built up at a grassroots level.

Corbynism was an electoral project of the radical left, whose aim was to enter government, implement a radical programme and, at the very least, leave behind a legacy that would leave the left and the labour movement in a strong position to try again. From all of these perspectives – in terms of expanding the electorate, convincing voters of radical policies, holding the Labour leadership to its principles and promises and creating an atmosphere of hope and rebellion – it was essential that an independent force existed which could push the electoral project from below. The point of Momentum was that it could take the mass movement that lay under Corbynism, build political agency at the lowest possible level and use it to exert pressure on the political system, subverting the logic of electoralism that had seen so many Labour politicians drift to the right as they neared power and forcing 'a new kind of politics' into the mainstream.

But, time and time again, the decisive pressure went the other way – from the top downwards. By and large, the new Labour left's activists focussed not on pushing the leadership, or on building trade union branches, but on cheering on whatever Corbyn was saying from week to week and, from the 2016 leadership challenge onwards, making war on the Labour Right in every available arena. Everyone looked upwards – constantly, expectantly. They became mesmerized by prime minister's questions and votes on the NEC and the ins and outs of drama in the parliamentary Labour Party. Corbynism's greatest heroes and spokespeople were not its most effective organizers and dedicated workplace militants but well-spoken commentators with lots of Twitter followers. Its most influential figures did not – with some notable exceptions – wield their influence by virtue of being talented or being elected but by virtue of personal connections, organizational patronage, loyalty and being in the right networks.

The transformation of Momentum made it much harder for anyone who wanted a different vision for the project to have influence or for ordinary activists to meaningfully change it from below. Clive Lewis had been on Momentum's original reference group and was touted as a potential successor to Corbyn but would now find himself dissenting from the Labour leadership's strategy on Brexit and would be pushed towards the margins of Corbynism. 'We made a pact with a section of the trade union bureaucracy', he says. 'And they basically said "yeah sure, we'll bail you out, but you need to kill this whole new left thing". It was more of a 'quid pro quo' than explicit agreement – at least as far as I knew – but that is the logic of what happened.'

In other words, despite its much more radical policy programme, Corbynism displayed all of the internal management practices of a conventional Labour Party leadership – and rather than the mass movement subverting the logic of the parliamentary process, the parliamentary process became the logic of the mass movement.

There was, then, one last great irony. Lansman, Corbyn and many of the most senior figures on the Labour left had stayed in the party during and after the 1990s and had defined themselves in opposition to New Labour's managerial style. But like the technocrats of New Labour, the leadership of Momentum and the Leaders' Office itself, regarded much of its own activist base with suspicion and sought to reach over their heads to a wider membership, often swapping democratic processes for consultations and hailing this shift as an act of modernization. Like them, it often viewed internal democracy in instrumental terms rather than as a guiding principle and used members primarily as doorknockers. In stoking up fears of a Trotskyist takeover, it even mirrored the rhetoric and narratives of the Labour Right. Corbynism was to a great extent an attempt to reboot Bennism for the twenty-first century, but in practice it just as often resembled a left-wing version of Blairism.

For me personally, the split in Momentum – and in particular the way in which it ended – was a moment of bitter demoralization. I had spent most of the past year poor and stressed to the point of breaking, having barely taken a day off from the beginning of the EU referendum campaign onwards. Most of my energy had been dedicated to Momentum: I had spent most days in its offices and had built friendships with its staff and volunteers who had, apparently, engineered the abolition of my role and of the organization's democracy behind my back. Now, the whole Corbyn project seemed to be closing down, Donald Trump was the US president and the nationalist right was on the march in Britain. I entered a period of black depression, trudging and chain-smoking around the parks of south London, and never set foot in the Momentum office again.

A world transformed, but marginalized

The narrowing down of Momentum posed an increasing problem for anyone who conceived of politics in broader terms than cheering on the Labour leadership and taking over committees. As a result, many of the social movement activists from the first half of the decade migrated to other projects. Soon after being effectively booted out of Momentum, I started working full time for Another Europe is Possible, whose main task in the coming years would be organizing a left-wing movement against Brexit and on migrants' rights, a role that would set me on a collision course with the Labour leadership. I also got involved in organizing the Stop Trump coalition, which was originally initiated by Owen Jones as an immediate reaction to Donald Trump's ban on arrivals from majority-Muslim countries but which would grow into a broad network of NGOs, unions and grassroots campaigns (including Momentum) that would later mobilize demonstrations against his visits to the UK.

Many others found a new political home not in campaigns but in a new political education project: The World Transformed (TWT). For Deborah Hermanns, who had arrived in Corbynism via a heavy dose of direct action and extra-parliamentary politics in the student movement, the story of TWT began in the summer of 2016. 'I got involved by accident', she says. 'I'd decided to leave student politics, and I needed something else to do so I'd started volunteering in the Momentum office. Around the time I started, lots of the people who were working on the project had to leave in order to work on the leadership campaign, and so very quickly I and other new people took on a lot of responsibility.'

The 'project' was Momentum's unofficial fringe at Labour Party conference, but under the stewardship of Hermanns and a number of other activists ('everyone pretty much was from the extra-parliamentary left') it quickly took on the dimensions of a festival in its own right. From the start, TWT was marked by its distance from the old Labour left, the trade union bureaucracies and the fixers who came to dominate the centre of the Corbyn project. 'The leadership campaign meant that the kids were let loose and allowed to run the show – so we had way more freedom to be creative', says Hermanns. 'We were in the same office as the leadership campaign, but we were at this desk in the corner and people didn't pay much attention to us.' Andrew Dolan also arrived in the Momentum offices for the first time. 'As activists, you sometimes need to have a level of autonomy in order to get something done,' he says, 'and that is what TWT immediately gave people who got involved, and it had a big cultural side to it which also drew me in.' In contrast to the leadership campaign and the Leader's Office which were awash with union money, TWT was staffed almost entirely by volunteers like Hermanns and Dolan, who in turn managed an army of volunteers at the event itself, all of whom seemed to work twenty-hour days.

The scale and success of the first festival took both the press and the party itself by surprise. Over the course of four days in September 2016, TWT welcomed thousands of party activists, conference delegates and members of the public to its first festival based at the Black-E building in Liverpool in what was a deliberate attempt to change the nature of Labour conference. 'For years the conference had been a stage-managed spectacle, more about the performance of the leader than about any kind of democratic process,' says Dolan, 'so I viewed

TWT as about trying to transform the atmosphere at what had become a very bureaucratic event.'

The agenda did not consist only of rallies with prominent figures from the Corbyn leadership – though these were popular – but also debates, workshops, organizing meetings, arts and crafts sessions, live music and a number of large late-night parties. In the main space, surrounded by banners from dozens of campaigns which hung above them, were stalls and an open social space in which Momentum activists, journalists, conference delegates and interested Liverpool residents mingled. Many of the sessions were handed over to, or co-managed with, external grassroots campaigns of one sort or another, giving a real sense of the breadth of the movement that lay behind the Corbyn moment – and this was deliberate. 'The idea was to bring together the movement with the parliamentary project in one event', says Deborah Hermanns. 'The media image of Corbynism from the beginning was always about "a new politics" and young people, and TWT was about trying to put that into practice and show what it meant. And the reality of that coming together in a physical space really shocked people I think, including a lot of people who were very sceptical of Momentum and Corbyn.'

When Momentum's leadership imposed a new constitution on the organization in early 2017, many of TWT's organizers looked on in horror, though the organization never took any position on Momentum's internal politics (it was, after all, a pluralistic left-wing events company, not a faction). With Momentum's internal politics increasingly toxic, TWT continued to attract a large number of young, outwardly focussed activists into its organizing collective. By spring 2017, they were helping left-wing Labour activists in Leave voting areas organize events under the heading 'take back control'. Beyond the confines of the Labour conference fringe, the following years would witness a plethora of local events and a network of local Transformed groups run in parallel to the official Momentum structures.

As the years went by, the annual festivals at Labour conference got bigger and evolved to meet the needs of the project. In the absence of any annual democratic conference of the left, TWT was one of the only spaces in which the Labour left could convene to debate controversial issues. There was a therapeutic and morale-building role, too. 'We always had an element of celebrating the movement', says Hermanns. 'Our first festival started with Corbyn getting re-elected, and in later years, as people got more divided and things got more difficult, it was about trying to give people energy and bring them together through collective experiences.' And then there was the role the events played in generating and profiling ideas, in an attempt to develop what Corbynism meant.

'We deliberately chose difficult issues,' Hermanns says, 'like prison abolition or migration or areas where it was important to hold the Shadow Cabinet to account.'

The Corbyn project was a moment in which all parts of the existing left collided, very often without much knowledge of each others' traditions and experiences. There was a desperate lack of spaces in which activists could have discussion and debates, and, in comparison to any other generation of left-wing influx into Labour, the levels of knowledge about history and theory were very low. TWT provided an answer to many of these problems, and as the movement developed and the demand for political education grew, it found itself advocating for its brand of pluralistic political education and acting as a consultancy to other organizations in the movement about how to put on events and programmes. Its local groups and centrally organized festivals offered a kind of informal mediation process between Corbynism's component parts and were, for many Corbyn supporters, the only physical manifestation of the project in which all of these parts were presented as a coherent and comprehensible whole.

But while TWT was undoubtedly a success on many levels, it also demonstrated a lack of direct political agency on the part of the new left that had been formed by the social movements of the first half of the decade. Its core organizers were almost all drawn from the student and anti-austerity movements, and the intellectuals to whom it looked for leadership – people like Hilary Wainwright and Jeremy Gilbert – were conscious partisans of a new left tradition that stretched back decades. The pluralistic organizing practices of TWT were a contrast to the culture official Corbynism and presented an implicit alternative to it, but rather than organizing around a coherent politics, many of the best and brightest veterans of recent social movements confined their efforts to organizing events and creating a space for Corbynism to breathe intellectually. In doing this, the project provided a great service to the movement as a whole and may well have laid the ground for a healthier left in the future, but it served as a retreat from intervening in the immediate battle for the soul of Corbynism.

Projects like TWT could ameliorate around the edges of Corbynism, but they could not substitute for the lack of a truly democratic organization and of a healthy democratic culture on the new Labour left. In the end, the absence of these two things would cause terminal damage to the project – not just to its internal life, but to its ability to take clear positions and win elections.

The machine strikes back

Brexit

Brexit is an issue which divides not just every part of society but every part of the left. Every tradition – mainstream social democrats, democratic socialists, the old Labour left, horizontalists and anarchists, Trotskyists, left liberals, Communists, social movementists – found itself on both sides of the EU referendum in 2016, even if the vast majority did back Remain. In the aftermath of the vote, the acrimony within Labour and the wider left deepened, as a vast number of strategies and policies were proposed and fought over. No one's analysis of the subject is uncontroversial and, as one of the new Labour left's most ardent Remainers, mine least of all.

And yet, whatever one's views on Brexit itself, it is the issue which best demonstrates the problems with Corbynism. At its heart was not just a disagreement about Britain's EU membership, but a lack of internal democracy, a culture of top-down party management and a tendency towards triangulation and short-term electoral calculation. We have seen how, in the aftermath of the financial crisis, a wave of social and industrial struggle created the conditions for a new left. The past two chapters were the story of how that half-formed new left was swept into Labour after 2015 and then defeated and marginalized within it. This chapter is about the consequences of that defeat: in the end, Corbynism was brought down not by its radical intentions but by its conventional, institutional methods.

Many left-wing activists and commentators regard it as a tragedy that the resurgence of the British left happened at the same time as the Brexit moment, as if these two events merely passively coincided. Whatever way one looks at it, Britain's departure from the EU – and, more pressingly, the shift in attitudes and public debate that took place alongside it – was in many ways the thing that killed Corbynism. The results of the 2019 election reflected the fate of a party that had lost comprehensively on both sides of the Brexit divide: an overwhelming number of the seats Labour lost had voted Leave; but, even with a policy supporting a second referendum, it still lost more voters to more pro-Remain parties than to pro-Leave ones, leading to significant Liberal Democrat surge in the popular vote. The nationalist and anti-migrant narratives behind the Brexit vote, and the shifting identities that went alongside them, cut right across the renewed class politics that the Corbyn project represented. For many years before Corbyn came into office, Labour had a problem in the North and the Midlands, where it was bleeding votes among older working class voters – the same voters among whom the Leave vote was highest and among whom Jeremy Corbyn was least popular – and the context of Brexit supercharged and accelerated this process.

However, the fact that Brexit and Corbynism occupied the same moment in time was not a coincidence. They were products of the same conditions and, in a sense, part of the same process. The failure of the neoliberal economic model to deliver material advances for most people and the social and political crisis that followed the financial crash in 2008 shattered the centre-ground of politics and created space for radical alternatives. The collapse of the global financial system also created a period of fragmentation, in which international institutions associated with the neoliberal economic order – including, rightly or wrongly, the European Union – became more fragile. Popular support for the privatization of public services, financial deregulation and liberalization of the labour market had never been that high, but in the period following the crash it collapsed entirely, and, in part because of the explosion of mass movements and social struggle in the first half of the 2010s, austerity also began to lose its electoral appeal. All over Europe and in the United States, new left-wing projects emerged, wielding a resurgent class politics twinged with generational injustice and posing a serious threat to ruling-class interests. In order to sustain a winning electoral coalition behind a continued policy of economic orthodoxy, a section of the ruling elite consciously turned towards a politics of right-wing nationalism, protectionism, anti-migrant scapegoating and racism.

In the United States, Trump was their answer. In the UK, it was Brexit – a project whose aim, in essence, was to deepen the deregulation of the British economy while blaming foreigners and migrants for the consequences of austerity and decades of right-wing economics. Many of the Labour voters who ended up voting Leave (leaving aside Leave's main base, which was home-owning Tory voters) had been subject to a process of de-industrialization, falling wages, atomization and disenchantment and had been drip-fed poison about immigrants by the tabloid press and the political elite for many years.

Brexit took this poison and attempted to put it on the winning side of history by means of a public vote. The idea that it is a passive tragedy that Brexit and Corbynism coincided rests on the premise that the new Labour left had a simple core task which the Brexit moment somehow interrupted. But the reality was that Corbynism and the Tories' Brexit project were born of the same moment of polarization, necessary parts of the same whole that could not both succeed. Far from being a peripheral concern, defeating the rise of right-wing nationalism was always going to need to be a core part of Corbynism's strategy – and that meant defeating Brexit or at the very least the narratives and politics it contained.

If the new Labour left understood the gravity of what was at stake in the EU referendum, this was not apparent to those of us who were trying to campaign in it. Another Europe is Possible was set up by a motley collection of left-wing academics and activists following David Cameron's victory in the 2015 general election.[1] In the face of what we knew would be an establishment-dominated Remain campaign, Another Europe existed in order to present an independent, explicitly left-wing case for staying in the EU, championing freedom of movement and open borders and warning of the dangers of Brexit for workers' rights, environmental protections and other areas of regulation. Having held a launch event in February 2016, we had a great deal of support from a layer of pro-European enthusiasts on the left, as well as fulsome support from the Green Party and a level of interest from some trade unions, most prominently the FBU.

We held a series of big rallies across the country (Owen Jones, Caroline Lucas, Matt Wrack and Clive Lewis all featured heavily) and put on a thousands-strong conference in central London with Yanis Varoufakis and John McDonnell which was the biggest event of the referendum campaign on the Remain side. Looking back, however, it is astonishing how ill-prepared and under-resourced we were and how little the organized Labour left did during the campaign. Another Europe only got the cash together to hire its first staff member – me – in April, just two months before the referendum on 23 June. Momentum, the left's only activist organization, only came out for Remain in late May after local groups pushed a motion through its National Committee. After that, our (by now four-person) staff team moved into the Momentum offices, where a handful of staff and volunteers did eventually throw their energies into the campaign.

Organizationally, however, the referendum was barely considered a priority at all in Momentum, and without much of a central lead, many of its local groups remained dormant. It was only in the final week or two of the campaign that we began to get a flurry of activity, with hundreds of thousands of leaflets landing in addresses all across the country.

As panic set in among all parts of the Remain coalition, the ideas got increasingly desperate and elaborate. In early June I found myself recruiting volunteers from Momentum networks to take part in a counter-flotilla against Nigel Farage's fishing fleet parade, an excruciatingly bad stunt which culminated in an irate Bob Geldof screaming abuse at working class fishermen on the Thames outside parliament. Hovering above the fray, I and a team of a volunteers dropped a gigantic banner off Westminster Bridge (it read 'Don't let Farage Sink Britain') while periodically scuffling with retired couples from English market towns who had come down to cheer on Farage and were determined to prevent us from displaying it.

In the final week of the campaign, Momentum was approached by a senior government official who had a number of wild attention-grabbing stunts that they thought we might be interested in pulling off. The most fanciful suggestion was hiring a lorry-load of animal dung, ditching it in the road outside Boris Johnson's Islington home and then press releasing the incident under the title 'you're full of shit'; the establishment press would, apparently, give us rave reviews.

Like most of its positions, Momentum's relative apathy during the EU referendum was handed down to it by the Labour leadership. During the second leadership campaign, I and other pro-Corbyn Remainers spent a lot of energy talking about how Corbyn had thrown everything into the referendum campaign, and perhaps I even convinced myself of this. With hindsight, it wasn't true: although senior Labour figures did speak at various rallies, the leadership took relatively little interest in owning and shaping a radical case against Brexit, and Labour's own Remain campaign was left in the hands of former New Labour minister Alan Johnson, who oversaw a centrist-sounding campaign focussed on abstract economic arguments. 'It was fucking amateur', says Laura Parker, who was Corbyn's private secretary at the time of the referendum. 'I went into the office on the morning of the result wearing my "Lambeth In" t-shirt, having – obviously – not slept, but it didn't feel to me like there was much understanding of what was at stake in the core team, or any of that determination or energy or connection to what our people must have been feeling on the ground.' The fact that Corbyn went onto live national television that morning to call for the immediate triggering of Article 50 was greeted by many Remainers with dismay, but it was as much as anything a product of a lack of preparation or agreed lines.

The result of the referendum presented Labour with a serious problem. While two-thirds of the seats it represented had voted Leave, two-thirds of its voters had voted Remain. The demographic base of support for Remain – which was young, urban and educated – was the same as that of the Corbyn surge itself, and much of this base saw Brexit as a defining issue of deep principle, bound up as it was with questions of transnational identity, migrants' rights and the wider culture war.

By and large, the Corbyn leadership viewed Brexit as an inconvenience which needed to be navigated around, and when the 2017 general election was called, its strategy was based on cold polling figures. Theresa May wanted to make the election about Brexit because it was the issue on which the Tories resoundingly beat Labour, but if the subject could be changed to the NHS, housing and public services, the project might just stand a chance. And so, as part of the 'change the subject' strategy, a policy of constructive ambiguity was adopted, in which Labour essentially gave no details on its proposed Brexit settlement. I and other Remainers on the left were sceptical of this strategy, and we were wrong. Along with a huge grassroots campaign led by Momentum and a fair bit of quiet tactical voting by centrist Remainers, it worked: the Corbyn project survived and was emboldened by the biggest increase in Labour's popular vote since 1945.

The high of the 2017 general election result was, on so many levels, an intoxication from which Corbynism never sobered up: in the eyes of the leadership and many of its supporters, it vindicated everything that had happened, most prominently the process of centralization that had occurred in Momentum and the party machine and the policy of not having a policy on Brexit.

In the long run, however, constructive ambiguity was a disaster. The success of Corbynism, and the reason why so many new people had flocked to join Labour to support it, was built on an authentic sense of principled, progressive politics. Where establishment Labour leaders had triangulated rightwards for electoral gain, Corbyn had spent decades standing up for what he thought was right and fighting to convince those around him of it. The turning point of the 2015 leadership election had been when Corbyn was the only candidate to break the whip when Harriet Harman instructed Labour MPs to abstain on the Welfare Bill. And yet on Brexit, the main issue of the day, the Corbyn leadership behaved exactly like an establishment Labour leadership would have done. In 2017, despite Corbyn's own views on immigration, Labour ditched support for freedom of movement and endorsed the use of 'no recourse to public funds' measures against migrants. When Ed Miliband's Labour Party produced mugs emblazoned with the slogan 'tough controls on immigration', many on the left roundly denounced it, but, in the sense that it abandoned freedom of movement, the 2017 manifesto was to the right of Miliband on immigration.

By the time the 2019 election was called, Labour had already lost. The country was already polarized beyond the point of no return, and many Leavers were simply never going to vote for Labour, a party that could never deliver the kind of hard Brexit they desired. With hindsight, we all made a mistake by focussing solely on Labour's formal policy position, rather than on the real task of combatting the political content of the Brexit project, its narratives and ideas. To have stood a chance, Labour would have had to have picked a position early on – either a Single Market position or a second referendum one could probably have won – and go out to win an argument in the country, putting forward a new class politics as the explicit and counterposed alternative to right-wing nationalism and border-building.

Instead, it shifted from policy to policy in the hope that it might draw voters towards it, meaning that from a distance, all that most members of the public could see was a series of handbrake turns. In 2017, it triangulated a position which committed it to delivering Brexit but softening the deal in an as yet largely undefined way. In February 2018, it announced that it would support a customs union with the EU, though it did not commit to retaining free movement or remaining inside the EU's wider regulatory framework. In September 2018, it shifted to supporting a labyrinthine policy in which 'all options were on the table'. And, after the disaster of the European elections in which it lost most of its seats because of a Lib Dem and Green surge, it finally committed to supporting a confirmatory referendum on the Brexit deal with an option to Remain – but only after it had spent the previous three years publicly campaigning against this very policy.

There are many explanations for why the Labour leadership failed first to campaign as vigorously as it could have done in the referendum and then to take a clear position on Brexit. While Corbyn was leader, his opponents in the press and the parliamentary party had a vested interest in holding up his own record of Euroscepticism as the main culprit, but this is if anything the least convincing of the available explanations. Corbyn's history of voting against the Lisbon Treaty and his various statements criticizing the EU are entirely consistent with a left-wing Remain perspective, even if his was a very passive one, and in any case Corbyn never really held the pen on Labour's Brexit policy. Much more influential, and much more easily identifiable, were the views of Corbyn's inner circle. Len McCluskey campaigned for Remain in the referendum, but it was widely known that his private views were more pro-Leave than he let on. Meanwhile, Andrew Murray and Seamas Milne, two of Corbyn's closest advisors, had always been perfectly honest about their views on Brexit. In 2012, they had even co-authored a book entitled *Building an Economy for the People* which argued for 'full withdrawal from the EU and a reorientation of the UK's priorities globally [to] enable Britain to take an independent approach to political and economic issues confronting the nation'.[2]

In the end, however, Labour's failures on Brexit policy were not caused by high-level wrangling in the court of Corbyn but by a much deeper and perennial set of problems within the project: a lack of proper internal democracy and an orthodox party management strategy in which trade union bureaucracies were encouraged to outmanoeuvre and overpower the wishes of members.

If the Labour leadership had wanted to pursue a strategy of clarity and campaigning on Brexit, all it had to do was let members decide its policy democratically. By the summer of 2017, when the party could have pivoted towards a more concrete version of soft Brexit in the aftermath of the general election, more than 80 per cent of Labour members wanted the UK to stay in the EU Single Market.[3] By September 2018, when it was probably not too late to adopt a second referendum position and campaign properly on it, support for such a position among the party membership was again at more than 80 per cent.[4] But instead of allowing these views to translate into party policy, the leadership consciously sought to prevent members from deciding, or even debating, the matter.

It is a common misconception that Labour's Brexit debate was a battle between fundamentalist Remainers and a compromising leadership. In fact, between the EU referendum and early 2018, Another Europe is Possible was primarily a campaign for soft Brexit and freedom of movement, and Open Britain, the legal successor to the official Remain campaign Britain Stronger In Europe, was a campaign for Single Market membership. Best for Britain was set up as the explicitly anti-Brexit alternative to Open Britain, but only just before the 2017 general election and only in April 2018 did Open Britain change its name to People's Vote and start fighting for a second referendum. Events at party conference in September 2017 reflected this reality. Following Labour's abandonment of freedom of movement in the 2017 general election, Another Europe and a number of allies had set up the Labour Campaign for Free Movement, which quickly gained the support of many thousands of members and organized the submission of a motion to the conference, which would have pledged the party to defending and extending free movement rights. It would also have introduced a wider set of progressive immigration policies such as the closure of all detention centres and the end of 'no recourse to public funds' policies. At the same time, a more centrist coalition, acting with the support of much of the parliamentary party, had set up the Labour Campaign for the Single Market, which also got its motion submitted, which would have committed Labour to campaign to stay inside the EU Single Market – an outcome that would have seen Britain leave the EU but keep all of the rights and protections that progressives held dear.

Taken together, or even on their own, these two motions presented Labour with an opportunity to take a clear enough Brexit position to take a campaign to the country that hit back against the Tories' key Brexit messages. And yet, high on the success of constructive ambiguity at the general election, the leadership decided that it would manoeuvre to keep the motions off the agenda. On the direct instruction of the Leaders' Office, Momentum – whose democratic structures were not consulted and were in any case now free of the kind of dissident voices which might object to such a plan – asked delegates to vote to prioritize other areas of policy to block discussion of Brexit and immigration. The Labour Campaign for Free Movement mounted a rearguard action by printing a special leaflet overnight and running up and down the Brighton seafront speaking to hundreds of delegates, but the loyalist urges of most delegates was too strong, and the motions were simply never heard.

By party conference 2018, the debate both inside Labour and more widely had moved on, and as the country polarized it became clear that the moment in which a soft Brexit was electorally viable had passed. A mass movement had formed to call for a second referendum, which had local groups under a variety of different banners in most towns and cities and would go on to mobilize the biggest protests since the Iraq War. The leadership of this new movement was dominated by the People's Vote campaign and centrist Labour figures, but at its rallies and protests were many left wingers and Corbyn supporters. Meanwhile, we had learned our lesson from the procedural fix of the previous year. Determined to get the issue on the agenda and demonstrate the level of grassroots support, Another Europe is Possible led a campaign which saw well over a hundred constituency Labour Parties submit text calling for a second referendum, breaking the record for the number of motions submitted on a single policy. This made the moral and political case for Brexit being on the agenda overwhelming, and we arrived in Liverpool confident that we would be able to achieve a decisive shift in the party's position away from the existing fudge.

But the tide of support we had mobilized did not prevent us from being pushed aside in a backroom. In order to make it to a vote at Labour Party conference, motions must first make it through a process called compositing, in which, to cut a long story short, representatives of each CLP or union which has submitted a motion on a given topic go into a room on an evening at conference for a gigantic argument. The entire process is designed to wear down ordinary delegates and, because it is aimed at producing a single motion text out of many contradictory motions, producing a fudge which can be waived through conference with neither opposition nor any real meaning. Compositing meetings are presided over by a member of the Shadow Cabinet (in this case, Shadow Brexit Secretary Keir Starmer), the chair of the meeting cannot be challenged from the floor and votes are taken by acclamation – that is, by shouting. The meetings can last for hours (in this case, six hours) with only a couple of breaks. Crouched outside the room with a laptop and a WhatsApp broadcast channel, I had access to the West Midlands Labour finger buffet, but the delegates inside had no such luck.

Knowing how difficult it would be to get a clear policy out of the process, Another Europe and a handful of allied organizations had run a big operation to intensively brief all of the more than a hundred delegates who were going into the room, and I had spent a number of hours in hotel rooms and lobbies with representatives of the trade unions who would be in the compositing meeting – the TSSA and the GMB – hammering out a motion that would commit Labour to supporting a referendum if it could not force a general election. Then, at the last minute, disaster struck. Unison, whose voting power on conference floor was essential to seeing through the strategy, pulled out because of some last-minute horse-trading, and, as they filed past me in the crowd of delegates on their way into the compositing meeting, the GMB informed me that they were following suit: 'sorry Michael, it's off.' As a result, the operation in the room had to be reassembled from first principles, and no matter how hard our delegates pushed, they would be unable to secure the crucial shift in policy. Receiving a steady stream of despairing reports from delegates in the meeting, I posted an angry tweet condemning the whole thing as a grubby stitch up by the party machine but then immediately deleted it and went back to staring at my phone and preparing to spin the result as a success. As I spoke to BBC Radio in the corridor outside, I was in my own way the perfect picture of the kind of zombie that is created by the Labour Party: I'd been outmanoeuvred by bureaucrats I couldn't even see, I'd had about eight hours' sleep in four days and I was now committed to talking up a dire, meaningless Brexit policy as some kind of great step forward.

We had done everything – mobilized an unprecedented number of motions, dominated the airwaves, run an intensive operation before and during the conference and negotiated so as to ensure we had a winning coalition when it came to the vote – but we still found ourselves ground down into supporting a weak compromise by the party's bureaucratic processes and the manoeuvring of major unions. We could, technically speaking, still have forced a split in the motions and put our own clear proposal to conference floor. Looking back, my failure to argue for this course of action – on the grounds that we would almost certainly have been defeated by trade union bloc votes, which accounted for 50 per cent of votes at conference and were almost all lined up behind the leadership – was probably the greatest political mistake I have ever made. Either our victory or our defeat would have been a better outcome for Labour than the mealy mouthed fudge that was eventually voted on. In the end, Labour was committed to a position of campaigning for a general election and, when that inevitably didn't happen, keeping its options open while reaffirming some warm words about international solidarity which we were forced to spin as a victory.

Following the 2018 conference, there were many more twists and turns and many more moments which seemed to symbolize what had happened to the left as it collided with the realities of running the Labour Party. At party conference the following year, Another Europe is Possible, whose activists were determined to allow no more fudge to happen, finally ended up going head-to-head with the leadership in an attempt to push Labour to adopt an explicitly pro-Remain position in any future referendum. In a tense meeting in the Leader's Office enclave on the first floor of the Hilton on Brighton's seafront, I found myself hammering out a last-minute deal with three senior members of Corbyn's team. The pro-Remain delegation to the meeting consisted of me and Simon Hannah – the same Simon Hannah who had marched next to me in hi-viz as the student protest neared parliament on the day of the parliamentary vote on tuition fees in 2010 – and the solution that came out of the meeting (which was to have a pro-Remain position for Labour but a neutral position for the Labour government) was unceremoniously overruled by someone higher up the food chain. We were defeated on the conference floor the following day after the Leader's Office went all in and turned the vote into a test of loyalty; the loudest cheers of the debate were reserved for speakers bellowing 'back your leader'.

But there is little point in elaborating in any great detail about these developments. The truth is that by the time of the 2019 conference, it was already too late to change the course of history in time for the December general election. The crucial fact to understand is that in order to survive, the new

Labour left had to defeat the Tories' Brexit agenda, and in order to do this it had to take a clear enough position early enough that it could mount a campaign to address the political content of the Brexit project, pushing back right-wing nationalist narratives in the minds of voters. Lots of things prevented this from taking place, and there were personal and political failings at a high level on both sides of Labour's Brexit divide, but the fundamental cause was the dominance of a politics of bureaucracy and triangulation that was essentially no different to what had existed in Labour before Corbyn. Despite Corbynism's promise to democratize the party and open up politics, its policy on the most important issue of the day, and the issue that cost it its existence, was decided exclusively and at all times by professionals in suits behind closed doors. The 'new kind of politics' and the machine politics of the labour movement establishment did not just exist in tension with each other: in the end, one quite clearly defeated the other, at least at the top of the project. And this fact was an electoral, as well as a democratic, disaster.

The party untransformed

One of the most basic demands of the Labour left, long before the Corbyn moment, was for the party to democratically decide its policy at conference. The fact that Labour's Brexit debate played out as it did demonstrated the fact that the democracy of party conference had remained largely unchanged from the model introduced by Blair in the 1990s. By 2019, a greater amount of time was given over to hearing motions than in the Miliband years, but the heavily managed process of compositing was the same and the conference itself was not sovereign – Labour's actual policies were still set by the leadership and the Shadow Cabinet.

Even more important was mandatory reselection: the right of party members to democratically decide the party's parliamentary candidates, including in seats which already have a sitting Labour MP. This practice was and is the norm in almost every centre-left party in Europe but has historically been energetically resisted by the parliamentary Labour Party (for whom it is a personal threat), the Labour Right (for whom it undermines the core belief in Labour as a professional parliamentary party independent of the wider movement) and most but not all trade union bureaucracies (for whom it is a threat to the system of patronage and back-room deals which constitute their power). From the start, the official position of the Corbyn leadership was not clear, as it balanced its in-principle commitment to party democracy with its aims of managing the party and appeasing the PLP. Prominent figures within the project, such as Owen Jones and Jon Lansman, were scolded when they independently put forward arguments for mandatory reselection during the 2015 leadership campaign.

But as radically minded members joined Labour to find their representatives in parliament stuck in the previous decade, the demand for change grew stronger and stronger. At party conference in 2018, Momentum found itself at the head of a campaign for mandatory reselection – which it had rebranded as Open Selections – and many constituency delegates arrived believing that the policy would pass. But then, remembers Jon Lansman, the major unions dug in against it. 'The "big 5" agreed at their meeting before conference that they would oppose it,' he says, 'and at that point Jeremy kind of caved in.' Using the power of the NEC, the unions put forward a different rule change, which merely altered the requirements for removing a sitting MP and organized the votes at conference in such a way that, if the NEC's position passed, Momentum's proposal for Open Selections would automatically fall without being voted on.

The Leader's Office directly intervened with Momentum's leadership in a private meeting on the eve of the vote in an attempt to get them to withdraw Open Selections entirely. 'To their eternal credit,' recalls Momentum's then-national coordinator Laura Parker, 'they stood their ground and absolutely refused to withdraw. But of course with the unions all on one side the balance of votes was just overwhelmingly against us.' Momentum did, however, recommend support for the NEC's proposal (much to the consternation of its own delegates) on the basis that if it fell, there might be no advance on the status quo. On conference floor the following day, FBU general secretary Matt Wrack found himself giving a rallying cry against the position of both his trade union colleagues and the Labour leadership he fought so hard to support:

> Jeremy Corbyn is not a Labour MP because he's called Jeremy Corbyn, or because he's fantastic, or because he makes jam. He's the local Labour MP because local Labour Party members selected him as the best candidate to stand for Labour in that constituency, and that should be normal practice after every election.[5]

He was cheered on, but the NEC's proposal passed, and the chance to introduce mandatory selections was gone – maybe, once again, for decades. For John McDonnell, the failure of party reform was bitterly disappointing on a personal level. His involvement in pushing for democratically selected MPs dates all the way back to the 1970s, when he was a student at Brunel University and moved the deselection of his local MP Neville Sanderson (Sanderson was reimposed on the constituency by Michael Foot, only to end up defecting to the SDP). He pushed hard within the Corbyn leadership for Open Selections but failed. 'There were too many people in key positions who were wedded to the old traditions and weren't willing to take the risk', he says. 'It was easier to try to control than it was to open it up. That's always the case – you don't have to read Trotsky on bureaucracy to understand that, you can just read Max Weber – it's what happens.'

As results of the vote became clear on conference floor in 2018, the hall erupted in booing and shouts of 'shame' from irate constituency delegates. Special ire was aimed at Unite, which as a union had a democratically agreed policy in favour of mandatory selection but in practice had played a crucial role in the stitch up that saw it defeated. On a panel at TWT later that day, Jon Lansman was heckled by attendees and in response was frank about the reality that 'the trade unions blocked it. One trade union in particular, which has a policy in favour of mandatory reselection. Unite, basically.'[6] This kind of public debate between Momentum and the leadership was not the kind of situation that Lansman felt comfortable in. 'Of course I had arguments with the leadership', he says now, 'but I was never going to turn against Jeremy publicly. So my arguments were private, but I had an awful lot of them with him or his senior staff.'

The battle over Open Selections came at the end of a period of extended tension between Momentum and the Unite-run Labour machine. Even after Momentum had abolished much of its internal democracy, it was still not quite imbued enough with the ethos of machine politics to be fully trusted. 'You've got to remember that it wasn't just a bunker,' says Laura Parker, 'it was a bunker within a bunker, and inside that another one, and Momentum wasn't in the inner ones.' When Parker first told her boss in the Leader's Office that she was moving on to head up Momentum's staff team at the end of 2017, she was flatly told that she was making a terrible decision, politically and personally.

In the months running up to the 2018 conference, both Lansman and Parker had got into hot water when they challenged the coronation of Labour's general secretary following the belated resignation of centrist fixer Iain McNicol. Unite's chosen candidate was its very own Jennie Formby, and they were not willing to engage in much of a discussion about it. 'I could see that they were just imposing their will on everyone', says Lansman. 'There was no debate about strategy, about renewal, no debate about the need to reform the party and why, and so I put myself forward to open it up.' His hope was that by standing himself for the position more candidates might come forward, and that it might be possible to argue that the position should be the subject of a proper election at conference rather than just an NEC appointment.

The personal conduct of the dispute that followed gives a flavour of the way in which the new party machine – which was supposedly operating on behalf of a mass movement built on 'a new kind of politics' – responded to having its authority challenged. Throughout the episode, figures in Momentum would be regularly summoned for bollockings in party headquarters and received what can only be described as menacing texts from senior Unite officials. On one occasion, Laura Parker happened to be in party headquarters for two meetings which were a few hours apart, and in between the two scheduled slots she bumped into a number of staff and politicians with whom she had coffees. She thought nothing more of it but the next day, she says, 'I get a text from a well-placed MP saying "you do know you're being watched don't you" and listing all of the people I'd met in order. It was like being followed around by the KGB.' In the end, Lansman withdrew under heavy pressure from the Labour leadership, and Formby was duly waved into the position by the NEC. The lack of democratic transformation in Corbyn's Labour left him exasperated: 'The reason why we needed to prioritise democratic reform in the party was because, with the parliamentary party always attacking us, we probably weren't going to form a government. The odds were *always* against it. Didn't we realise that? So what was our plan? What was our legacy?'

With us or against us

The point of recounting incidents of control freakery and bullying within the Corbyn project is not to demonstrate insider knowledge or to showcase what is by now stale intrigue but to argue back against the lazy narrative that is prevalent among so many commentators: that the radical left, because of its uncompromising politics, is predisposed to such behaviour, and that the moment it gets a whiff of power, a culture of bullying and aggression will rear its head. On the contrary, the unpleasant culture that prevailed in many parts of the Corbyn project was nothing on the personal conduct of many Blairites and enforcers during the New Labour years.

For many of its activists, myself included, Corbynism became an unpleasant place to be: by 2019, I had stopped attending my local Labour left group because the atmosphere had become so toxic, and my outspoken dissident position on Brexit made me a figure of genuine hate among many fellow

Corbynites. Things became this way not because of Corbynism's break with Labour's establishment but because of its proximity to and domination by it. There was, to be sure, unpleasant behaviour on all sides of pretty much every dispute over policy and party reform. But certainly in my experience, the worst behaviour came almost universally not from the party's radicals and movement builders but from its conservatives and bureaucrats – on both right and left. The modus operandi of Labourism – of fiefdoms, loyalism, top-down decision-making, position filling, an intolerance for dissent, an obsession with rules, the subordination of everything to immediate task of defeating one's internal opponents and winning elections – gave the new Labour left an unhealthy internal culture that got worse with time. The more that Corbynism resembled a conventional Labour Party project, the more unpleasant and dysfunctional it became.

For everyone who supported it, the Corbyn leadership represented an unprecedented opportunity to reshape British politics and renew the left. The fact that the project was born not as the result of a long march through the institutions or a concertedly connected struggle outside, but of a sudden miracle in summer of 2015, underlined to us all just how fragile this opportunity was. A sense of collective peril was constantly reinforced throughout the Corbyn years by a campaign of demonization in the media and sabotage by the left's internal opponents. This constant pressure, combined with the pre-existing urges of some of Corbynism's key lieutenants, had an impact on an organizational level: it accelerated the professionalization and centralization of the project, entrenching the power of Unite in the Leaders' Office and precipitating the transformation of Momentum from messy democratic movement to disciplined praetorian guard.

The praetorianism that took hold had, above all, a cultural impact. In the new Labour left, there was very often no higher argument than the opinion of the Labour leadership, nothing more important than 'what Jeremy wanted'. On every issue of the day, grassroots activists, and an army of party hacks and commentators, would dedicate substantial energy to deciphering what it was that Jeremy wanted and then defending it. This was true of issues on which the party leader at least had a clear position, but it was also true of Brexit, an issue on which the man himself was non-committal and on which the position of the broader leadership would change from week to week. Doing debates on Brexit at Labour Party and Momentum branches – and indeed watching the output of the project's media outriders – I would regularly come across people arguing in favour of a second referendum who, a few months previously, had castigated the idea as an affront to democracy that was wrong on principle –

or, even more surreally, defending 'Jeremy's position' on Brexit, without ever defining what it was.

This loyalism had a double existence, for while it may have stemmed from a deep sense of personal affinity for Jeremy Corbyn, it functioned in practice as an allegiance to the layer of bureaucracy around him. For the loyalists, and for leaders of organizations like Momentum, it was rarely, if ever, permissible to dissent once the leadership had made up its mind, even if it was public knowledge that Jeremy Corbyn himself was not the person deciding the policy in question. Corbyn's long record of standing up for migrants and supporting freedom of movement was well known, but after the Labour Campaign for Free Movement was launched in the summer of 2017, it regularly faced the charge of 'undermining Jeremy', and with the exception of Clive Lewis, no prominent Corbynite MPs signed up to support it as it launched.

Corbyn had also been a loud and proud advocate of mandatory reselection for a number of decades, but when the major unions blocked Open Selections at party conference in 2018, you could have been forgiven for thinking he opposed it. When Len McCluskey took to the pages of the *Morning Star* to defend Unite's position in the face of a substantial backlash, it is striking that he did so not by arguing the actual reasons for which the unions had driven through their agenda but by invoking the idea that the union was merely acting on behalf of Labour leadership. It was, he said, 'simply false' to say that the union had voted against its own policy. 'Unite has indeed got a policy in support of mandatory reselection', he wrote. 'But we have another policy [. . .] we support Jeremy Corbyn.' And not only was it disloyal to Jeremy to criticize Unite's opposition to mandatory reselection at conference, it was – conveniently – also an act of disloyalty even to criticize the methods which they employed to do so: to use 'ultra-leftist terminology like "machine politics" and "bureaucratic machine" risks undermining the wishes of Jeremy Corbyn and the unity he has created', McCluskey concluded.[7]

Corbynism's internal culture was such that, by and large, it was not possible to have an honest disagreement with the party leadership: as far as many were concerned, you could either defend Jeremy or betray him. Nowhere was this culture clearer than on the issue of Brexit. 'Some people have an understanding that in the left and the labour movement you need iron discipline, and that needs to be policed', explains Owen Jones. 'So with Brexit, the sense is that the People's Vote campaign is this millionaire bankrolled hostile threat to Corbynism which, if it's successful, will prevent the left from ever coming to power – and so whether people are acting in good faith or bad faith in campaigning for a second referendum, all of them are the same existential threat. And that's how some people saw it – they saw Another Europe is Possible as left cover for a right wing assault on the Corbyn project. And the tradition of iron discipline that had seen Corbynism through multiple assaults on its leadership – that kicked in.'

Opposing a second referendum, or arguing that Labour should not support one for electoral reasons, was of course an entirely legitimate position to hold. The problem was that the internal culture of Corbynism meant that anyone on the left who dissented from the leadership on Brexit was liable to be treated not as a comrade to be debated but as a heretic to be shunned and as a collaborator with the project's enemies. This culture was often encouraged and initiated at the very top, using networks of online influencers and left-wing websites such as Skwawkbox, which effectively functioned as a notice board for some members of Corbyn's top team. 'It's an ugly way of doing politics', reflects Owen Jones. 'A lot of the so-called digital outriders who were in a WhatsApp group with some senior figures from the Leader's Office were encouraged to target people not just on the right but within the Corbyn project, including even people like John McDonnell.' As Jones points out, this way of doing things has a self-fulfilling, and self-destructive, effect: 'The thing about that form of conspiratorial, with-us-or-against-us politics is that will never attract any more than a hardcore of people, who tend to be quite unpleasant people.'

A young movement without a youth movement

It is one of the misnomers in the popular understanding of the new Labour left that there is a clear and easy generational divide in the political culture of Corbynism, and that its younger activists were uniformly more open in their outlook. To a great extent, this misunderstanding stems from the fact that, for political journalists who look at the project from the outside, there is an overwhelming temptation to replace political analysis with crude aesthetic judgements. Seeing fresh-faced volunteers from afar, or relying on interviews with a selection of bright young people hand-picked by press officers, one might draw the conclusion that loyalism and machine politics were things that old people did. But smoking roll-up cigarettes, attending music festivals and organizing innovative social events did not, on their own, make someone more inclined to a culture of healthy pluralism or give them a perspective more inclined to build social movements.

On the contrary, some of the youngest recruits to the new Labour left were prone to developing an outlook which was entirely focussed on party politics, canvassing and defending the leadership – not because this was automatically their way of doing politics but because Corbynism was the first political project in which they had been involved and, because of the lack of democratic spaces within Corbynism and the lack of social movements going on outside it, they knew no alternative. In this sense, there was a noticeable difference between the activists who had experience of the 2010 student movement or the years after it – especially those who had been involved in less hierarchical organizations like UK Uncut or the student left or new media projects like Novara Media – and those who had come to Corbynism with no prior experience.

The youth politics of the Corbyn project was one of its most dramatic battlegrounds, and to understand what was at stake we must take a brief look back at Momentum's development. The whole reason I had got involved in Momentum at a national level was that I wanted it to build a democratic, independent youth wing for the new Labour left. The aim was to do so by holding a founding conference, open to all young and student Momentum members, which could elect a committee and start to run campaigns on its own terms. This proposal passed at Momentum's very first National Committee meeting in February 2016 but was energetically resisted by both the Momentum leadership and the existing group of young activists – most of them drawn from a very small pool of those already involved in organizations like CLPD before the Corbyn surge – who had been centrally hand-picked to head up Momentum's youth operation. As far as they were concerned, the task was to assemble a slate for Labour's official youth elections (a slate which, needless to say, they would be in charge of choosing) and any sense of Momentum having its own youth wing was superfluous. After navigating my proposal through the various bureaucratic obstacles placed in its way, we set a date for Sunday, 5 June 2016, and booked the University of Manchester Students' Union for the founding conference of Momentum Youth and Students (MYS).

What happened on the day, and what became of MYS, was a blunt illustration of wider problems. After finally managing to get a couple of national emails out, we managed to get about 300 people along for a conference with motions, elections, themed workshops and an opening plenary starring local MP Rebecca Long Bailey. But making democratic events happen in Momentum was never that easy, and instead of running the conference, I spent most of the day locked in tense negotiations with Momentum chair Jon Lansman and Steering Committee member Sam Wheeler. As the opening plenary began, I was summoned to a side room in the student union office where, the discussion mediated by one of Momentum's staff members, I was presented with an ultimatum. If the

conference went ahead as planned, I was told, the Steering Committee would
not recognize MYS. And over the course of three protracted meetings, I also
reached a second conclusion. Manchester was home to many open-minded and
action-focussed activists, but it was also home to a faction of young activists
who had been strongly hostile to the existence of MYS. This faction had quite a
number of people at the conference, and while they might not have had the votes
to stop us from holding elections and forming a new organization, they certainly
had the numbers to disrupt proceedings so comprehensively that we couldn't do
it. In the end, we agreed a deal in which elections would take place (in which I
agreed not to stand) and a constitution agreed, but both would be understood to
be provisional and to be repeated in six months' time.

In any case, they needn't have worried: the committee elected by the
conference did their job for them. Hattie Craig had been present at Millbank
during the 2010 student protests while a sixth former had come up through
student activism in Birmingham and was now an activist with TWT. She was
elected to the MYS committee but found herself in a minority. 'I had high hopes
for it initially', she says. 'I thought it could do lots of education and student
campaigning, and also push Labour on policy. But it quickly became clear that
there were two camps on the committee, and that the other side would basically
rather shut MYS down than become anything that might be remotely critical of
the Labour leadership. One of the things that I took from the student movement
was the importance of democracy in organising, and that was a big difference.
The people who came out of the old Labour left or trade unions or via more
traditional routes just weren't that bothered about it.' Under the stewardship of
its new committee, MYS did nothing, and Momentum never held another youth
conference. MYS's only contribution to future developments came in January
2018, when its output on social media became so much of a liability – so full
of vitriol and paranoid sectarian gossip – that Jon Lansman was obliged to
intervene and formally disband it. 'Momentum shuts down youth wing because
of online trolling', read the *Sun's* headline.[8]

The experience of what happened to youth politics during the Corbyn years
demonstrates the limits of distinct generational approaches to politics within
the left. 'Corbynism was always the networked generation plus the defeated
babyboomer generation', explains Paul Mason. 'The politics of many people of
the boomer generation has an unbroken adherence to hierarchy, and not just to
formal hierarchy, but to fixing and rigging things on the orders of others. What
they have ingrained in their DNA is that you set up these quasi-democratic
structures, and then in the background you have these cabal-like meetings

where you decide what's really going to happen. A majority of the networked generation are very turned off by that kind of politics, but, and this is the tragedy, it turns out that a significant number of them were never really that opposed to hierarchy at all – and as soon as somebody wanted to offer them a job, or some status, or some kudos in the movement, they were very happy to accept all the Stalinist manipulative methods.'

The horizontalist movements, the direct action, the years spent building power built from below: all were liable to be eaten up by the juggernaut of the institutional left, its patronage and its promises of power. And, like so many of the problems facing the left today, the core of the problem comes back to this generation's unique lack of history and, owing to the weakness of the organized left, its lack of connection to the traditions that might give it the tools to critique the political practices in which it became ensnared. 'I don't think it's just venality', says Mason. 'It's a problem of the politics of modern leftism: because if it isn't rigorously anti-hierarchical, like autonomism and anarchism are, for instance, then what is it? I think the default political of many younger activists are inspired by post-structuralist Marxism. It tells them that history is, as Althusser said, "a process without a subject" – where human agency doesn't really matter. It can be very anti-humanist, and has no real democratic sentiment, no understanding that the spontaneity of the masses is the thing from which everything else comes.'

The new Fabians

Corbynism claimed the mantle of Bennism and was very often administered by either the veterans of the Labour left's struggles in the 1980s or by people who were too young but nonetheless called themselves Bennites. And yet from so many perspectives, the realities of the new Labour left of the 2010s represent a major departure from that of the 1980s. Bennism marked itself out from previous generations of the Labour left with its recognition that the parliamentary road to socialism would have to happen in tandem with an orientation towards social and industrial struggle outside the arena of conventional party politics. It viewed as outrageous the domination of Labour's politics by a narrow elite and wanted to throw open the doors of decision-making. It focussed not only on matters of party programme but also on structural democracy, fighting for a sovereign Labour conference and an accountable, recallable parliamentary party. It viewed as crucial the task of transforming and radicalizing the wider labour movement and trade unions at the top and in the rank and file and was willing to routinely upset trade union leaderships. Benn was an outspoken pluralist and risked much to fight for the rights of dissidents within the left, including those with whom he profoundly disagreed, such as Militant.

The promise of Corbynism was to do all of this and more: at its head was a man whose political career was, much more than third-generation parliamentarian Tony Benn, built outside the parliamentary arena. The backdrop to its existence was a movement against austerity which surged into the party from the outside, sucked in by the strongest inward tide in Labour's history. The veterans of this movement knew first-hand the inadequacies of the trade union bureaucracies and the dire need to rebuild the trade union movement. The generation that comprised Corbynism's youth had, a few months prior to its existence, never considered Labour as an organization they might join. The nascent new left produced by the struggles of the first half of the decade brought horizontal and anti-hierarchical politics seemingly closer into the heart of Labour than ever before. They joined forces with older generations of the extra-parliamentary left and veterans of previous attempts to fuse Labour with social movements – people like John McDonnell and Hilary Wainwright.

The Corbyn project was a huge and hugely diverse moment, and there are counterexamples to almost every evaluation of it. But by and large, the opposite evolution occurred to the one that was promised. The historic lows of industrial struggle and the low ebb in social movements were to an extent beyond Corbynism's control, but it nonetheless occurred as the large bulk of Britain's activists were consumed by a battle for control of the party. There was barely any attempt to transform or democratize the wider labour movement, and trade union bureaucracies were treated not just as stakeholders but as the project's key enforcers and managers. On a day-to-day basis, a culture of fixing and elite decision-making largely prevailed, and messy processes of internal democracy were routinely shut down. There was no meaningful democratization of the party and certainly no sovereign conference or mandatory reselection. The internal culture of Corbynism was patchy – and there were spaces, cultivated by new left projects like TWT, in which pluralism and a genuine discussion of ideas flourished – but it tended towards loyalism at the base and control freakery at the top. In contrast to Benn's pluralism, the official Labour left in the 2010s often incubated an almost McCarthyite attitude towards other organized socialist groups, in particular Trotskyists. Corbynism was a beacon of hope and could yet be the starting point for a shift to the left in British politics. But if it was an attempt to carry forward the Bennite project of transforming the Labour Party and the wider labour movement, it was an exceptionally bad one.

To a great extent, the differences between Corbynism's promise and its real outcomes were the product of the context in which it found itself. Whatever its ambitions to carry forward the mantle of Bennism, the project that was born in the summer of 2015 had a much more basic task: in a moment in which no concerted alternatives to the neoliberal economic model had surfaced in more than twenty years, it was charged with reasserting the left's right to exist in mainstream politics. By the time that Corbyn entered the Labour leadership, the organized left and the labour movement had spent decades in a state of seemingly terminal decline, and rather than focussing on rebuilding their strength and health, the new leadership was forced to spend all of its energy pushing back the consensus around austerity. In this task it excelled, aided by the backdrop that had been painstakingly constructed by the mass movements of the previous five years. It also faced a campaign of sabotage not just from the hostile press but from the pre-existing Labour establishment, and this state of siege created the conditions for both a bunker mentality and a tendency towards centralized bureaucratic decision-making that ultimately betrayed the project's promise of a 'new kind of politics'.

To stop there, however, would be to surrender to a passive tragedy – and to accept the idea that the fate of the left will always be determined by the establishment in its various guises. On the contrary, things could have been different, and it is within our collective power to make them different in future. In order to do so, we must recognize that, much more than the left changing the Labour Party, the Labour Party changed the left. In the end, the chaotic, creative forces that opened the door to the creation of Corbynism were defeated within it, and the project came to be dominated by an orthodox perspective which saw the future entirely in terms of electing a Labour government, with the levers of power and policy resting in the hands of experts and fixers.

At the heart of this process was an elitist socialist tradition indigenous to the Labour Party since its inception. To its more conscious adherents, the centralization of the project which occurred following the 2016 leadership challenge – in the shutting down of Momentum's internal democracy and the tightening grip of the Unite bureaucracy over the party machine – was not a necessary evil but a positive outcome and a step towards the kind of professionalized politics that would be needed to legislate socialism from the commanding heights of government. The messy world of grassroots democracy was not just something that needed to be put on hold, or sublimated into a million set-piece rallies and canvassing sessions, but which needed to be managed out of existence. Dissent was not something to be engaged with, or even tempered, but something to be stigmatized and rubbed out.

By the time Corbyn left office, it had become a regular feature of media coverage to use adjectives like 'Stalinist' to describe the Labour leadership and 'Kremlinology' to describe the art of understanding how it operated. There was some truth to this description, though perhaps not in the superficial way that it was understood by commentators and tabloid editors with little real knowledge of the left's traditions. Over time, Corbyn's inner circle did come to be populated by conscious partisans of the orthodox communist tradition – people like Seamas Milne and Andrew Murray. However, tempting though it is to use these more eye-catching labels, I think that the best way to understand the political tendency that came to dominate the Corbyn project is as the continuation of an establishment Labourism that runs right through the party's history, from the New Labour years all the way back to the early Fabians.

The Fabian Society is these days more of a networking opportunity for party activists and aspiring politicians than it is an organized political tendency, but that was not always the case. The name the Society's patrons gave it in 1884 – taken from the Roman general Quintus Fabius Maximus Verrucosus, whose patience defeated Hannibal on the battlefield – is indicative both of the gradualist approach they took to politics and the middle class, Classics-familiar world from which they were drawn. Sidney and Beatrice Webb, the couple at the heart of the early Society, had originally seen no need to create an alternative to the Liberal Party, which they attempted to 'permeate' – that is, influence intellectually. Eventually, however, the Fabians were persuaded of the case for Labour and were one of its founding Socialist Societies when the party formed.

Although the Webbs were anti-Marxist – and presented their ideas as a British-born constitutionalist road to socialism – the political programme of the early Fabians would be regarded today as extremely radical and went further in terms of state ownership than Labour would ever go in power. They even wrote Labour's original Clause IV, which Blair would abolish in the drive to create New Labour. But to a great extent the legacy of Fabianism, and the long series of traditions which it informed once its ideas got into Labour's bloodstream, was less about policy and more about, in Hilary Wainwright's words, its 'paternalistic political methodology'.[9] However radical it might have been in a crude statist sense, Fabianism was conservative in terms of its organizational politics and theory of change. The Webbs proudly referred to themselves as bureaucrats. For them, the state was the instrument of transformation, and agency was to be located among those at the top who pulled its levers for the grateful masses. Some Fabians, most prominently George Bernard Shaw, even fleetingly spoke positively of the big-state endeavours of fascist Italy and Nazi Germany. The Webbs were strong opponents of democratizing the Labour Party and regarded its members with disdain. 'We have little faith in the average sensual man', wrote Beatrice Webb in 1948. 'We do not believe he can do much more than describe his remedies . . . We wish to introduce the professional expert.'[10]

Throughout Labour's history, this tradition has provided intellectual ballast and political justification for the methods of various Labour leaders of the right, who required top-down and centralizing methods to deliver manifestos quite at odds with the views of party members. Working class self-emancipation and grassroots democracy are not just a messy, alien concept from an elitist Fabian perspective – they are also a total liability if your aim is to win elections by a process of triangulation and establishment appeasement. Blairism was the pinnacle of this way of doing politics, but its echoes can be heard in every corner of the labour movement, conveyed up its long veins by the bureaucracies of trade unions, the parliamentary cliques and the common sense of the sensible, suited people to whom you might look if you were in a tight spot. It is a tradition that has always been grateful for the mass movement's efforts on the Labour doorstep but which has never trusted that movement's judgement.

Within the Corbyn project, it was the force which sought at every turn to manage and control; to pat its activists on the head while denying them internal democracy and democratic reform; to confuse trade unionism with the personal fiefdoms of its largely unelected officials; to reduce the complexities and differences of opinion to the level of loyalty and heresy; and to subordinate everything (even Corbynism's own soul) to the task of being in charge and taking over the state. To the new left – the social movement veterans, horizontalists, revolutionaries and extra-parliamentary radicals who had come through the mass movements from 2010 onwards – this was our opposite and our kryptonite. Some of us realized too late the force with which it would hit us, and some of us never realized at all.

And we should not be surprised that the essentially conservative labour movement tendency within Corbynism forged alliances, and shared practices, with the orthodox communist tradition. After all, if your agent of change is not working class self-emancipation but 'the professional expert', all sorts of authoritarian practices become justified. The original Fabians were quite opposed to the Russian Revolution, but when Stalinism took hold of the Soviet Union – and instituted an authoritarian and bureaucratically administered society based on state ownership – the Webbs and their co-thinkers became enthusiastic about the Soviet Union. The American Marxist Hal Draper summed this journey up succinctly when he wrote that 'the swing of Fabianism from middle-class permeation to Stalinism was the swing of a door that was hinged on Socialism-from-Above'.[11] While Labour's right wing has always been the natural home for machine politics, there is a tradition of elitism that cuts across the party and which shares a common strand of political DNA.

Warts and all, the rise of Corbynism and the rebirth of the left over the course of the 2010s is the most significant advance for progressive politics in Britain in my lifetime. In the space of ten years, we went from being a laughable anachronism to a movement which challenged for power and mobilized hundreds of thousands of people. Among all the defeat, despair and cries of betrayal – and the simultaneous rise of a nationalist right that we have yet to find an effective means of combatting – there is a story of hope and inspiration, not just a story of happy tales to be related to future generations, but a concrete base on which we may yet build a movement that transforms society. To do that successfully, we must extricate the transformative potential of the Corbyn project from the quagmire of Labourism, machine politics and elitism and relaunch the politics of socialism from below.

Conclusion

What now?

The death of Corbynism represented a moment of strategic crisis for progressives in Britain. The new Labour left produced by the period immediately after 2015 was a movement almost uniquely dependent on central direction. It had a clear figurehead (Jeremy Corbyn) and a clear immediate aim (to win an election), and the loss of both of these had immediate consequences. Keir's Starmer's election as Labour leader in April 2020 – with a mandate even bigger than that achieved by Jeremy Corbyn in his leadership elections – marked another turning point in Labour's history. The years immediately after the general election defeat of 2019 did witness a number of significant mobilizations, most notably the flourishing of Black Lives Matter and an ever-growing climate justice movement. But the endless lockdowns during the pandemic, in which face-to-face political meetings were largely banned and protests happened only sporadically and without the backing of major unions, compounded a sense of stagnation from which we are in some senses still emerging.

The need for a continued revival of the left has rarely been more pressing. The 2010s were a decade in which, through the collective effort of millions of people, radical political alternatives finally returned to the political mainstream. These alternatives were a response to the crises of the day: the bankruptcy of the neoliberal consensus; the threat of catastrophic climate change; and the rise of authoritarian nationalism. The 2020s will be a decade in which many of those crises are resolved – one way or another. By 2030, we will likely have a good idea as to whether we have either transformed the logic of the global economy or else rendered large parts of the world uninhabitable. Either the onward march of civil rights and civil liberties will continue or it will be halted and reversed by demagogues and razor wire. New technologies will either be used to liberate us or to surveille and control.

With the stakes so high, it is essential that we talk not just in terms of a revival of the left in general but also about what kind of left we need. We cannot hope that simply returning to a period of social struggle, on the one hand, or repeating

Corbynism, on the other, will suffice. Across the whole of the centre and left of British politics today, however, there is one ubiquitous strategy: 'one more heave'.

In the 2010s, the Labour left was the beneficiary of a wave of social movements that changed the political landscape and surged in to renew the party; of more than a decade of leftward shifts in the leaderships of many trade unions; of the intellectual death of New Labour; and of a perfect storm which allowed Corbyn to first reach the ballot paper and then win the leadership for the left for, by most definitions, the first time in the party's history. But so many of its leaders and activists are wedded to a narrative of excuses: if only we could try a bit harder, if only it wasn't for Brexit, if only it wasn't for the Corbyn project's traitors and heretics, then next time it will be different. One more heave, comrades.

The answers to the strategic dilemmas of the 2020s lie with a new left that was created by the upheavals of the 2010s. Its existence was informed by the inadequacies of the existing left – of its official institutions, the ailing socialist grouplets and the traditional passive modes of dissent. It was defined by the experiences of a cohort of young people for whom generational identity was a means of expressing class politics rather than an alternative to it and who had been cut off from the history and traditions of the left by the defeats of the 1980s and 1990s. This new left existed outside of mainstream politics and was suspicious of leaders and hierarchies, until in 2015 the social movements were flipped on their heads and dragged into Labour.

This new left was in pockets influential in shaping the politics and aesthetics of Corbynism. But in the end, its spirit was defeated as the Corbyn project came to be dominated by more institutional forces, robbing the project of the democracy and collective imagination it needed to succeed. Drawing on the experiences and human material from the social movements of the first half of the decade, the conditions exist for the regrouping of a left which is up to the task of transforming politics. So what should that left do, and what lessons should we draw from the 2010s?

The centre could yet hold

Labour's centre and right offer little more than their own versions of 'one more heave'. The Corbyn leadership went down to a marginal defeat in 2017 and a dreadful one in 2019, but its radical social and economic programme was about the only genuinely popular thing it had. In spite of this, so many of Labour's leading lights remain stuck on the fact that the only time the party has managed to win an election in the past forty years was when it moved so far to the right that it became on many issues indistinguishable from the Conservative Party. In the absence of any popular demand for a genuinely Blairite political programme, their plan amounts to conjuring up something resembling a hand-wringing re-enactment of the Miliband years. It is always possible, of course, that Labour could win the next election by default or by virtue of a crisis in the Conservative Party – but it is in principle hard to imagine a less popular strategy for the party than middle-of-road respectability and acquiescence to right-wing economic narratives.

There is a temptation to look back at the past decade and conclude that centrist politics is finished. After all, Joe Biden's victory against first Bernie Sanders and then Donald Trump may have represented a superficial return to 'politics as normal', but the Biden administration has in fact presided over a gigantic expansion of state spending not seen since the New Deal of 1930. Keir Starmer could only rise to become Labour leader by promising to retain the radical domestic agenda set out by the Corbyn leadership. But any progress on policy will only be temporary if it merely consists of establishment politicians using radical economics or anti-establishment rhetoric to gain support while marginalizing the left politically.

Just because the traditional politics of the Labour establishment is unelectable does not mean that it will disappear. The question of which ideas come to dominate politics is not resolved by which ideas are best but by which ideas can mobilize the strength they need to dominate. The class of professional politicians, journalists and advisors that tend to be in charge of the Labour Party still cling to the narratives that defined Blairism: they still think that Labour can only win elections when it can convince the ruling class that it is a safe pair of hands, and they think that in order to achieve this, they must re-enact Neil Kinnock's policy of performatively marginalizing the Labour left and its ideas, as if reading back a script from the late 1980s.

The defining claim of centrists in the time of Kinnock and Blair was not only that left-wing alternatives were irrelevant and untenable but also that they *always would be*, and once made this claim cannot easily be withdrawn. Whole careers and political identities have been built on pillorying and demonizing the left.

To understand the resilience of this kind of politics, it helps to understand the subjectivity of a cohort of ageing Generation X-ers. Cultural analyst Jeremy Gilbert has for some time theorized the idea of the 'long 1990s', a period of superficial cultural stasis which has made it impossible for many of his peers to accept that politics had changed. 'For my generation, growing up in a culture that was already saturated by Boomer nostalgia, there was this idea that what historical change looked like was dramatic, highly visible and audible change in music and fashion', he says. 'The great political struggles of the twentieth century had come to an end, but at least we had music that couldn't have been imagined ten years previously. That isn't necessarily how things work any more – music and fashion now work according to very different cycles of change and continuity.'

The absence of a dramatic shift in youth culture like punk or rave in recent decades has meant that a comfortably off section of Generation X, a demographic sometimes disparagingly referred to as 'centrist dads', has become convinced that politics hasn't changed since the 1990s either. 'But of course things have changed, especially for younger people', Gilbert says. 'And so these people can't understand that young people weren't supporting Corbyn just because they were mad or immature – but because the housing market is totally fucked, the labour market is totally fucked. These centrists are not able to grasp the extent to which the political strategies and the policy programme of the 1990s are just not going to work any more, even on their own terms.'

In 2010, we inherited a world in which class politics was regarded as an anachronism and in which the legacy of New Labour held a tight grip on the political imagination of most of Labour's politicians and voters. The rise of the Corbyn project changed that picture. The popularity of the policies contained within its manifestos was such that, once said out loud, they could not entirely be put back in their box. On another level, however, the change affected by Corbynism was a narrow one. Unlike the movements that created it, it was not focussed on 'politics from below' and did very little to deliver lasting or structural change – either in the party or in the wider labour movement.

It also failed to address the depoliticization of civil society. The rolling back of the state in previous decades meant that charities and quangos stepped in to fill the space. Rather than viewing social problems as the result of political choices and seeking to organize people in an oppositional way, these bodies tend to focus on ameliorating life, navigating stakeholders and consulting people rather than give them direct democratic ownership over any given project. This methodology got deep into the bloodstream of the left's institutions, with many trade unions focussing service provision, and this trend has simply continued. Even Momentum became a kind of NGO: it was led from an office with a professionalized campaign plan, and its engagement with grassroots activists was mostly at the level of consultation and training. The fact that the structure of politics remains largely unchanged leaves the legacy of the great left revival of the 2010s in a precarious position.

The adults aren't coming to save you

The story of the 2010s is a story of relentless institutional failure. When students went into revolt in 2010, the NUS condemned them. In the following years, those who marched and rallied and occupied their Town Halls, and the thousands camped in the cold at Occupy all over the country, looked up to the Labour Party for an alternative to the despair of endless cuts and for a mirror to their anger and energy. They found a party at war with its own conscience which was engaged in a desperate, unending attempt to look and sound as it thought electable politicians might look and sound, half-heartedly mimicking the policies and rhetoric of its opponents.

In the absence of the left's grown-ups – its officials, leaders and technocrats – it was left to hundreds of thousands of young people, radical retirees, public sector workers, benefit claimants, squatters, weirdos, precarious migrant workers, single mums and concerned citizens to throw themselves at the austerity consensus in the hope that it might break. It is from these people, not the celebrities and icons of the left, that we ought to draw our inspiration. As the wave of the movement broke and gave way to a grinding, seemingly inevitable defeat, the human material created by the social movements looked around for somewhere to go, and in the summer of 2015 it magically, miraculously, found its political expression.

In the end, however, Corbynism was not an exception to the unbroken chain of institutional failure on the left. Under siege from the political establishment inside and outside Labour, the project turned to the grown-ups and to the long tradition of machine politics that has run through Labour since its inception. We might have given the grown-ups credit if the turn towards institutional politics had merely meant sacrificing some of the transformative essence of Corbynism in return for some electoral success, but in the long run this is not what happened.

Democratic reform in the party, 'a new kind of politics' and a transformation of the trade unions were all casualties of this process. But so too were Labour's electoral prospects. By closing down democratic decision-making in favour of an endless fudge, the adults made finding a clear and credible Brexit policy impossible. The closing down of Momentum's democratic structures made the organization a more efficient machine, but it also meant that its local groups collapsed. There was only ever so much that Momentum could be expected to achieve by bussing in hundreds of people from the outside whenever election time came around, however dynamic its operation was.

The standard history of Corbynism records the professionalization that the project underwent in the wake of the 2016 leadership challenge as a moment of growing up which enabled Labour to do so well in the 2017 election and then ends there. I think this narrative is standing on its head. If your aim is to achieve radical change, one of the worst mistakes you can make is to confuse jargon and officialdom for effectiveness and seriousness and to assume that loyalty and order will deliver better results than the chaotic, creative mess of a genuine activist democracy.

Now that we are in a new era of Labour Party's history, many politicians and commentators will assert that the takeover of the party by the group of insurgent radicals from the former fringes of politics was a blip, and that now it is time to trust once again in the world of focus groups and even tighter party management. But if we have learned anything from the past decade, it is that not only do the grown-ups and professionals tend towards control freakery and conservatism, it is that they are – on a deep, political level – incompetent for the task at hand.

Build decentralized movement which can speak for themselves

The paradox of Corbynism is that the rebirth of the political left came alongside a decline in social movements and the lowest industrial struggle on record. The suddenness with which the anti-establishment and extra-parliamentary left of the first half of the decade flipped into becoming the new Labour left, and the lack of collective strategy and organization that they had when they did so, made this contrast all the more stark. A great number of the veterans of the social movements had no conception of being 'in and against' the Labour Party: they were first against it and then just in it.

Perhaps this process will naturally unravel, and just as I have written a book now about how social movements built Corbynism, another book will be written in five years' time about how Corbynism laid the ground for another era of social movements. I think this is overly optimistic. The Corbyn moment has structured the left almost exclusively around parliamentary politics. It has taught activists the virtues of not rocking the boat, fighting over positions on committees that do nothing, and throwing everything into a narrow burst of activity to get your people – whom you very often had no say in choosing – elected. It has also given us an addiction to parliamentary leadership, a prevailing sense that we must find the next great figurehead around which to structure ourselves. To rebuild a politics of pluralism and social movements, much of the culture and practice of Corbynism will have to be consciously unlearned.

There has been a pattern in the fortunes of left-wing movements over the past decade. The strikes of 2011 were led from above and could be switched off like a tap – as indeed they were. This happened not just because of the conciliatory impulses of some union leaderships but also because there was no adequate organization among trade union activists who wanted to carry on the dispute. Momentum's formidable centralized electoral machine came at the expense of deeper movement-building capacities. The student movement of 2010, on the other hand, and UK Uncut in its heyday, and the Occupy movement that spread across the globe: all owed their disruptive capacity to their decentralized nature – to the fact that, in a thousand different meetings and assemblies, millions of people took their fate in their hands, without waiting for permission, following a strategy that they and their wider network had themselves devised. One of the veterans of the Millbank riot sums up the spirit of these movements with the old punk slogan: 'Do it here, do it now, do it yourself.'

There is no contradiction between building activist networks with the freedom to act and having an organizational centre for the movement which can seek to coordinate. So many of the decade's attempts at networked movement-building failed because they realized, too late, that a purely horizontal method was liable to burning out and being eclipsed by better-organized institutional models of dissent. Aside from a few explosive moments, the predominant activities remained the passive A to B march and the symbolic one-day strike, followed by a turn into conventional electoral politics. The NCAFC developed into a sustainable organization but only after the 2010 student movement had died. The anti-austerity movement sprouted several competing anti-cuts coalitions but, owing to the controlling method and sectarianism of much of the left, these never had the breadth of appeal to play the role that was needed at the height of the struggle. Only when the movement was on the decline did the People's Assembly Against Austerity emerge, and it existed more as a coalition of important people and organizations than as a federation of networked local activist groups.

The task for the left in the next cycle of protest movements, then, is to rediscover autonomous action and the capacity to disrupt while building the infrastructure that might make this sustainable. The organizational centres of the movement will have to be non-sectarian, open and rigorously internally democratic, in contrast to what has come before them.

The past decade has proven, not for the first time, that any rebirth of the left that does not come with a transformation within the trade union movement is doomed to failure. It has not been enough for the likes of PCS, Unite and the NUT to have left-wing general secretaries, and it was beyond the valiant efforts of general secretaries like Mark Serwotka to rescue the pensions dispute in 2011. It is remarkable just how little the new Labour left has impacted the unions in terms of militancy and democratization, and as a result, most trade unions in Britain today remain institutionally conservative. Not for nothing have recent years witnessed a growth of nimble, action-focussed unions like the UVW and the IWGB. During the Corbyn period, on matters such as Open Selections, and on the culture of fixing and stitch-ups on policy and in selections, most unions largely reverted to their historic role as a counterweight to a more radical membership. Without a bottom-up transformation of the trade union movement, the left's chances of success in winning basic advances in the coming years are much diminished, and our chances of permanently shifting the Labour Party are precisely zero.

If we are even moderately successful in these tasks – building sustainable decentralized social struggle and transforming the wider labour movement – the new movements will need to have a political expression. In the 2010s, when the movements flooded into Corbynism, they lacked any collective organization or strategy within it. They trusted their fate to the old Labour left and to the professionals who were, in effect, the left wing of the party establishment. Next time around, they must consciously build a political expression on top of themselves, rather than walking into someone else's; we must build political projects which – inside or outside Labour – enable us to speak for ourselves.

Recruit activists, not foot soldiers

The crowds that the Corbyn project assembled were unprecedented in the recent history of British politics, but for all the radical policy content the task in which they were engaged was a conventional electoral project and in the end an unsuccessful one. To build a sustainable new left, the veterans of Corbynism will have to move beyond the logic of following, and to do that, they must be empowered to be critical, thinking activists.

Throughout the Corbyn era, there was a widespread realization of the fact that the sudden influx into the left had created imbalances of knowledge and skills. The answer to this problem was an increasing emphasis on training and political education, though what was meant by this was patchy. From 2017 onwards, Momentum turned its focus towards training local activists, but it largely trained them in electoral campaigning. Many activists picked up an education in factional politics and fixing via their work taking over constituency parties. There was an endless proliferation of panels and talks on economics, history and various different issues and a whole new cast of left-wing celebrities and intellectuals to populate them. If you looked for it, you could find strategy discussions and debates taking place on crucial issues. Fundamentally, however, many of these attempts at political education reinforced a top-down logic of politics and were aimed at making activists more efficient within it. Those projects which were aimed at cutting across this logic – as TWT was, to an extent – were incapable of doing so successfully on their own. It didn't matter how many books they'd read. To nurture activists rather than foot soldiers, the recruits must have real power to change their own movement and the world, on their own terms. In other words, it's about agency.

And agency is complicated. The norms of the professional political world teach us that agency is found among leaders and spokespeople; but what is striking, looking back at the decade, is how little agency those at the top often have. Corbyn didn't even want to be Labour leader. Those around him made many blunders and strategic mistakes which were avoidable, but they spent much of their five years making forced errors, surrounded by a hostile party. Momentum's leadership dramatically altered the course of Corbynism when they decided to abolish the organization's democratic structures in January 2017, but many of those involved felt like they had no choice, as if their hands were being forced by the situation or the decision had already been made somewhere else up the food chain. When I was running the campaign to get Labour to adopt a second referendum position, I probably had as much influence as I have ever had to shape real-world events but still found myself being helplessly pushed into supporting a fudge by the machinery of the party, an outcome which proved disastrous.

The place where left-wing activists have most agency is at the lowest level. So much of history is made in the cracks between great events. The precarious worker organizing a strike has in many senses more agency than the famous commentator who visits their picket lines. Looking back, maybe the most important thing I will ever do was, at the age of twenty, helping to set up the NCAFC prior to the 2010 student movement. This activity did not feel glamorous at the time and often consisted of bringing together tiny numbers of activists to have long, irrelevant-seeming rows about the future of the student movement. The point is that the collective agency of the project had far-reaching consequences.

The Labour Party trains people not to seek to change the movement and the world as part of a collective but to seek promotion and position and to pursue power and influence in the way that it is conventionally understood by professional politics. Jeremy Corbyn and John McDonnell found their way to the top by being principled and isolated figures who dedicated their lives to unfashionable causes, but that is not the rule, and within the Corbyn project it was, inevitably, the conventional Labour method that prevailed. By and large, you gain position by keeping your head down, being in the right networks, not rocking the boat and disciplining unorthodox opinions in yourself and others. The second half of the 2010s educated a whole new generation in this manner of doing things.

Developing a more critical, and a more democratic, internal culture will have to run alongside a moment of ideological reckoning. Corbynism's mass base was brought together because it identified with the left – but what did that mean? Socialist was the movement's prevailing adjective, but its immediate policy programme was mostly about reasserting the basics of social democracy, and there was little or no collective discussion inside Corbynism about what a truly socialist or anti-capitalist programme might look like in the future. Such a discussion would have opened deep divisions about the role of the state, the autonomy of workers and the overall strategy of the left. Other deep divisions – on borders, nationalism and the urgency of fighting climate change – have been papered over by a uniting central project in which dissent and collective organization was very difficult. The task now is developing a culture that is healthy and pluralistic enough to manage the left's inevitable fragmentation while retaining a collective focus for action in social movements and the political realm.

Fight the battle against amnesia

The great unique effect that Thatcherism had on my generation was a subjective one. The 'generation without a history' turned with great suddenness into Labour, without much in the way of a coherent critique of the party as an institution. The long-term defeat of the labour movement and the onward march of Blairism combined to isolate us from the left's traditions and collective memory.

One of the main symptoms of amnesia is nostalgia, and the British left is full of it. Our endless obsession with the 'spirit of 45' functions as a means of forgetting the austerity and paternalism of the post-war period and maintaining illusions in a two-dimensional politics of state ownership which later generations of radicals set themselves against. Between 2015 and 2019, nostalgia for Bennism allowed much of the leadership of the new Labour left to sing the praises of party democracy while failing to support it. If we are not careful, nostalgia for the Corbyn period will soon become a means of forgetting its flaws and repeating its mistakes.

The left is strongest not when constructing its own historical myths but when shattering other peoples'. Despite being attacked by the press as a re-enactment society for the 1970s and 1980s, the Corbyn leadership and Momentum set out to look and sound like the future, both in policy terms and in terms of methods and aesthetics – and in this they were often successful.

What is needed now is a campaign against amnesia, not just with an attempt to teach and share history – essential though this is – but by rebuilding a space for ideological traditions and collective memory in a practical sense. The new left must assert itself, putting forward a politics of pluralism, social progressivism, internal democracy, opposition to rising borders and an outward turn towards social movements and industrial struggle. The coalition behind this approach to politics is very diverse. It includes many people who, like me, have never quite fitted in to any single tendency as well as a hodgepodge of social movement veterans; those influenced by anarchism and autonomism; many Greens; some of Labour's less instutionalized social democrats; some old Bennites; and some inheritors of Britain's Marxist traditions.

I am of course not the first person to talk about the need to cohere this broad political space. In an influential article in early 2020, Jeremy Gilbert observed 'the emergence of a distinctive, radical-left current that is democratic, green and internationalist in its socialist aspirations'. He counterposed the Radical Left to both the more moderate Soft Left and to the Orthodox Left, the latter of which 'still basically wants to implement the Communist party's 1951 plan, The British Road to Socialism, with its vision of socialism being implemented in one country by a strong, centralised national government'.[1]

The most frustrating feature of the new left of the 2010s (and the same can be said of Gilbert's Radical Left) is its chronic lack of organization. It exists so often at the level of networks and cliques, or in campaigns that come and go, and is often squeamish about formalizing itself. What is needed is a conscious big tent project to bring its fragments into constellation.

Brexit is still the problem

It is easy for the left to tell itself the story of how it defied the odds and defeated the centrist establishment of the Labour Party for three magical summers in a row. What is much harder is to acknowledge, or at least to seriously reflect upon, is that the elevation of Jeremy Corbyn to the labour leadership was not the beginning or the end of the collapse of the neoliberal centre but one of a series of connected shocks. What almost no one within the Corbyn project understood – and this is evident from how seriously it took the EU referendum in 2016 – is that the nationalist right was preparing its own shock, one which was perfectly calibrated to divide and destroy Corbynism. The new Labour left failed in large part because it simply refused to recognize the dangers presented by the Brexit project.

On one level, Labour's failure on Brexit was a failure of internal democracy. Intoxicated by the success of the 2017 election campaign, the leadership came to fetishize ambiguity and empowered an army of party managers in order to hold onto this strategy against the will of party members. And so Labour went through years of zigzagging, with its activists (me more than most) fighting an obsessive war over the party's formal position and spending almost no time on the task that might have saved the Corbyn project: countering the political content and narratives of the Brexit project in wider society.

But the problem was political as well as procedural. There was always a perfectly reasonable left-wing case in favour of Brexit, much though I may have disagreed with it. The real problem for Labour was the existence of a body of opinion within the left, which exists across the Western world, which essentially regards the 'culture war' as a distraction from the real business of class politics. This tendency diagnosed Brexit as a container for a lot of issues – such as migrants' rights and transnational identities – which were essentially marginal to the main task of electing a left Labour government which would enact a radical economic programme. Aside from misunderstanding the nature of Brexit, which is about economic deregulation just as much as it is about culture wars, this version of reality is often built on a very narrow view of who the 'real' working class is. Running in parallel to this outlook in the minds of many left-wing activists ran the internalization of a right-wing populist argument that hamstrung the debate within the party: that the outcome of a single referendum constituted the immutable 'will of the people' which could not be revisited, even with another referendum.

The question of 'in or out' is now settled (for the moment), but the project that began on 23 June 2016 was not about Britain's membership of the European

Union: it was about a campaign of deregulation, nationalism and dividing the left's coalition. Either we defeat this project or we spend the next thirty years fighting a losing war with the *Daily Mail.*

The first thing we must do is reassert working class unity in all its diversity. The working class does not consist only of old white people with regional accents: it is also young, urban, Black, trans, gay and female. If you are a Black nurse, or a trans barista, or a migrant cleaner, the culture war is not a luxury. The fight for liberation and equal rights is not a distraction from class politics but an integral part of them.

Second, we must tackle the anti-migrant content of the Brexit project head-on. The Labour Party has a long and proud history of throwing migrants under the bus for the sake of electoral calculation – under leaders of all stripes – and, as well as being an abject failure of solidarity, this strategy also hasn't worked. The left will never be able to compete with the Tories on border controls, and accepting the premises of the nationalist right only ever serves to strengthen their narrative. The case against migrants in our national debate today is a simple one, based on the lie (which is uniformly rebutted by all reliable statistics) that migration is responsible for falling wages and on the exploitation of racism by the political establishment. There can be no squeamishness about 'talking down to working class people' when it comes to this debate: Labour claims to be the party built by and for the working class. If it cannot have an honest argument with its traditional voters about a fundamental moral issue, it has no right to exist.

Third, the radical economic agenda forced into the mainstream by the Corbyn project must remain at the heart of Labour's programme. There can be no defeat of the nationalist right without dealing with the material legacy of Thatcherism on wages, housing, infrastructure and public services.

Fourth, the left must deal with the crisis of meaning fuelling the Brexit project and the broader cultural legacy of the past few decades. The legacy of neoliberalism and de-industrialization was not just a fall in living standards but an ever-present crisis of alienation, loneliness, atomization, loss of community and loss of purpose. This sensation is not unique to 'left behind' communities. Britain as a whole has developed a national policy of underregulating capital while overregulating almost everything else, in particular public space and collective leisure – both of which are core aspects of identity and community. We retain the paternalism of the post-war settlement, while keeping none of its social security. Our parks close at sunset because we regard having fun in a public place as a moral problem. What little public space remains in our cities is aggressively monetized and subject to a blizzard of permits and regulations – whether you are organizing a protest or just want to have a picnic. We have a political class that likes to blame 'the public' for its public health disasters and which talks in a language of 'making the right choices' rather than actually improving people's lives. Meanwhile, our incomes stagnate and our public services fall away. The endless inflation of assets, property and land has washed away many of our independently run social spaces. The corporate takeover of culture has homogenized our existence and stripped meaning out of people's lives. It is like living in a nanny state, only without any of the caring capacities.

The nationalist right has a clear, if cheap, answer to this situation: to reinvent the nation as an exclusive community with a content of nostalgia, both post-war and imperial. Since Boris Johnson took over the Conservative Party, this has come alongside a promise of state investment. In Labour, centrist politicians and advisors will have their answer: to wrap the Labour Party in the flags and symbolism of this nationalist vision, without – supposedly – taking its content to heart. There are already many thinkers and activists engaged, in one way or another, in developing and popularizing a left response to this problem – one which goes beyond both a hollow imitation of the right's flag-waving and a shopping list of top-down economic interventions from central government – and it is one the most important tasks that we now face.

Labour must die

A familiar debate is now playing out in meetings, on zoom calls and in people's heads.

Person A argues that the Labour Party is umbilically linked to the task of managing the state and is dominated by bureaucrats who create a conservative drag on the labour movement. In every generation, it draws in the activists of wider movements, offers them a glimpse of state power and sucks them dry, leaving them as passive spectators and foot soldiers. To some it hands medals, positions and fiefdoms, and to others it hands endless grunt work, charges of heresy and the illusion of agency. It is now moving back, inexorably, away from the radical moment of Corbynism, and, given that we have missed the window for much-needed party reform, there are precious few levers which the likes of us can pull to change its course. If the miracle of 2015 and the leadership of someone so left-field as Jeremy Corbyn cannot transform Labour, nothing can.

Person B will argue that almost all progressive advances since the Second World War have come from Labour governments, and that the potential of Labour governments will be much weaker if there is no Labour left there to push them. The link between Labour and the trade unions is the only organic link between working class self-organization and high politics in Britain. Any movement that wants to achieve reform requires a political project from which it can draw some realistic hope that its goals may be achieved. Outside of Labour, the organized left in Britain is marginal and is cut off from the mass of progressively minded people who naturally gravitate towards Labour. Most concretely, the First Past the Post electoral system means that any attempt to set up an electoral alternative to Labour in Westminster elections is simply doomed. The Green Party has one MP after thirty years in existence. Left of Labour alternatives like the Trade Union and Socialist Coalition and Left Unity have only ever received derisory vote shares.

The problem with these perspectives is that they are both right. We could go further, in fact. Over the course of the 2010s, almost every strand of the left has hit the buffers. The networked and horizontal movements of 2010 and 2011 ran out of steam. Across much of the world, they were crushed by the state and a wave of nationalist reaction, and in Britain they were devoured by the juggernaut of an electoral project. The Trotskyist left, which was the dominant organized left force in Britain between the 1970s and 2015, began the 2010s at a historically low ebb. We might expect the organized socialist left to grow exponentially in a period of such upheaval, but it ended the decade in a worse position than it started it.

The left's debate about Labour has barely changed in decades. In each generation, the tides have drawn the movements into and out of the party. The pendulum has swung back and forth between social movement and electoral turn, from the doorstep to the streets and back again. The most recent tide was the sharpest and most extreme yet and was marked also by its rollercoaster emotional journey: from the seeming quiet of the immediate post-crash period to the explosion of 2010 and the grand awakening of 2011; through the bitter failures of leadership and the defeat of the anti-austerity movement; into the despair of 2015 general election; up to the heights of elation with Corbyn's election that summer; the shock and grief of Brexit; the attrition of Labour's civil war and the battles in Momentum; then again the euphoria of near-victory in the general election of 2017; the deepening splits and divisions; the democratic disappointments; and, finally, the black despair of December 2019.

There is a view of history that sees these changes almost like seasons, as part of the natural rhythm of the British left. But while there may be an inevitability to a changing emphasis of the left's activities in different historical contexts, I think the time has come to view Labour's tidal system less as a fact of life and more as a recurring nightmare from which we need to awake. The sharpness of the tides reflects a situation in which, outside a few dwindling socialist groups, the left has no overall strategy. Without such a strategy, we are like moths being drawn to the brightest lights.

The Labour Party needs to split. In no circumstance other than a First Past the Post electoral system would it make sense for the advocates of Private Finance Initiatives in the NHS and the Iraq War to share a political project with Marxists and anti-war activists. In this context, changing Westminster's voting system stops being a dry or peripheral matter and starts being a crucial strategic question for the left. The sharply differing world views within Labour had an obvious and profound effect on the fate of the Corbyn project. Its lack of democracy and culture of loyalism owed much to the fact that its activists and leaders felt obliged to close ranks and focus on fighting a Labour Party establishment which seemed determined to prevent it from taking power.

Corbynism was so attractive because it seemed to offer a shortcut through the enormous task of rebuilding the left after its defeat by Thatcher and Blair. The past five years have vastly expanded the number of people in Britain who call themselves socialists and mainstreamed some of the left's economic narratives. The crucial task now is to take this legacy and turn it outwards, and that will mean having an argument with the prevailing wisdom of the new Labour left. Who cares about the handful of new left-wing MPs – no matter how charismatic they might be – if there is no movement underneath them? Even if the left won the Labour leadership tomorrow, it would simply be repeating a failed strategy unless it changes the balance of the situation in some other way.

Despite all the setbacks of recent years, the conditions are now in place for a revival of the left for which Corbynism was only the beginning. To build such a moment of renewal, we will need to develop a way of doing politics, in Hilary Wainwright's words, 'through which we're neither vanguards nor the supporting spectators'.[2] We will need to find a way to wake up from the nightmare of being sucked into the Labour Party and washed back out again and a political culture which is pluralistic and conversant with history. We must find a way of organizing that cuts across the old divides that separate the extra-parliamentary left from electoral politics and the revolutionaries from the reformists. The new left that resurfaced in the 2010s is as diverse as the struggles that built it. It is time now for it to wake up and realize its strength.

Notes

Introduction

1   ONS data: https://www.ons.gov.uk/employmentandlabourmarket/peopleinwork/
    earningsandworkinghours/bulletins/annualsurveyofhoursandearnings/2019#:~:text
    =Median%20weekly%20earnings%20in%20real,reduction%20from%2043.3%25
    %20in%202018.

2   'Child Poverty in the UK: The Report on the 2010 Target', published by The UK
    Government 17th June 2012: https://www.gov.uk/government/publications/child
    -poverty-in-the-uk-the-report-on-the-2010-target and https://cpag.org.uk/child
    -poverty/child-poverty-facts-and-figures and 'Ending Child Poverty', published by
    The Children's Society: https://www.childrenssociety.org.uk/what-we-do/our-work/
    ending-child-poverty.

3   Trussell Trust: End of Year Stats: https://www.trusselltrust.org/news-and-blog/latest
    -stats/end-year-stats/.

4   Fair Society Healthy Lives (The Marmot Review), published by the Institute of
    Health Equity: http://www.instituteofhealthequity.org/resources-reports/fair-society
    -healthy-lives-the-marmot-review.

5   'Child Health in 2030 in England: Comparisons with Other Wealthy Countries',
    published by Royal College of Paediatrics and Child Health: https://www.rcpch.ac
    .uk/sites/default/files/2018-10/child_health_in_2030_in_england_-report_2018-10
    .pdf.

6   Toby Helm, *Observer Report*, 1 June 2019: https://www.theguardian.com/politics
    /2019/jun/01/perfect-storm-austerity-behind-130000-deaths-uk-ippr-report.

7   Prescribed Medicines Review: Summary, published by the UK Government: https://
    www.gov.uk/government/publications/prescribed-medicines-review-report/
    prescribed-medicines-review-summary.

8   Labour lost 1.9 million of its 2017 Remain voters and 1.8 million of its Leave
    ones. These statistics are Datapraxis analysis of YouGov data for Labour
    Together's *Election Review 2019*, published by 18 June 2020. https://electionreview
    .labourtogether.uk/.

Chapter 1

1 The only currently existing feature-length history of the 2010 student movement is Matt Myers's oral history *Student Revolt: Voices of the Austerity Generation* (Pluto, 2017). I am indebted to it for some of the detail that appears in my own account.

2 'Kettle Tactics Risk Hillsborough-Style Tragedy – Doctor', published by Shiv Malik and Mark Townsend for *The Observer*, 19 December 2010: https://www.theguardian .com/uk/2010/dec/19/police-kettle-risk-crush-hillsborough.

3 I was unaware of this detail until the release of Matt Myers's book in 2017.

4 *Daily Mail, Reports*, 10 December 2010.

5 *The Times, Reports*, 9 December 2010.

6 Frederick Jameson: *The Seeds of Time* (Columbia University Press, 1994).

7 Mark Fisher: *Capitalist Realism* (Zero Books, 2008, 2009), p. 2.

8 Statistics cited in Leo Panitch and Colin Leys: *Searching for Socialism* (Verso, 2020), pp. 153–5.

9 Ibid., p. 156.

10 The *Daily Mail* published a full list of the Cabinet and their personal wealth on 22 May 2010: https://www.dailymail.co.uk/news/election/article-1280554/The -coalition-millionaires-23-29-member-new-cabinet-worth-1m--Lib-Dems-just -wealthy-Tories.html.

11 See Kanja Sessay: 'Education, Cuts, Class and Racism', in *Springtime: The New Student Rebellions*, edited by Clare Solomon and Tania Palmeiri (Verso, 2011), p. 25.

12 ONS Labour Market Statistical Bulletin, March 2011, p. 17.

13 James Meadway: 'The Rebellion in Context', in Ibid., p. 20.

14 Des Freeman and Michael Bailey: *The Assault on Universities: A Manifesto for Resistance* (Pluto, 2011), Kindle Edition location 103.

15 Myers, p. 31.

16 Ibid., p. 34.

17 Laurie Penny: 'Out with the Old Politics', published by *The Guardian* on 24 December 2010: https://www.theguardian.com/commentisfree/2010/dec/24/ student-protests-young-politics-voices.

18 The demands were published on *Indymedia*: 'Occupation at Birmingham', 24 November 2010: https://www.indymedia.org.uk/en/2010/11/468456.html.

19 A video of the speech is on YouTube on the UCL Occupation channel: https://www .youtube.com/watch?v=DyYLNaEHcDg&ab_channel=ucloccupation.

20 James Butler: 'Image of the Year', 2 January 2011: https://piercepenniless.wordpress .com/2011/01/02/image-of-the-year/.

21 The Arts Against Cuts statement explaining book bloc is still online: *Book bloc Comes to London*, 9 December 2010: https://artsagainstcuts.wordpress.com/2010/12 /09/book-bloc-comes-to-london-2/.

22 See Andrew McGettigan's blog 'RAB Hits 45% – But What Does That Mean?', published by 21 March 2014: https://andrewmcgettigan.org/2014/03/21/rab-hits-45 -but-what-does-that-mean/.

23 Keir Milburn: *Generation Left* (Polity, 2019), p. 45.

24 Owen Hatherley: 'The Occupation of Space', in *Fightback: A Reader on the Winter of Protest*, edited by Dan Hancox (Open Democracy, 2011), p. 121.

25 Dan Hancox: 'This Is Our Riot: POW', in *Fightback*, p. 265.

26 The full video of the speech can be seen on the *Guardian* website: https://www .theguardian.com/politics/video/2010/nov/23/nick-clegg-hugo-young-full-lecture.

Chapter 2

1 Ipsos Mori polling: https://www.ipsos.com/ipsos-mori/en-uk/how-britain-voted -october-1974.

2 Ipsos Mori polling: https://www.ipsos.com/ipsos-mori/en-uk/how-britain-voted -2010.

3 See *The Future Is Ours: Labour's Youth Manifesto*, 2019: https://labour.org.uk/ manifesto-2019/the-future-is-ours-labours-youth-manifesto/.

4 See Milburn, p. 37.

5 *Guardian Report* by Katie Allen and Larry Elliott, 27 July 2016: https://www .theguardian.com/money/2016/jul/27/uk-joins-greece-at-bottom-of-wage-growth -league-tuc-oecd.

6 Laura Gardiner for the Resolution Foundation: *STAGNATION GENERATION: The Case for Renewing the Intergenerational Contract*, July 2016: https://www.resolutionf oundation.org/app/uploads/2016/06/Intergenerational-commission-launch-report .pdf.

7 Jonathan Cribb, Andrew Hood and Jack Hoyle for the IFS: *The Decline of Homeownership among Young Adults*, 2018: https://www.ifs.org.uk/uploads/ publications/bns/BN224.pdf.

8 Robert Booth for *The Guardian*, 15 November 2016: https://www.theguardian.com/ uk-news/2016/nov/15/more-than-7m-britons-in-precarious-employment.

9 ETUC Report: *Young People and Precarious Work*: https://www.etuc.org/en/young -people-and-precarious-work.

10 See Greece Youth Unemployment Rate at Trading Economics: https:// tradingeconomics.com/greece/youth-unemployment-rate#:~:text=Youth %20Unemployment%20Rate%20in%20Greece%20is%20expected%20to%20be %2039.40,37.60%20in%2012%20months%20time.

11 See Milburn, pp. 37–56.

12 See Ibid., pp. 59–66.

13 'The Graduate with No Future' Is a Term First Coined by Paul Mason on his BBC blog in 2011: '20 Reasons Why it's All Kicking off Everywhere': https://www.bbc.co .uk/blogs/newsnight/paulmason/2011/02/twenty_reasons_why_its_kicking.html. It was later turned into a bestselling book (Verso, 2012, 2013).

14 Len McCluskey: 'Unions, get set for battle', in *The Guardian*, 19 December 2010: https://www.theguardian.com/commentisfree/2010/dec/19/unions-students-strike -fight-cuts; and press statement earlier.

15 *Generation Left* (Polity, 2019) is, despite its brevity, a seminal contribution to theorizing the leftward trajectory of the millennials, and I draw on its analysis a number of times here.

16 Panitch, pp. 72–7.

17 Jason Deans for *The Guardian:* Steel in the UK: A Timeline of Decline, 30 March 2016: https://www.theguardian.com/business/2016/mar/30/steel-in-the-uk-a -timeline-of-decline.

18 John Kelly: *Contemporary Trotskyism* (Routledge, 2018), p. 67.

19 *Independent Leader Column*, 21 May 1998: https://www.independent.co.uk/voices/ leading-article-a-modest-victory-for-the-workers-1158009.html.

20 Kelly, p. 66.

21 Herbert Marcuse: *One Dimensional Man* (Sphere, 1964), p. 32.

22 Ibid., p. 19.

23 'The End of the Long 1990s' by Jeremy Gilbert, published in 2015: https://jeremyg ilbertwriting.files.wordpress.com/2015/09/the-end-of-the-long-90s1.pdf.

24 Laurie Penny: 'Out with the Old Politics', *The Guardian*, 24 December 2010: https:// www.theguardian.com/commentisfree/2010/dec/24/student-protests-young -politics-voices.

25 Mason is writing in the Preface to *Student Revolt* by Matt Myers.

26 Paul Mason: *Why it's All Kicking off Everywhere* (Verso, 2012, 2013), p. 45.

27 Pablo Iglesias: 'Understanding Podemos', in *New Left Review*, May/June 2015: https://newleftreview.org/issues/II93/articles/pablo-iglesias-understanding -podemos.

28 'The Open-Sourcing of Political Activism: How the Internet and Networks Help Build Resistance', in *Fightback: A Reader on the Winter of Protest* (Open Democracy, 2011), pp. 44–60. *The Cathedral and the Bazaar* (O'Reilly Media, 1999) is a book by software developer Eric S. Raymond based on an essay written one year previously.

29 Ibid., p. 48.

30 *Why it's Kicking Off*, p. 77.

31 Ibid., p. 77.

32 'The Open Sourcing of Activism: How the Internet and Networks Can Help Build Resistance', in *Fightback*, pp. 50–60.

33 David Graeber: *The Democracy Project* (Penguin, 2013), p. xxi.

Chapter 3

1 *Financial Times* report by Valentina Romei, 3 January 2020: 'Living Standards Grow at Slowest Rate since Second World War': https://www.ft.com/content/44401594 -2ca0-11ea-bc77-65e4aa615551.

2 'If the UK is high tech, why is productivity growth slow? Economists weigh in' by Ethan Ilzetzki for the LSE Blogs: https://blogs.lse.ac.uk/businessreview/2020/03 /07/if-the-uk-is-high-tech-why-is-productivity-growth-slow-economists-weigh -in/.

3 TUC analysis, 10 January 2020: https://www.tuc.org.uk/news/unsecured-debt-hits -new-peak-ps14540-household-tuc-analysis.

4 *Independent Report*, 28 December 2017: https://www.independent.co.uk/news/uk/ home-news/disability-benefit-claimants-attempted-suicides-fit-work-assessment-i -daniel-blake-job-centre-dwp-a8119286.html.

5 'Austerity, sanctions, and the rise of food banks in the UK' by Rachel Loopstra, Aaron Reeves, David Taylor-Robinson, Ben Barr, Martin McKee and David Stuckler in *BMJ 2015;350:h1775:* https://www.bmj.com/content/350/bmj.h1775.

6 Government statistics: 'Statutory Homelessness: April to June Quarter 2015 in England': https://assets.publishing.service.gov.uk/government/uploads/system/ uploads/attachment_data/file/463017/201506_Statutory_Homelessness.pdf.

7 Taken from '169 evictions in Britain a day: "I knocked every door, and no one helped me"' in the *New Statesman* by Samir Jeraj. Jeraj is citing Ministry of Justice statistics - *Mortgage and Landlord Possession Statistics in England and Wales, October to December 2017*. https://www.newstatesman.com/politics/uk/2018/03 /169-evictions-britain-day-i-knocked-every-door-and-no-one-helped-me.

8 'At least 135,000 children in Britain to be homeless at Christmas' by Patrick Butler in *The Guardian*, 3 December 2019: https://www.theguardian.com/society/2019/dec /03/at-least-135000-children-in-britain-will-be-homeless-at-christmas.

9 See Child health in 2030 in England: comparisons with other wealthy countries' published by Royal College of Paediatrics and Child Health: https://www.rcpch.ac .uk/sites/default/files/2018-10/child_health_in_2030_in_england_-report_2018 -10.pdf; and 'Fair Society Healthy Lives' (The Marmot Review), published by the Institute of Health Equity: http://www.instituteofhealthequity.org/resources-reports /fair-society-healthy-lives-the-marmot-review.

10 The King's Fund: 'What Are Health Inequalities?' by Ethan Williams, David Buck and Gbemi Babalola, 10 February 2020: https://www.kingsfund.org.uk/publications /what-are-health-inequalities.

11 Prescribed medicines review: summary, published by the UK Government https:// www.gov.uk/government/publications/prescribed-medicines-review-report/ prescribed-medicines-review-summary.

12 'Antidepressants prescribed far more in deprived English coastal towns' by Damien Gayle for *The Guardian*, 14 April 2017: https://www.theguardian.com/society/2017 /apr/14/antidepressants-prescribed-deprived-seaside-towns-of-north-and-east -blackpool-sunderland-and-east-lindsey-nhs.

13 Fire Brigades Union, 4 September 2019: https://www.fbu.org.uk/news/2019/09/04/ firefighter-numbers-crisis-after-chronic-underfunding.

14 'The Austerity Generation: the impact of a decade of cuts on family incomes and child poverty', published by the Child Poverty Action Group, November 2017: https://cpag.org.uk/sites/default/files/files/Austerity%20Generation%20FINAL.pdf (point 34, page 11).

15 *BBC Report*, 27 March 2014: https://www.bbc.co.uk/news/uk-26766345.

16 *Independent Report*, 28 December 2017: https://www.independent.co.uk/news/uk/ home-news/disability-benefit-claimants-attempted-suicides-fit-work-assessment-i -daniel-blake-job-centre-dwp-a8119286.html.

17 Adam Tinson for the New Policy Institute: 'The rise of sanctioning in Great Britain', June 2015: https://www.npi.org.uk/files/1314/3444/4908/Sanction_report _1606.pdf.

18 *Guardian Report*, 27 October 2016: https://www.theguardian.com/society/2016/oct /27/benefit-sanctions-food-banks-oxford-university-study.

19 *Guardian Report*, 20 January 2020: https://www.theguardian.com/society/2020/jan /20/youth-services-suffer-70-funding-cut-in-less-than-a-decade.

20 *Guardian Report*, 5 April 2018: https://www.theguardian.com/society/2018/apr/05 /1000-sure-start-childrens-centres-may-have-shut-since-2010; and *BBC Report*, 4 June 2019: https://www.bbc.co.uk/news/education-48498763.

21 TUC report: 'Breaking Point: The Crisis in Mental Health Funding', https://www .tuc.org.uk/sites/default/files/Mentalhealthfundingreport2_0.pdf; and 'Austerity and NHS cuts: Wrecking our Mental Health' from Keep Our NHS Public: https:// keepournhspublic.com/austerity-wrecking-mental-health/.

22 The King's Fund: 'How Serious Are the Pressures in Social Care?': https://www .kingsfund.org.uk/projects/verdict/how-serious-are-pressures-social-care.

23 See Allyson Pollock's blog: https://allysonpollock.com/?p=1872.

24 Statista: Number of people on a zero hours contract in the United Kingdom (UK) from 2000 to 2020: https://www.statista.com/statistics/414896/employees-with-zero -hours-contracts-number/.

25 Vince Cable in the *Daily Mail*, 9 February 2009: https://www.dailymail.co.uk/debate /article-1138673/VINCE-CABLE-Bring-guillotine--bankers.html.

26 https://www.youtube.com/watch?v=oL2phKBnXNM&feature=emb_title.

27 https://www.youtube.com/watch?v=dNwgMXkk75I&ab_channel=AdrianCousins.

28 At the time of writing, the website for 'Turn Trafalgar into Tahrir' was still online: https://march26tahrir.wordpress.com/the-call/. The call was primarily the initiative of the SWP but was taken up by a broader layer of anti-cuts activists.

29 https://www.youtube.com/watch?v=F_f6U4NyjjI&ab_channel=TradesUnion Congress%28TUC%29; https://www.theguardian.com/society/2011/mar/27/tuc -march-ed-miliband-labour-rally.

30 Graeber: *Democracy Project*, p. 22.

31 Ibid.

32 EDM (Early Day Motion) 2253: tabled on 17 October 2011: https://edm.parliament .uk/early-day-motion/43336.

33 'Riots broken down: who was in court and what's happened to them?' by Simon Rogers on *The Guardian Datablog*, 4 July 2012: https://www.theguardian.com/news/ datablog/2012/jul/04/riot-defendants-court-sentencing.

34 Ibid.

35 *Channel 4 News Blog*, 18 November 2011: https://www.channel4.com/news/occupy -london-protesters-take-over-third-space.

36 'Jeremy Clarkson Apologises over Strike Comments', *BBC Report*, 1 December 2011: https://www.bbc.co.uk/news/uk-15993549.

37 'Public sector workers to be offered further concessions in pensions row' by Nicholas Watt in *The Guardian*, 11 November 2011: https://www.theguardian.com/ society/2011/nov/11/public-sector-concessions-pensions-row.

38 Mark Fisher: 'THE LONDON HUNGER GAMES' on *K-Punk*, 8 August 2012: http://k-punk.abstractdynamics.org/archives/011918.html.

39 Interview: 'Mark Serwotka: no one should take lectures from privileged Tories' by Dan Milmo and Rajeev Syal for *The Guardian*, 20 March 2012: https://www .theguardian.com/society/2012/mar/20/mark-serwotka-unions-pension-reforms.

40 Interview: 'Ed Balls: George Osborne's Plan Is Failing but Labour Cannot Duck Reality' by Patrick Wintour for *The Guardian*, 13 January 2012: https://www .theguardian.com/politics/2012/jan/13/ed-balls-george-osborne-plan-failing.

41 Kelly Rogers successfully sued West Midlands Police for unlawful arrest. A number of other cases are ongoing at the time of writing.

42 Kelly: *Contemporary Trotskyism*, p. 37.

43 Mark Steel: 'Oh Good Lord, What Has the SWP Gone and Done NOW?', 13 March 2013: https://marksteelinfo.com/2013/03/oh-good-lord-what-has-the-swp-gone -and-done-now/.

Chapter 4

1 https://www.youtube.com/watch?v=DK36ps3L-aU&ab_channel=Diwonisojo.

2 See 'The Unravelling of Hollande's "anti-austerity" programme and the Crisis of French Socialism' by Sean McDaniel on the University of Sheffield's website: http:// speri.dept.shef.ac.uk/2017/01/26/the-unravelling-of-hollandes-anti-austerity -programme-and-the-crisis-of-french-socialism/.

3   See Momentum's submission to the *Labour Together Report*: https://
    peoplesmomentum.com/wp-content/uploads/2020/04/Momentums-Labour
    -Together-Submission.pdf.

4   Yougov data: 'Nationalisation vs Privatisation: The Public View': https://yougov
    .co.uk/topics/politics/articles-reports/2017/05/19/nationalisation-vs-privatisation
    -public-view; and 'Majority Support for Rent Controls': https://yougov.co.uk/topics/
    politics/articles-reports/2015/04/27/majority-support-rent-controls.

5   'Labour's Left Flank Must Ask Itself: Is it Time to Walk Away?', by Michael Chessum
    for *The New Statesman*, 28 May 2015: https://www.newstatesman.com/politics/2015
    /05/labours-left-flank-must-ask-itself-it-time-walk-away.

6   Monica Poletti, Tim Bale and Paul Webb for the LSE Blog: 'Explaining the pro-
    Corbyn surge in Labour's membership': https://blogs.lse.ac.uk/politicsandpolicy/
    explaining-the-pro-corbyn-surge-in-labours-membership/.

7   Hilary Wainwright: *Labour: A Tale of Two Parties* (Hogarth, 1987), p. 1.

8   *Parliamentary Socialism* by Ralph MIliband (Merlin, 1961, 1972), p. 13.

9   Ibid.,.p. 376.

10 Panitch, p. 81 – quoting from CLPD's 'Priorities for 1979' document.

11 Race said these words in a speech delivered at 'the Debate of the Decade' in March
    1980. The debate was later published as a short book by Pluto and was edited and
    introduced by Peter Hain.

12 Owen Jones: 'Labour Has a Membership Surge. Now it Has to Build a Mass
    Movement', on *The Guardian*, 29 September 2015: https://www.theguardian.com/
    commentisfree/2015/sep/29/labour-corbyn-membership-momentum-movement
    -voters.

13 'Revealed: The Radical Hard-Left Momentum Activists Mounting a Ruthless Purge
    of Labour' by Andrew Gilligan, 13 September 2016 for *the Telegraph* https://www
    .telegraph.co.uk/news/politics/labour/12156177/momentum-activists-jeremy
    -corbyn-labour-purge.html.

14 A full transcript of the debate was later released as a book by Pluto Press, with an
    introduction by Peter Hain. All speech from the debate quoted here is lifted from it.
    The Crisis and Future of the Left / The Debate of The Decade (Pluto, 1980).

15 "See *The Crisis and Future of the Left / The Debate of The Decade* (Pluto, 1980)".

16 See Tariq Ali: 'Why I'm Joining the Labour Party', in *Socialist Review, No. 38*,
    14 December 1981. pp. 20–1.

17 Wainwright: *A Tale of Two Parties*, p. 65.

18 McDonnell is consciously referring to the title of the classic 1979/80 title *In and
    Against the State* by Jeanette Mitchell, Donald MacKenzie, John Holloway, Cynthia
    Cockburn, Kathy Polanshek, Nicola Murray, Neil McInnes and John MacDonald
    aka the London Edinburgh Weekend Return Group (Pluto, 1979, 1980). The
    book crystallized an anti-statist perspective on the crisis facing the left at the
    beginning of the 1980s using a number of case studies from the public sector. It was

republished as a second edition in the summer of 2021, with an introduction by Seth Wheeler.

19 Wainwright: *A Tale of Two Parties*, p. 99.

Chapter 5

1 'Former MI6 boss labels Jeremy Corbyn a danger to national security unfit to lead the country' on *Politics Home*, 24 November 2019: https://www.politicshome.com/news/article/former-mi6-boss-labels-jeremy-corbyn-a-danger-to-national-security -unfit-to-lead-the-country.

2 'Jeremy Corbyn is neither nice nor decent – he is a nasty bully and an embarrassment to the country' by Tom Harris in *The Telegraph*, 1 July 2016: https://www.telegraph.co.uk/news/2016/07/01/jeremy-corbyn-is-neither-nice-nor-decent- -he-is-a-nasty-bully-an/.

3 The Campaign for Free Education (CFE) was founded in 1995 and was in many ways the predecessor of the 2010 coalition NCAFC in terms of the political coalition it brought together. Between the end of CFE and the founding of NCAFC in 2010, the analogous organization was Education Not for Sale, in which fellow Labour MP Lloyd Russell Moyle was also active.

4 'Owen Smith told Leanne Wood she gets invited on Question Time because she is a woman', *Wales Online Report*, 14 July 2016: https://www.walesonline.co.uk/news/politics/owen-smith-told-leanne-wood-11613820.

5 See the article of that name on *Vice* by Angus Harrison, 16 September 2016: https://www.vice.com/en/article/3bw4a9/owen-smith-penis-leadership-campaign.

6 Commons Briefing Note, 9 August 2019: https://commonslibrary.parliament.uk/research-briefings/sn05125/.

7 ONS data: 'Workplace Disputes and Working Conditions': https://www.ons.gov.uk/employmentandlabourmarket/peopleinwork/workplacedisputesandworkingconditions/.

8 These were Jeremy Corbyn's words at the time of the launch of the Community Organising Unit. See 'Corbyn launches community campaign unit', *BBC News Blog*, 8 January 2018: https://www.bbc.co.uk/news/uk-politics-42599895.

9 The alliance between us was not always an easy one: we came from very different political backgrounds and had clashed over various issues (particularly Labour's anti-Semitism crisis) – but we shared a commitment to what we saw as honouring the democratic process.

10 A few weeks after the new constitution was imposed, Barnet, Blyth and Wansbeck, Brighton and Hove, Broxtowe, Cambridge, Camden, Cheshire West and Chester, Coventry, Darlington, Derbyshire, Enfield, Harrow, Hexham, Hounslow, Kirklees, Lambeth, Leicestershire, Leeds, Lewisham, Liverpool, Medway, Newham, North

Tyneside, Northamptonshire, Richmond Park and Twickenham, Rotherham, Sheffield, South Tyneside, South East Kent, Southwark, Thanet, Tower Hamlets, Truro and Falmouth, and Wandsworth had voted to condemn it; and those supporting it were Calderdale, Stockport, Teesside, Manchester and Trafford, and Sheffield (the latter of which in the end passed motions in support of both sides). Many more groups later passed motions of censure.

Chapter 6

1   The campaign was initially created after a conversation activist-academic Luke Cooper (who had been heavily involved in the anti-austerity movement and had recently played a role in setting up the new left party Left Unity) and Green Party deputy leader Amelia Womack, though it quickly drew in broad range of support. I didn't get involved until late in 2015.

2   See *Building an Economy for The People* (Manifesto, 2012), p. 43. A PDF is available here: https://21centurymanifesto.files.wordpress.com/2018/03/an-economy-for-the-people-free.pdf.

3   'Big majority of Labour members 'want UK to stay in single market'' by Anushka Asthana for *The Guardian*, 17 July 2017: https://www.theguardian.com/politics/2017/jul/17/most-labour-members-want-uk-to-remain-in-single-market. The original data is from the ESRC Party Members' Project.

4   'Poll shows 86% of Labour members want new Brexit vote' by Jim Pickard for *The FT*, 22 September 2018: https://www.ft.com/content/dc56ee36-bea4-11e8-95b1-d36dfef1b89a. The original data is YouGov.

5   https://www.facebook.com/watch/?v=939197699859907.

6   *Guardian Report* by Jess Elgot, 24 September 2018: https://www.theguardian.com/politics/2018/sep/24/labours-left-divided-against-itself-over-reselection-reforms.

7   Len McCluskey: 'Unite will always work towards democratic reform' in *The Morning Star*, September 2018: https://morningstaronline.co.uk/article/unite-will-always-work-towards-democratic-reform.

8   'RED REPRISALS Momentum shuts down youth wing because of online trolling by far-left youngsters', *The Sun*, 10 January 2018: https://www.thesun.co.uk/news/5312426/momentum-shuts-down-youth-wing-because-of-online-trolling-by-far-left-youngsters/.

9   Hilary Wainwright: *A New Politics from the Left* (Polity, 2008), p. 13.

10 Beatrice Webb: *Our Partnership* (Longman, 1948), p. 120. This quote is taken from Wainwright in *A New Politics from the Left*, Ibid.

11 Hal Draper: *The Two Souls of Socialism* (Independent Socialist Committee pamphlet, 1966), p. 16.

Conclusion

1 Jeremy Gilbert: 'The Labour leadership contest has exposed new factions in the party', published online on 1 March 2020: https://www.theguardian.com/commentisfree/2020/mar/01/labour-leadership-contest-new-factions.
2 See Wainwright's speech at 'Debate of the Decade' in 1980, p. 29.

Further reading

Below are a limited set of recommendations on further reading, split up thematically and chronologically.

It would be a fool's errand to try to give a full list of classic theoretical texts relating to the themes covered in the book, so I will focus instead on highlighting books which are more or less contemporary and designed for the general, as opposed to the academic, reader. So, **from a theoretical perspective**, Mark Fisher's *Capitalist Realism* (Zero, 2009) is short in length but essential reading. Keir Milburn's *Generation Left* (Polity, 2019) is a concise and excellent summary of the radicalization of millennials. Hilary Wainwright's *A New Politics from the Left* (Polity, 2018) is another concise bringing together of many years of thinking about a new left. Meanwhile, *Hegemony Now: How Big Tech and Wall Street Won the World* (Verso, 2022), Jeremy Gilbert's latest book (written alongside co-author Alex Williams), develops the theme of the 'long 1990s' touched on in our interview. Similarly, those interested in exploring debates around technology and the future of capitalism touched on in interviews should read Paul Mason's *Postcapitalism* (Penguin, 2015) and *Clear Bright Future* (Allen Lane, 2019); Aaron Bastani also released a book on the subject, *Fully Automated Luxury Communism* (Verso, 2019). *In and Against the State* is not a contemporary text, but the new edition (Pluto, 2021) contains insightful and timely reflections from John McDonnell and the book's editor Seth Wheeler.

There remains relatively little general literature on **the student movement of 2010**. Matt Myers's oral history *Student Revolt: Voices of the Austerity Generation* (Pluto, 2017) remains the only authoritative account. *Fightback: A Reader on the Winter of Protest* (Open Democracy, 2011, edited by Dan Hancox) contains a diverse range of articles and essays from participants in the movement. For anyone interested in primary sources on the movement in a more global perspective, *Springtime: The New Student Rebellions* (Verso, 2011, edited by Clare Solomon and Tania Palmieri) is also worth a look. Those interested in the higher education policy landscape at the time would do well to read *The Great University Gamble: Money, Markets and the Future of Higher Education* (Pluto, 2013) by Andrew McGettigan and *The Assault on Universities: A Manifesto for Resistance* (Pluto, 2011 – edited by Michael Bailey and Des Freeman).

For wider texts on the **global revolts of 2011**, there is much more available. In terms of the events themselves, the classic text is Paul Mason's *Why It's Kicking Off Everywhere: The New Global Revolutions* (Verso, 2012). *The Democracy Project: A History, a Crisis, a Movement* (Spiegel & Grau, 2013) is David Graeber's first-hand account of the start of the Occupy movement. The specific history of **the UK anti-austerity movement** is a much less covered area, however. By and large the sources that go into any kind of detail, or engage with the movement on its own terms, are to be found in academic journal articles, blogs and position statements from the time – though accounts of it can be found in passing in mainstream print (for instance, in Owen Jones's *This Land: The Story of a Movement*, Allen Lane 2020; and Andrew Murray's *The Fall and Rise of the British Left*, Verso, 2019). One of the reasons why Chapter 3 is the longest chapter of this book is an attempt to fill some of these holes in the literature – though much of that work remains undone.

There are no shortage of accounts of **the rise of the new Labour left and the Corbyn Project**, though the vast majority of these are focussed on the high politics of the moment rather than the broader picture behind it. Two accounts of the Labour left's rise, by Owen Jones and Andrew Murray, are already listed above. Alex Nunn's *The Candidate: Jeremy Corbyn's Improbable Path to Power* (OR Books, 2018) remains a good inside story of the campaign. For a less involved journalistic take, *Left Out: The Inside Story of Labour Under Corbyn* (Vintage, 2020) gives a detailed and entertaining court history. David Kogan's *Protest and Power: The Battle for the Labour Party* (Bloomsbury, 2019) also provides an outsider's perspective, including a great deal of detail and historical background.

There are a wealth of texts on **the general history of the Labour Party and the Labour left**, but two recent titles in particular are worth mentioning. Leo Panitch and Colin Leys's *Searching for Socialism: The Project of the Labour New Left from Benn to Corbyn* (Verso, 2020) is an unmissable account. So too is Simon Hannah's *A Party with Socialists in It: A History of the Labour Left* (Pluto, 2018), which covers a longer chronology and is written from a more critical and politically engaged perspective.

Finally, there are a number of **forthcoming books** which should be mentioned because they relate to key themes that this book contains and are written by people who feature as protagonists in this book. These include Ash Sarkar's debut book and take on the culture war, *Minority Rule*, published by Bloomsbury; Owen Jones's *The Alternative and How We Built It*, published by Penguin, which may cover some of the same ground as this book; James Schneider's *Our Bloc: How We Win*, a strategic manifesto for the British left published by Verso; and James Meadway's *Pandemic Capitalism*, also with Verso.

Index

1968 movements
  comparison to youth movements of
    2010s   50–2
  influence on 2010 student
    movement   36
  influence on key activists   129–30,
    146

Abbott, Diane   15, 115, 126
academization   14
ACORN   100, 160
Alexander, Heidi   157
Ali, Tariq   146–50
Alternative Economic Strategy   49
Alternativ fuer Deutschland   117
anarchism, anarchists
  in the anti-austerity movement   80–1,
    87, 90–3
  and Brexit   176
  future organising   211
  prominence in young people   55–7,
    61, 77
  relation to Corbynism   6, 107, 123–5,
    195
  in the student movement   24, 47, 53,
    56
Anderson, Perry   54
Another Europe is Possible   145, 160,
  172, 178, 182–5
anti-fascist movement; Anti-Nazi
  League   16
anti-trade union legislation   49, 72, 84,
  103, 158
Arab Spring   1, 26, 43, 58, 81–2, 87, 123
austerity
  and Labour under Corbyn   121, 157,
    197
  and Labour under Miliband   6, 18,
    24, 42, 55, 82, 99, 105, 116–17, 120,
    134, 180
  as a policy   18–19, 38–42, 65, 71–3,
    108–9
  public support for   40, 177

  social and human impact   2–3, 66–71,
    139

baby boomers   16, 34, 64
Bakers, Food and Allied Workers' Union
  (BFAWU)   133, 152, 163
Balls, Ed   99, 105
banking sector bailout. See financial crisis
Barber, Brendan   96
Bastani, Aaron   30, 58–60, 107, 137
Battle of Seattle   47
Beach, Ben   6–7, 123–4
Benn, Tony
  alternative Economic Strategy   49
  in the anti-austerity movement   15,
    44, 73, 102
  deputy leadership and leadership
    elections   132, 136, 148, 151
  party reform   115–16
  speaking at the Debate of the
    Decade   146–8
Bennism
  comparison to Corbynism   5, 147,
    150, 172, 195–7, 211
  comparison with Bevanism   147
  contemporary context   120, 148, 167
  presence within Corbynism   133–4,
    136–7, 144
Bergfeld, Mark   24, 79
Bevan, Aneurin; Bevanism   5, 136, 147,
  150–1
Biden, Joe   203
Binette, George   74, 101
Black Bloc   54, 81
Black Lives Matter   160, 202
Blair, Tony   14, 18, 42, 49, 127
Blairism. See New Labour
Bloomsbury Social Centre   94
Blower, Christine   84, 127
Book Block   31
Brand, Russell   107–8
Brexit
  anti-Brexit protests   160, 172